Slaying Brexit Unicorns

The truth about our decision to leave the EU

Edwin Hayward

Illustration by Liquid Faerie
LiquidFaeries.com

Layout by Polgarus Studio

First edition.

ISBN: 978-1-9162713-0-2

Contents

Introduction

We are in a terrible mess right now. Brexit is chaos incarnate.

More than three years after the referendum, we still don't know what Brexit really means. We face a bewildering range of scenarios, but are no closer to choosing one.

Positions have become entrenched. Compromise is history. Think back to where you stood on Brexit before the referendum. Can you say hand on heart that your own view hasn't hardened? In May 2016, a month before the Brexit vote, Nigel Farage warned: "In a 52-48 referendum this would be unfinished business by a long way."[1] Remarkable prescience.

It wasn't meant to be like this. Brexit was supposed to be easy, and our future outside the EU bright and shiny, at least according to prominent Brexiters.

Back in April 2016, Michael Gove said: "The day after we vote to leave, we hold all the cards and we can choose the path we want."[2] A month later, he claimed: "If we vote to leave then I think the union will be stronger."[3] A few days after the referendum, Boris Johnson assured us: "There will continue to be free trade and access to the single market."[4] As recently as July 2017, Liam Fox said: "The free trade agreement we will have to do should be one of the easiest in human history."[5]

The politicians weren't the only ones talking up our prospects. The Vote Leave campaign promised: "After we Vote Leave, British businesses will trade freely with the EU"[6] and also "there won't be a sudden change that disrupts the economy."[7]

Seen from the perspective of October 2019, a resolution to Brexit remains as elusive as ever. The UK stands weeks away from crashing out of the EU without a deal. Businesses stockpile supplies in an economy that has started shrinking for the first time since 2012.[8] Consumers worry about food and medicine shortages.

Meanwhile, the Tory party has lost its parliamentary majority, trust in politics is at an all-time low, and calls for independence are rising in Scotland and Wales.

Politics as usual is dead.

Politicians used to listen to each other. Not all the time or on every subject. But they would at least have real debates during which they would try to convince each other with facts and reasoning. And then they'd get things done. But when it comes to Brexit, they lose themselves in endless slanging matches. Faces redden, fingers point, voices turn shrill.

The normal work of Parliament has ground to a halt. Key issues get ignored. Vital legislation languishes. Nothing moves in the Brexit quicksand.

Brexit has smashed political allegiances and driven MPs to desert their parties in droves. The composition of the House of Commons has changed remarkably since the 2017 general election. We have new political parties (Brexit Party, The Independent Group for Change) and looser groupings within the established ones. Over 30 MPs now sit as independents. No other issue has caused anything close to this level of disruption in our lifetimes.

The corrosive influence of Brexit is everywhere. TV news and panel discussions have become take-no-prisoners battlegrounds. (Some of the fiercest fights involve proponents of different forms of Brexit.) Newspaper front pages bellow and scream. Everything is extreme. Brexit will be glorious or apocalyptic – there is nothing in between. It has destroyed friendships, soured workplaces, and split up families.

Even the language surrounding Brexit has coarsened. Those with opposing views are betrayers, saboteurs, traitors, enemies of the people. The Daily Express warns: "Ignore the will of the people at your peril."[9] War metaphors abound. A failure to leave the EU means surrender. And if we hit some bumps in the road, we should rely on Blitz spirit. Arron Banks (the millionaire who bankrolled UKIP and the Leave.eu campaign) made the comparison explicit: "Brexit was a war. We won."[10]

The epithet "undemocratic" gets bandied about a lot. Remainers say it is undemocratic to deny people a chance to think again now that we have more facts. We vote in general elections every few years. What makes this *advisory* referendum so special the result must be set in stone for all time? Leavers say it would be undemocratic to hold a second referendum before implementing the first. Politicians told us they would implement whatever we chose.

Many action films contain variants of the same cliché scene. The bad guy or gal starts the timer on an explosive device. Shots of glowing digits punctuate the rest of the film. The final act finds Our Hero facing the bomb as the last few seconds trickle away. Tick tock. *Is it the green wire or the red?* Tick tock. *Wish I wasn't colour blind.* Tick tock. 3... 2... 1... Snip! Phew. Fade to black.

In the case of Brexit, detonation is currently set for 31 October 2019 at 11pm UK time. One heartbeat we're in the EU. The next we're out. Bang go all our trade agreements and other arrangements. Without a deal there will be nothing to replace them. Yet Boris Johnson insists we must leave "do or die, come what may."[11] (If we ask the EU for an extension and they grant it, we can reset the timer a little. But the no deal bomb will not be defused short of a deal, or cancelling Brexit altogether.)

The Government's hard-line approach to the Brexit negotiations has never properly reflected the narrow 52% to 48% margin of the referendum. But now many of the 52% are being sidelined too, in this case by the pursuit of no deal, an outcome that was never on the cards in 2016. As Michael Gove wrote in the Daily Mail in March 2019: "But we didn't vote to leave without a deal. That wasn't the message of the campaign I helped lead."[12] Only a small minority of voters will be happy with no deal yet that seems to be what the Government is steering us towards.

A pursuit of Brexit at any cost risks leaving us weak. The UK is a lever. Our EU membership is a fulcrum that lets us take that lever and multiply our strength. Take away the fulcrum, and the lever becomes a useless stick.

Foreign powers are rubbing their hands as our negotiating position crumbles. Without a deal with the EU, we will have to sprint to countries such as the US and China to replace some of our lost trade. They will exact a hefty toll in return for helping us. That toll may be selling us chlorinated chicken or hormone-treated beef. It may be letting their private sector snap up pieces of our NHS. It may be something else. Whatever it turns out to be, we won't enjoy paying it.

What a mess. What a tragic mess. The UK used to be a sensible country with a well-deserved reputation for cooperation and fair play. Our democracy was a model for the world. Not for nothing is our Parliament known as the Mother of Parliaments.[13] But now we're laughed at or, worse, pitied. Our closest allies in the EU are losing patience with our dithering and in-fighting. It's as if Brexit were a hallucinogen in the water supply causing us all to take leave of our senses.

Time to snap out of our collective trance.

About this book

Move over, Project Fear. Here comes Project Fact…

For those who identify as Remainers, this book will remind you what you're fighting for. It will reveal the extent of the hole the UK is digging for itself, and confirm you are right to fear Brexit. But it will also bust the myth that there are no benefits to leaving the EU.

If you support team Leave, you may be led up unfamiliar paths. You will find out exactly what we stand to lose by giving up our EU membership. You will learn what trading exclusively on WTO terms would mean, and why being the only country in the world to do so isn't something to aspire to. You will also see why no deal is a really *really* bad deal.

If you're in neither tribe, this book will show you what's on both sides of the Brexit fence. Maybe you could coax Jeremy Corbyn off it if you happen to see him?

Although this is a serious book about a serious subject, it contains a sprinkling of gallows humour. If we don't take the opportunity to laugh as the end of the world approaches, it will be too late afterwards.

(PS: this book quotes facts and statistics, economists and other experts. And many, many politicians. No animals will be harmed, except for Brexit unicorns. They won't stand a chance.)

Preamble: an appeal to the politicians

Brexit dominates politics like a black hole, all other initiatives frozen in its gravitational field. It is spreading like a cancer through every aspect of life in the UK. The damage has already begun: we are becoming poorer, less competitive and more isolated. The IFS estimates that Brexit has already cost the UK between £55 billion and £66 billion as a result of slower economic growth.[14] Jobs are being lost, and firms are downsizing, or moving operations and assets abroad. And the Government has funnelled £6.2 billion in taxpayer money into Brexit preparations, with billions more poised to follow.

Hold on a minute. Isn't unemployment close to a record low? And hasn't the economy grown in recent years? True. But imagine trying to fill a bucket with a hole in. If the flow from the tap is strong enough, you might still be able to. But you'll waste an awful lot of water in the process. Everything is relative. We're surviving. Without the hole created by Brexit, we'd be thriving.

We tend to be bad at talking about money. The subject leaves us flustered and tongue-tied. That could be why we shy away from the uncomfortable truth that every flavour of Brexit is likely to leave us poorer. This matters, because there are so many things we ought to be doing as a nation to improve our collective lot in life. But they all depend on having the means to pay for the changes.

Compassion won't improve the NHS or transform mental care. Positive vibes won't deliver better children's services or sort out Universal Credit. Optimism won't reduce inequality or help the low paid. Patriotism won't build better road and rail links. A million good intentions and a pound will still only get you one item from Poundland.

We need cold hard cash to begin fixing our problems – and lots of it. Unromantic? Sure. Reality often is. But we must face the world as it is. So many of the arguments around Brexit are financial in nature because such impacts affect millions of lives now and into the future.

The UK is an economic powerhouse. As the sixth largest economy, we punch well above our weight on the world stage. And we should feel deserved pride in doing so. But there's almost no slack in the system. Our finances operate very close to the limit, like an engine rattling at maximum revs. Our Government spends every penny it collects in taxes, and more. It relies on borrowing to make ends meet, like the friend who's always skint a few days before payday.

The austerity programme pursued by successive Tory governments exemplifies this. Austerity suppressed UK growth by about 2% over the last decade.[15] That may not sound like much, but it translates into tens of billions of pounds in lost tax revenue. Money which could have been spent instead on our NHS or other national priorities.

How does Brexit impact UK finances and livelihoods? Millions of jobs have been created by attracting foreign firms and inward investment. They come for our educated workforce and English language business environment. But more than anything, they come because we're the perfect "gateway to Europe".

Brexit threatens to brick up that gateway. Companies will face delays, queues at the ports, and a mountain of new red tape. In the absence of a deal, they will face new tariffs too. All these factors translate into extra cost and hassle, destroying the frictionless border arrangements that allow for just-in-time production.

Many firms have already put in place expensive contingency plans in the hope of mitigating the worst effects of Brexit. Warehouses across the UK bulge with stockpiled goods, as if all our Christmases have come at once. Which is unfortunate, given that Christmas itself is fast approaching, and with it a huge spike in goods needing to be stored somewhere. Santa may run out of room for all his presents. Other businesses are in "wait and see" mode, fearful, unsure how to prepare.

Uncertainty drags on investment. Why expand a factory or deploy new machinery when Brexit may upend everything in short order? Individuals face similar concerns. Why take on a mortgage or buy a car if you don't know whether you'll still have a job in a few weeks? (New car registrations peaked in 2016, and have declined every year since. Some blame can be laid at diesel's door, but it's too simplistic to dismiss the effect of Brexit entirely.)

All our free trade agreements will end the instant we leave the EU. These include our membership of the single market and customs union, as well as the EU's deals with other countries we share in as EU members. Together, they govern over 60% of all our international trade. If we manage to conclude a Brexit deal, it will carry over the effects of the trade agreements during any transition period. But the agreements themselves will no longer apply to the UK, deal or no deal, after Brexit Day. Liz Truss managed to roll over a smattering of trade deals, as did her predecessor, Liam Fox. Despite their efforts, we are nowhere near replacing what we are poised to lose.

Multinational firms are likely to flee, taking jobs and investment with them. Our economy will be hit under every Brexit scenario according to both Government and independent forecasts. The heaviest burden will fall on the most disadvantaged communities. Less money will mean less to spend on all the things that really matter. And it will mean a return to austerity – definitely for years, likely for decades.

Hauliers warn that Brexit will destroy their livelihoods. Farmers warn of fruit and vegetables left to rot in the fields as their seasonal workforce dries up. The NHS warns of delayed operations and severe staff shortages. Universities warn of lost funding and the end of shared research partnerships. Nobel laureates warn that our leading position in science will be under threat. Car manufacturers warn that Brexit will force them to shift production overseas. Airlines warn that flights will be affected. Representatives from sector after sector have contributed their own warnings.

Perhaps their concerns could be dismissed in isolation. Taken together, they paint a damning picture of our post-Brexit future. If enough people report smelling smoke and seeing the flicker of flame, the simplest explanation is that the house really is on fire.

Given all the above, you can see why Brexit will have such an effect on our prosperity and our ability to improve public welfare. But it's not just about the money. UK citizens in Europe fear what their lives may become. Will they still have access to their pensions, and to affordable or free healthcare? Will they even have the right to remain in the countries they now call home? EU citizens in the UK – our friends and neighbours, often doing vital jobs or those we choose not to do – find themselves equally in limbo. Millions of people, all waiting to see how and where the Brexit Sword of Damocles will fall.

So far, we have but scratched the surface of Brexit. The Irish border, Gibraltar, the gutting of the UK service sector… Brexit raises so many critical issues, it's hard to keep track of them all.

Meanwhile, our Government is requisitioning ferries and turning motorways into car parks. It is stockpiling food, and renting cold storage for thousands of pallets of medical supplies. The police force is formulating plans to deal with civil unrest. A role has been pencilled in for the Army too, with 3,500 soldiers expected to be on call.[16] There has been serious talk of the need to impose martial law in the guise of the Civil Contingencies Act 2004.[17]

Take a step back, a really big step back. Is any of this normal? Isn't it extraordinary the extent to which Brexit is forcing us to reconsider what we think of as everyday life? The pursuit of Brexit feels like a march into darkness, every grim headline taking us further from the light.

The EU has its problems, plenty of them. But you wouldn't tear down a tower block because you don't like the colour of the bricks or the leaky roof gutter. No, you'd fix the issues, adapt, find workarounds, improve things.

Brexit sows division. It sets friend against friend, colleague against colleague, family against family, young against old. The referendum fired the starting pistol on a seething resentment that's still gathering pace. It also fanned the flames of intolerance and racism. We see this reflected in the sharp rise in hate crime since 2016. Brexit will not unite us, no matter how often politicians insist otherwise. It is the disease, not the cure.

We are on a course that leads straight to Brexit. It was set when we triggered Article 50 over two years ago. We can see Brexit through, leave with or without a deal, and endure the consequences. At the moment, we're due to leave on 31 October 2019. That deadline might slip if we can persuade the EU to give us another extension. Or we can abandon the idea of Brexit, revoke Article 50 and stay in the EU on our current membership terms.

You can't be a little bit out of the EU. That would be like being a little bit pregnant. No, we will be out as soon as the deadline mandated by Article 50 passes. Rebuilding our international relationships after we've left will take many years. And if subsequent events prove we made the wrong choice, rejoining the EU could take a decade or more.

Although we voted to leave by a narrow margin, our future is not yet set in stone. Are our interests best served by damaging our economy? By cutting ourselves off from the rest of the world at a time of increasing globalisation? By facing climate change and other massive challenges alone rather than as part of a strong team?

While any form of Brexit will damage the UK, a no deal scenario is likely to prove catastrophic. Brexit with a deal is like a heart transplant in which a patient receives a temporary replacement until a permanent solution can be found. The surgery leaves them weakened, but they have a decent chance of surviving it. No deal is like ripping their heart out of their chest, leaving a ragged hole. (Note: most top surgeons maintain the original heart is healthy.)

The hour is late, but there is still an opportunity to understand, learn, think again. To channel Yes Minister's Sir Humphrey: "If you're going to do this damn silly thing, don't do it in this damn silly way."

As individuals and collectively, as employees or company owners, as nurses or carpenters or bankers or carers or retirees, we all have important but minor roles to play in Brexit.

But the influence of MPs over the Brexit process is immense. It is no exaggeration to say that 650 men and women hold the future of our country and of the Union in their hands.

So let me make this plea directly to the politicians. All the information you could ever need is already at your disposal. You have access to House of Commons briefings, Select Committee evidence, impact assessments and preparedness notices. You also have a wealth of material prepared by the EU. This is not the time for gut instinct and reflex action, but for sober reflection and informed analysis. This is the challenge of your professional life. You have the power to save us or doom us. For all our sakes, please make the right choice.

The awkward relationship between Brexit and facts

Facts are immutable. Yesterday's football result is not open to interpretation. It will never change, no matter whether you're a die-hard fan of the winning team or the losing team.

In other words, facts exist independent of the views of the observer. They are not affected by feelings, belief, optimism or patriotism, nor do they get any less true because you don't like them. As Byline Times puts it: "while everyone is welcome to their own opinions, you cannot have your own facts".[18]

You can't vote to win the lottery. You can't vote to sprout wings and defy the force of gravity. Cause and effect don't work like that. Similarly, the outcome of the 2016 vote does not affect the chance of Brexit being a success. The referendum result prompts us to attempt Brexit. But it does not and cannot make Brexit itself a better idea.

Many aspects of Brexit are as factual as football scores. Yet most news outlets still blur the issues. Rather than explain each situation as it truly is, they opt for the absurd alternative of presenting two competing views as if equal in value.

Newspapers with an agenda tend to begin their Brexit analyses with a headline based on a statement by an MP on one side of the debate. The piece explores their point of view further. Next, there's a rebuttal from a different MP or subject matter expert. Battling quotes litter the text like discarded shell casings. The article disintegrates into a he-said she-said slanging match. There is no overarching editorial voice, nobody stepping in to say "this is true, and this is not". Readers are left none the wiser. They see competing claims from two people of a certain standing. But the presence of both claims wrongly suggests different opinions are possible. In reality, one position has the facts behind it. The other is empty assertion, i.e. worthless. Balance is unnecessary when there is only one correct answer. Indeed, a false attempt to introduce it hinders understanding.

Take for example the issue of tariffs. The EU's WTO tariff on cars is 10%. That's a fact and shouldn't be open to question. But an article on tariffs might include a quote from an MP saying they don't expect UK manufacturers to face tariffs in a no deal situation. There is no logic to support such a claim. By including their denial, the article acquires unnecessary bias.

The TV channels are no better. They often invite guests with opposing stances onto current affairs programmes and grill each one on the detail of their position. Falsehoods are allowed to stand after repeated challenges. ("OK, let's move on.") At no point does the anchor cut the discussion off on the grounds that a guest is exploiting their soapbox to propagate lies. We get views when we should get news.

Sometimes, guests are given free rein to fight it out like dogs in a ring. (You can almost hear a voiceover bellowing "Are you not entertained? Is this not why you're here?" in the manner of Russell Crowe in Gladiator.)

The BBC's misguided attempts at balance colour the wider Brexit debate. In striving to avoid accusations of favouritism, the organisation has surrendered its impartiality. It ignores the weight of evidence supporting each side of Brexit issues. Instead, it allocates equal airtime and website column inches to both sides. Such false equivalences are neither fair nor neutral. They boost specious arguments in defiance of the facts. The BBC has exhibited this pattern of behaviour time and again. For example, the day before the referendum, 1,280 business leaders backed EU membership in a letter to the Times. The BBC reported on the content of the letter. It provided "balance" by quoting two pro-Brexit representatives. One contributor came from Tate & Lyle. The other was the entrepreneur James Dyson. Combined, their rebuttal took up half the news piece.[19] The BBC took a similar approach when 13 Nobel prize-winning economists warned over Brexit. It gave the same amount of attention to rebuttals from people connected with Vote Leave.[20]

A similar problem arises with Brexit vox pop pieces. Comments from the public do not distinguish between clichés, misinformation and the truth since they are usually broadcast without interpretation. Such segments give equal weight to unequal matters by presenting the same number of voices on both sides. They also breathe new life into discredited statements, such as the £350 million for the NHS on the side of the bus. (The BBC is not alone in falling foul of this.)

The BBC's "balance where no balance is required" approach applied for decades to its reporting of climate change too. But recently, the organisation has accepted that the scientific evidence for climate change is overwhelming. As a result, it no longer provides a platform to climate change deniers. Instead, it brings together guests with differing views of how to solve a problem acknowledged by all concerned. By rights, it ought to take a similar stance on aspects of Brexit that are not open to interpretation. Sadly, there is no sign of it doing so.

Many proponents of Brexit exploit the confusion created by the denial of core truths mercilessly. They present the latest half-baked theories as if channelling the direct word of God. *Of course there's a technological solution to the Irish border. Yes, it can be in place by October.* (Even though no such solution operates on any border anywhere in the world at present). *You just have to squeeze your eyes shut and believe. Every time you deny it, a fairy dies.* They know they can get away with falsehoods because nobody is holding them to account.

That's where this book comes in...

In the beginning was the vote...

How do you get to grips with a subject as big as Brexit? "One bite at a time," as per the old joke about eating an elephant. And the first few nibbles must surely take in that fateful vote...

On the 23rd of June 2016, the UK held a referendum to see if we should remain in the EU or leave. David Cameron organised it largely to placate the Eurosceptic wing of his party, which had been agitating to "leave Europe" (sic) ever since the UK joined the Common Market in 1973.

Spoiler alert. The Leave camp won.

It won by 17,410,742 votes to 16,141,241, taking 51.89% of all votes cast vs 48.11% for Remain. That's a margin of victory of 3.78% – slim, but real. Across the UK, 72.21% of registered voters took part in the referendum.[21] The turnout was higher than in any General Election since 1992, when 77.7% of people voted.[22] (It was not however "the largest democratic mandate ever", a frequently repeated exaggeration.)

The outcome of the referendum seemed to come as a surprise. Thrilling for some, shocking to others, but a surprise for all concerned. In the immediate aftermath, Remain couldn't quite absorb the idea that the vote had gone the other way, that people had made the "wrong" choice. But many on the Leave side seemed equally nonplussed. The ashen faces of Boris Johnson and Michael Gove as they faced the media the next day testified to that.[23] (From fellow Brexit campaigners to bitter rivals, and now in power together – what a journey!)

Never ask an open question of the electorate.

There was a fatal flaw at the heart of the 2016 referendum: the single word "Leave" concealed a vast range of outcomes. Something that simplistic and ill-defined should *never* have been on the ballot paper.

The referendum produced a majority for Leave, but not for any single post-exit scenario.

The poor formulation of the original question guarantees that far more than half of voters will be disappointed by whichever Brexit we end up with. Remainers were always going to be unhappy if the vote went against them. But not all Leavers will be satisfied with the ultimate outcome of the referendum either. Why? Because each voter had their personal idea of the form of Brexit they were voting for. But only one type of Brexit is possible, so the final choice won't match the expectations many had when they made their cross on the ballot paper. It may land us too in too close a relationship with the EU for their liking, or too distant a one. And it may not address the bugbears they had with our EU membership.

Indeed, it is even possible that a majority of all voters would prefer staying in the EU to the Brexit we end up enacting, were they to be given a say on the matter.

The fault does not lie with the electorate. People who chose "Leave" did so in good faith. They cannot be held responsible for the dreadful formulation of the original question. The issue would have been moot if Remain had won because no action would have been needed. But Leave's victory compelled us to ask what the "Leave" option actually meant. And nobody had (or has) a definitive answer.

The referendum was like saying "Would you like to stay at home or do something?" The "Do something" option won. And that's when the fight started. We can only choose one thing.

Some people wanted to go for a meal, others to hang around down the pub, catch a film, even go to the zoo. Before long, discordant voices started drowning out the realistic suggestions. Why don't we ride a rocket to the moon? I want to travel back in time. Who's for Hogwarts?

Ever since the vote, the political mood has swung further and further from realism. "A meal? The pub? The zoo? Give me a break! None of those represent 'doing something'. They're the same as staying in. Now bring me a DeLorean so that I can crank it up to 88 mph…"

Many have forgotten – genuinely or conveniently – that the more extremist, fringe ideas of what "Leave" meant (such as No Deal) were never advocated during the referendum itself. Not by anyone close to the Leave mainstream, anyway. As Vote Leave put it in its campaign materials: "Taking back control is a careful change, not a sudden stop – we will negotiate the terms of a new deal before we start any legal process to leave"[24].

The journey towards radicalism began as soon as the referendum result was clear. People who had spoken of moderate Brexits (like the Norway option) only days earlier suffered collective amnesia. Notions of staying in the customs union or the single market evaporated. Then Theresa May invoked Article 50, locking us into leaving to a timetable. That freed the most radical to unleash their full fanaticism. They dismissed more and more Brexit scenarios as BRINO: "Brexit in Name Only". Now, the only acceptable form of Brexit appears to be a hard Brexit, the harder the better. If it won't scratch diamond, it's not Brexit.

This change in attitudes to Brexit wasn't driven by the wider population, but by a small number of politicians and their media backers. If anything, the mood in the country has swung the other way. Polls show that the appetite for Remain overtook Leave soon after the referendum. Remain has stayed ahead almost ever since; it now maintains a comfortable lead.[25]

Only a minority want Brexit at any cost. By rights they shouldn't be setting the agenda for everyone else. Unfortunately, Boris Johnson chose to stuff his Cabinet with Brexit believers. They have their hands on the levers of power and can almost taste their dream Brexit.

Thousands of hours of video and millions of words dating from the referendum campaign are available to prove those who wanted us out of the EU supported a wide range of positions. They never came close to coalescing around just one. Yet the loudest voices now profess to know what everyone voted for when they voted Leave. "We all chose time travel." (Meaning: "I chose time travel and I want it very, very much.") Their vision of Brexit is the One True Brexit. A patently false claim.

We are more stuck than a leaky tube of glue. Politicians generally want to implement the referendum result, but the only options left on the table are unrealistic or damaging.

One pragmatic approach would be to call a halt to Brexit. MPs could look the British population in the eye and tell us the truth: "We tried. We really did. We spent billions of pounds and millions of hours on getting ready for Brexit. But we still can't agree on a course of action. And all the evidence suggests that every form of Brexit will damage the UK to some extent. There seem to be no good Brexits. That's why, with the greatest reluctance, we are revoking Article 50 and staying in." Such a move would clear the logjam that has brought politics to a standstill these last three years. The issue of Brexit would not go away (the Brexit Party would see to that). But we would gain precious time. Time for reflection. Time to reach out across parties and all four nations of the UK to determine what Brexit would make the most sense. Time for proper planning. Time for politicians to start fixing the UK and concentrating on huge challenges such as climate change.

A second referendum might also offer a route out of our current impasse as long as it steered clear of the mistakes of the first. All choices on the ballot paper would have to be logical and achievable. The defined Leave option would need to have the support of a majority of MPs and of the EU too. This would guarantee that if Leave won again, we could proceed with Brexit without delay.

In other words, it would no longer be a choice between "staying in or going out". It might be "staying in or going to watch Avengers: Endgame" or "staying in or visiting Alton Towers". If the vote is to stay in, we know what that means. If it is to leave, we know what that means too: a blockbuster with popcorn, or an afternoon of roller-coaster rides.

No more prevarication. No more uncertainty.

We made a big mistake once. Let's own up and try to fix it, rather than repeat it again.

Leave exploited a deliberate absence of plans.

In advance of a General Election, all major parties release manifestos setting out what they will do if elected. These are substantial documents, not something dashed off at the kitchen table. They cover a wide range of issues, with key policies costed. Manifestos are seen as pledges to the electorate. Inevitably, some commitments they make fall by the wayside and become "broken promises". But anyone who takes the time to read these competing visions understands what they're voting for. They know their cross on the ballot paper should mean more money for the NHS, school reform, or a higher minimum wage – if their party wins.

The Brexit referendum was completely different.

The Liberal Democrats, Labour, the SNP, the Green Party and Plaid Cymru were all in the Remain camp. The governing Conservative party took a neutral stance; David Cameron allowed individual MPs to campaign for either outcome.[26] Most Tory MPs sided with Remain, including 23 out of 30 Cabinet ministers.[27] UKIP was the main political party on the Leave side, as was the DUP in Northern Ireland. (A few Labour MPs went against their party's official stance and sided with Leave too.)

This meant most advocates for Leave were not part of the Government going into the referendum. And since the referendum didn't involve any political realignment, they knew they would have no responsibility for implementing the outcome of the vote.

Remain had no plan. In fairness, it didn't need one. Had Remain won, life would have continued as usual on the morning of 24 June. The UK would have maintained its existing EU relationship. It would have confronted all the same issues of inequality, austerity, homelessness etc. as the night before. And the Eurosceptics would still have been grumpy about Europe. In short, nothing would have changed.

Leave had no plan either. Faisal Islam spoke to a pro-Leave Conservative MP within 48 hours of the referendum result. "I said to him, so where's the plan? Can we see the Brexit plan now?" The MP replied: "There is no plan. The Leave campaign don't have a post-Brexit plan." Pointing towards the Houses of Parliament: "Number 10 should have had a plan."[28]

But those in Government didn't see it as their responsibility to plan for an outcome they were campaigning hard against. As George Osborne told LBC: "Britain does not have a plan for Brexit. It's not for me to come up with [Leave's] plan."[29]

Adding to the confusion, there wasn't just one Leave campaign. Instead, a wide range of entities competed to espouse leaving the EU. Vote Leave was the official Leave campaign group, as designated by the Electoral Commission. But there were other major Leave groups too, such as Leave.EU, an organisation with deep pockets bankrolled by Arron Banks.

Each one offered different, often contradictory, visions of life outside of the EU. They had immense freedom, because they knew they wouldn't have to implement the referendum result. It's easy to say whatever takes your fancy when someone else has to face the consequences.

Dominic Cummings, who would later become Vote Leave's Campaign Director and is now Boris Johnson's closest advisor, made much the same point in a 2015 blog post about a (then) hypothetical referendum: "Does [the leaving the EU camp] need to have a unified plan for exit? There is much to be gained by swerving the whole issue." He expanded on the notion: "Different people have different ideas about the best way to leave. For example, some people suggest we should leave the EU but simply remain in the Single Market while we negotiate a new deal. Others have different ideas. Global rules set by the World Trade Organisation provide some guarantees against European countries discriminating against British trade. But none of this is the real point. We are not a Government. We can't negotiate anything."[30]

Or, as Tony Travers (a professor of government at the London School of Economics) put it to the New York Times less than a week after the referendum: "There was no coherence, because it wasn't a political party fighting for government, but an odd coalition fighting against something, but with no consistent view of what it was fighting for."[31]

(There were many Remain groups too, but they sang largely from the same hymn book because Remain so clearly meant the then status quo. They differed mainly in their approach to trying to convince voters to back Remain.)

Consider the Scottish independence referendum of 2014. In its run-up, the SNP produced a 650 page white paper that explained much of the detail of how leaving the UK might work.[32] Some criticised its lack of specificity over matters such as the plan for sterling. But it was a clear, coherent document. Voters knew what they were being offered.

In the Brexit referendum by contrast, the claims made by the various Leave campaigns blurred together like a massive Rorschach inkblot. Voters could see whatever they liked in it. That gave Leave a unique advantage by allowing it to unite factions that were not natural bedfellows. Leave drew in those who wanted to leave the EU but remain very close to it, those who wanted a clean break, even those who chose it as a form of protest at David Cameron's government.

If a manifesto represents what a party commits to doing if elected, what should we call the pledges made by those who knew in advance they would be in no position to deliver anything they were promising? Lies? Confidence tricks? Serving suggestions?

Although his comment caused controversy, European Council President Donald Tusk summed things up beautifully when he said in February 2019: "By the way, I've been wondering what that special place in hell looks like for those who promoted Brexit without even a sketch of a plan how to carry it out safely."[33]

Will of the people? More of a suggestion really...

We need to briefly address the advisory nature of the referendum.

There is no doubt that the referendum was advisory from the standpoint of UK law, i.e. the government has no legal obligation to implement the result.[34]

By default, UK referendums are *always* advisory. Explicit provision has to be made in legislation to ensure they are binding.[35] The European Union Referendum Act 2015 which underpinned the Brexit vote did not contain such a provision.[36] As the Briefing Paper that accompanied the bill which became the Act noted: "This Bill requires a referendum to be held on the question of the UK's continued membership of the European Union (EU) before the end of 2017. It does not contain any requirement for the UK Government to implement the results of the referendum, nor set a time limit by which a vote to leave the EU should be implemented. Instead, this is a type of referendum known as pre-legislative or consultative, which enables the electorate to voice an opinion which then influences the Government in its policy decisions."[37]

But there's more to life than the law, though lawyers might be loathe to admit it:

- A 2010 report by the House of Lords Constitution Committee into the conduct of referendums in the UK stated: "it would be difficult for Parliament to ignore a decisive expression of public opinion."[38]

- The leaflet distributed to all households in advance of the 2016 vote included the phrase: "The Government will implement what you decide."[39]

- The Attorney General, Geoffrey Cox, observed in Parliament on 25 September 2019: "The law in relation to the referendum is that it was not binding upon this Parliament. It was binding in every moral sense upon those who promised the British people it would be implemented. But it was not binding as a matter of law."[40]

In other words, the referendum result places a non-legal but still real obligation on the government to try to implement the outcome.

This means that...

A) Anyone who says that the referendum is legally binding and must therefore be enacted is either misinformed or lying.

B) Anyone who says that the referendum result can simply be ignored is liable to meet the freight train of public perception head on.

Our stated commitment to leave can be legally overturned. As we will see later, the ECJ's finding on Article 50 provides a mechanism to do just that. But any such attempt is likely to incur huge PR and other consequences. There needs to be an ironclad mechanism to check that such a reversal is acceptable. A second referendum, for example. Or a general election in which parties that favour remaining in the EU win a majority of seats.

There's a nasty stain on my nice new referendum result.

Although the Government has committed to implementing the referendum result, it is not clear it should be bound by the outcome at all given the many irregularities on the Leave side. Within days of winning, prominent Leave campaigners backed away from the infamous message on the side of the Vote Leave bus. ("We send the EU £350 million a week. Let's fund our NHS instead.")

Then a flood of questions began to pour in about the referendum itself. About Cambridge Analytica's use of personal data, harvested in bulk from social media. About possible Russian interference. About spending irregularities involving various core Leave campaign groups. About dubious sources of campaign funds. Here are some of the highlights:

- In May 2018, the Electoral Commission (EC) fined Leave.EU £70,000 for multiple breaches of electoral law, including overspending.[41] (Both sides in the referendum faced strict limits on what they could spend.)

- In July 2018, the EC fined Vote Leave £61,000 and referred several matters to the police.[42] Vote Leave appealed against the EC's findings but dropped its appeal in March 2019. A spokesperson for the Electoral Commission said: "Vote Leave was the designated lead campaigner for the leave outcome at the referendum. We found that it broke the electoral rules set out by Parliament to ensure fairness, confidence and legitimacy at an electoral event. Serious offences such as these undermine public confidence in our system and it is vital, therefore, that they are properly investigated and sanctioned."[43]

- In October 2018, the Information Commissioner's Office (ICO) fined Facebook £500,000 for their joint responsibility in enabling personal data to be syphoned from 87 million of its users.[44] Some of this data was later found to have been used by entities connected with the Leave side in the referendum.

- In February 2019, ICO fined Leave.EU £45,000 for sending unsolicited direct marketing emails without obtaining the necessary consent.[45] In a separate enforcement action, it fined Leave.EU £15,000 for sending almost 300,000 unsolicited communications in a single day.[46] It also informed Leave.EU that it faced an audit into its data protection practices.[47]

- In March 2019, ICO fined Vote Leave £40,000 for sending 196,154 unsolicited text messages during the 2016 referendum campaign.[48]

- ICO also undertook a wide range of investigatory and enforcement actions against other companies and entities connected with the Leave campaign, some of which are still ongoing. These were detailed in its report to Parliament in November 2018.[49]

Many of the issues touched on above are still being investigated. The wheels of justice may grind exceedingly fine. Unfortunately, they also turn at a glacial pace. We are likely to leave the EU long before a line can be drawn under every last allegation of wrongdoing. But international treaties don't come with rewind buttons. So once Brexit day has passed, the inquiry outcomes will mainly be of relevance to historians. Even in the extreme case that the referendum is declared so tainted as to be void, we will still be out of the EU.

That's not to suggest that justice should not be served. Each allegation must be pursued to the full. But we should be under no illusions about the impact doing so will have on the referendum's consequences: none whatsoever.

Remain were not snow-pure either. Various minor irregularities were noted and some small fines levied. None of the problems uncovered were of the same order of magnitude as those identified in entities associated with Leave.

It is imprudent to dwell on these matters further here given that investigations are still running. One day, a definitive account may be produced of the conduct of the referendum. We may well look back in shock at how dirty the campaign was. But it will be cold comfort to know that the perpetrators of illegal acts were finally held to account. Because they will already have got what they were after.

The ref may have been nobbled and the tactics underhand, but the game still produced a result. We are where we are.

So where does the referendum leave us?

- We had an advisory-yet-binding vote, conducted under murky circumstances.
- No specific actionable outcome of Brexit was ever defined.
- The desired course of action remains disputed to this day.
- We have an electorate split down the middle and constantly at each other's throats.

After such a promising start, how could anything else possibly go wrong?

What has the EU ever done for us?

We have a share and a major say in the policies of the largest and strongest trading block in the world. It can be hard to grasp how unique the EU is because it's all around us. We're so used to the freedoms it gives us, we have stopped acknowledging them. But there is no other construct like it anywhere else. No other group of countries allows its citizens to work, live, travel and settle freely in each other's territories. Nor firms to trade goods and services without any barriers across such a wide market.

Much of the discussion surrounding Brexit centres around the financial. As noted earlier, this is because everything we should be doing as a country (improving the NHS, boosting police numbers, tackling mental health, etc.) requires the means to do so. It's perhaps also because economic effects are easier to predict, measure and understand than, for example, sociopolitical change.

But our membership of the EU is about more than pounds and pence. It is about the things we take for granted, like peace and stability. And it's about the things we don't even realise the EU is doing for us, like protecting the quality of the air we breathe and the cleanliness of our beaches.

In the tradition of Monty Python's "What have the Romans ever done for us?" sketch, it's time to take a stroll through a couple of key aspects of our EU membership.

Peace

Peace is at the heart of the EU's raison d'etre.

Over the centuries, we've been rubbish at getting along with our Continental neighbours. A lot of blood has been spilled. In respites between battles, we watched from the sidelines as other European nations fought each other.

But since the horrors of WW2, there has never been a conflict between states of what is now the EU. (The atrocious wars in the Balkans in the early 1990s were civil wars.) This long period of peace came about by design, not by accident. When the European Community (precursor of the EU) was set up in the 1950s, it was with the overt aim of intertwining the affairs of its members to such an extent that war between them became unthinkable. The idea was that countries which traded together and worked together and pooled their strength in common cause would be much less likely to fight each other.

The concept worked. Peace has become the norm, so much so that we rarely consider just how unusual the lengthy period of calm we live in is by historical standards. The EU even won the Nobel Prize in 2012 in recognition for its role in preserving what has been dubbed the Pax Europaea.[50] Nowadays, the closest we get to war in Europe is the parade of films glorifying our past victories, and Dad's Army as a fixture on TV.

But the world is getting darker. Russia is exerting itself again, and China is flexing its muscles. The USA has largely abandoned its role as global policeman. Against such a geopolitical backdrop, European peace, assured by EU membership, has never been more important.

Freedom of Movement

Freedom of movement is a core aspect of EU membership and one of the indivisible "4 freedoms" of the EU project. It lets us live, work, study and retire in the EU. With a British passport, you're good to go. No complex immigration processes, no paperwork, no hassle.

Freedom of movement lets UK holidaymakers travel in the other 27 EU countries with ease:

- They don't need a visa, and can use the "EU Citizen" lanes at the border.
- UK driving licenses are valid across the EU, and UK car insurance provides the necessary cover to drive on the Continent.
- They can use their mobile phone without paying extra roaming charges for calls, texts or data. Under the EU's "roam like at home" rules, the costs are the same as if they were in the UK.
- If they fall ill or need hospital treatment, they can show a European Health Insurance Card and receive free or discounted care. (This is of enormous value to dialysis patients, who can holiday abroad without worrying about exorbitant costs.)
- They can binge their favourite shows on Netflix, play their music on Spotify, and access other streaming services. (EU law forbids firms from discriminating between local users and those travelling from other EU states.)
- Four-legged friends can come too using the simplified pet passport scheme.
- If something goes wrong with a flight, they can claim a fixed amount of compensation based on the EU's Air Passenger Rights.

Freedom of movement enables UK citizens to work anywhere in the EU. You don't need a visa or a prior job offer to move to another EU country and start working. Instead of being limited to the UK job market, people can go wherever their skills are in demand or wherever they simply fancy living. This is a boon for younger workers looking for a good start in life. For example, they can join a tech start-up in Berlin or Barcelona as easily as one in Birmingham. Those with professional qualifications, such as accountants and lawyers, can take advantage of the EU's mutual recognition rules to offer their services anywhere. EU law protects them once they find work because companies are forbidden from treating workers from other EU states differently from their own nationals when it comes to pay and working conditions.

British firms can send employees abroad for a few days – or a few years – without having to deal with a stack of paperwork. UK citizens can set up companies overseas and open local bank accounts. And they don't have to go alone. Freedom of movement rules apply to family members and dependants too.

Through freedom of movement, the whole of the EU has become like a series of interconnecting rooms. We can move between countries as easily as passing from the dining room to the kitchen, and back again. We can go as we please anywhere in the house, spending as long as we like in any room.

We enjoy a wide range of privileges in the rest of the EU, and EU citizens are accorded the same ones here. Friends, family, colleagues and neighbours from the EU enrich our society and add diversity. They fill vital jobs in understaffed industries and take on work we do not care to do.

Note that freedom of movement and open borders are not the same thing. Within the Schengen Area, people can travel between countries without showing documentation. But the UK is not in Schengen. We check passports and other travel documents at our own borders so we know exactly who is coming in and going out. It is also worth noting that the UK will not have to join Schengen in the future because we have a firm opt-out from that aspect of the EU.

What Remainers are fighting for

"You lost. Get over it." is a common chorus in certain Leave circles. It paints Remainers as sore losers harping on about a football match that ended the wrong way three years ago. ("Why are they *still* going on about it?")

This narrative ignores the massive levels of public concern swirling around Brexit. Never before have so many fought a political decision with such single-minded passion for so long.

Expecting Remainers to get over Brexit is like expecting them to ignore the impending loss of a limb. Brexit isn't a game. It's very real. And it's very frightening. They're not upset because they lost. They're worried, angry and terrified *because of what Brexit is doing to their country*.

Remainers are battling to save jobs and businesses. Defending themselves, family, friends, colleagues and neighbours from a hostile immigration environment. Striving to preserve the Irish peace process and the integrity of the Union. Fighting for the future of their children and grandchildren.

They know if things go wrong once we are out of the EU, there will be no going back on the decision to leave. Unlike the outcome of a general election, we can't reverse Brexit after a few years. To paraphrase the famous slogan about a dog: Brexit is for life, not just for Christmas.[51]

Remainers dread what Brexit will bring. And they burn with white-hot fury at those willing to heap the horrors of no deal on everyone in the UK, and on British citizens in the EU.

It would be a different story if Brexit were only going to affect those who voted to Leave. But it will impact everyone from newborns to centenarians, with no regard for their politics. It will also harm UK citizens in the EU, EU citizens here, and our European allies.

Perhaps greater understanding might prompt greater empathy. With that in mind, here's a whistle-stop tour of Remain concerns. Some apply to all Brexit scenarios, others in the case of no deal.

Now, it may be tempting to dismiss the below as more "Project Fear". But there's a world of difference between the following two warnings:

- "Be careful when you go out or you might break your leg."
- "Be careful when you go out. There's black ice along the pavement all the way to the newsagents. Wouldn't want you to break your leg."

The first example is Project Fear, the second explains why the concern is legitimate. And so it is with Brexit. The loss of our treaties and trade agreements with the EU has clear consequences leading to undeniable problems. And it's an absolute given that we *will* lose them when we leave.

The economy

Loss of our existing trade deals: We have an unbeatable trade deal with the EU itself. We also share in dozens of trade deals with other countries (Canada, Japan, South Korea etc.) as EU members. In the event of no deal, we will have to rely on weak WTO terms for trade with the entire world.

Complex customs procedures and costly red tape: At present, exporters sending their wares to the EU don't have to do much more than pop their goods on a lorry and wave it goodbye. After a no deal Brexit, they will face stringent new customs processes. They will have to assign commodity codes to everything they're sending and fill out export declarations. They will have to declare all exports to HMRC and attach commercial invoices. They will need to present goods and paperwork to customs. (Many shipments will be subject to inspection.) They will then have to submit a departure message to HMRC's CHIEF system. Finally, firms will have to keep six years worth of records.[52] A similar level of complexity will apply to imports. HMRC estimates new red tape resulting from Brexit will cost UK firms trading with the EU an extra £7.5 billion a year. EU firms will also face similar costs on their transactions with us. These costs (in total, more than we pay for our EU membership) are likely to fall on businesses and consumers.[53]

New tariffs on exports: UK-made goods do not incur tariffs when exported to the EU, or to the many countries the EU has trade deals with. This will change in a no-deal situation. Overnight, we will become subject to WTO-level tariffs. These range from 0% on some products to over 50% on certain agricultural goods.

Collapse of the pound: The value of the pound has fallen significantly since the referendum. Brexit will likely see it fall further. Many analysts believe it could drop to parity with the US dollar in a no-deal situation. (It has never been that low before.)

Failure of large-scale UK manufacturing: Sectors from automotive to aerospace rely on just-in-time delivery of parts and materials. Firms often keep only a few hours' worth of components on hand. They've never needed more because our ports have been free-flowing for decades. Their business model will break if Brexit introduces significant logistics delays. It's just too expensive to build and stock warehouses with large amounts of inventory. They will have to consider drastic options, such as moving production elsewhere in the EU. (Hundreds of manufacturing companies have tried to warn of this danger ever since the referendum.)

Sudden spike in the cost of living: The Government has confirmed that a no deal Brexit will bring food, fuel and energy price rises. It acknowledges that the burden will fall most heavily on the poor.[54] The falling pound will push up the cost of imported goods.

Lower direct investment: When we're no longer a gateway to Europe, the UK will be less attractive to overseas firms, especially if they face tariffs and other barriers to setting up shop here. Why would they pick us over the remaining 27 EU countries in such circumstances?

Rising national debt: The falling pound will make servicing our national debt more expensive. At the same time, the Government has indicated it plans a stimulus package in the event of no deal. This will add to our overall debt at a time when we were just beginning to balance our nation's finances.

Destruction of parts of the UK agricultural sector:

- Farmers rely on tens of thousands of seasonal migrants from the EU to pick crops and gather the harvest. There is already clear evidence of workforce shortages. After Brexit, with a harsher immigration regime in place, these will get much worse.
- After a no deal Brexit, WTO tariffs will make exporting many agricultural products uneconomical. Beef and lamb farmers will be amongst the worst affected. They will not be able to survive with their main export market closed off.
- After a no deal Brexit, we will no longer have an automatic right to land fish in EU ports. (We export two thirds of all the fish we catch to the EU.)

Departure of financial firms: Financial passporting allows firms in any EU country to sell their services all over the EU. Once we leave the EU, UK firms will lose access to the passporting regime unless we can reach a deal to preserve it. Already, many banks and investment firms have established branches elsewhere in the EU. They have also moved over

£1 trillion of assets and 7,000 jobs away from the City of London.[55] Many are waiting for Brexit to become clear before making major moves. Once Brexit happens, nothing will stop them executing their contingency plans.

Rise in bankruptcies: The level of UK bankruptcies is at its highest for several years.[56] It has kept rising since the referendum. From the potential for disruption outlined above, it's clear this trend is likely to accelerate rather than reverse after Brexit.

Widespread job losses: Brexit will bring job losses to manufacturing, agriculture, financial services and other sectors. Firms will not be able to absorb the burden of new red tape, transport delays and changes in regulations and tariffs. They will have to make cost savings. The obvious place to start will be payroll. It is quicker and easier to cut staff than it is to shutter factories.

Shortages and privations

Food shortages and restricted choice: The UK government has acknowledged that a no deal Brexit is likely to impact the supply of fresh food, much of which we import from the EU.[57] Transit delays will mean that produce arrives less fresh, and some things will no longer be viable to transport. Overall, there should be enough to keep us fed, but we will have less choice. As Dominic Raab put it when he was still Brexit secretary: "We will look at the issue in the round, and make sure there is adequate food supply."[58] Or as Michael Gove stated more recently: "Everyone will have the food they need."[59] Which is not the same as saying they'll be able to buy the food they *want*.

Disrupted medical supplies: We import 37 million packs of medicine from the EU each month. No deal Brexit disruptions at the ports will affect this supply.[60] The Government is preparing to activate a serious shortage protocol. It will order pharmacies to issue alternative prescriptions, different strength formulations or smaller batches.[61] Some medicines with short shelf lives will be flown in. The Government acknowledges that these measures may be insufficient to alleviate all shortages.[62] The EU faces issues too. We export around half a billion packs of medicine a year, worth £12 billion. Regulatory changes and customs delays may interrupt this supply. They could also affect the drug precursors used to manufacture medicines.

No money to reverse the cuts in public services: Boris Johnson has declared his ambition to put more police on the streets, and pump funds into education and other sectors. But if Brexit constrains public finances, these spending plans will have to be put on hold. As the Tories used to be fond of repeating: "There is no magic money tree."[63]

A return to austerity: Thanks to Boris Johnson's willingness to dip into the Treasury's wallet, we are starting to see the back of the Tory austerity project. But Brexit will mean a lower tax take. Company profits will fall, reducing corporation tax, and there will be fewer people in work and paying income tax. With less money in their pockets, consumers will spend less, meaning less VAT will get collected. The burden on the public purse will rise as the ranks of the unemployed swell. All these factors imply more cuts to keep the nation's finances balanced. Austerity may return with a vengeance.

Potential benefits to leaving the EU

Our impending departure from the EU isn't all bad news. There are potential upsides to Brexit too, depending on the nature of the eventual deal we reach (or the absence of one). But it's too simplistic to record them all as straightforward wins. Change often comes at a cost. It is important to consider the overall balance, and highlight the consequences alongside the gains.

Control over taxation: We will have greater freedom to set taxes, including corporation tax levels. We would be free to turn ourselves into a low tax jurisdiction like Singapore to attract more foreign firms. Such an approach risks antagonising the EU, which could sour negotiations on our future relationship. It would also mean foregoing some Government revenue. Alternatively, we could decide to raise corporation tax to pay for more public services. We could also reduce or get rid of VAT on things like domestic gas and electricity, though at the cost of less money to the Treasury.

Ability to vary product safety standards: Outside the EU, we will no longer be subject to EU standards on product safety. We can set our own rules instead. Note that if we lower domestic standards below the EU's own then UK manufacturers may be prevented from exporting their products to the EU (assuming they only produce to our lowered standards).

Independent trade policies: We will be able to strike our own trade deals rather than limit ourselves to the EU's existing ones. However, we will lose all our existing trade deals when we Brexit. So there will be a huge amount of ground to make up before our situation improves over where it stands at the moment.

Control over tariffs: In the case of a no deal Brexit, we could reduce or eliminate tariffs on products we don't make or grow in the UK. This would make such imported products cheaper. (Note that our exporters would face tariffs for the first time on much of their exports.)

Tailor our farming sector to our needs: The EU prevents farmers from growing genetically modified crops. We could decide to relax our rules on GM farming. Free of the Common Agriculture Policy, we can choose rules and subsidies more appropriate to our situation. Of course, farmers would take a financial hit if our current Government (or a future one) cuts the level of subsidies to the sector below EU levels.

Set our own food production standards: We could relax our food hygiene and animal welfare standards to make it easier to import food from the rest of the world. Many countries do not produce to the high standard the EU requires, so we cannot import from them while we're an EU member. By relaxing our rules, we could gain access to cheaper food. We would also face a greater risk of food poisoning. Significant ethical concerns could surround lowered animal welfare standards.

Flexibility in public subsidies: We would face fewer restrictions on the public subsidy of companies and sectors. This could make it easier to rescue failing businesses, and to nationalise certain industries. (By doing so, we would be exposed to the possibility of disputes at the WTO.)

Control of immigration: We will be able to formulate our own immigration policy, based on our unique requirements. If we want, we can put people from the EU and the rest of the world on an equal footing.

(Note however we already have more control of EU immigration than we choose to exercise.) Or we can favour immigrants from Commonwealth nations to tighten historic links. We can also offer generous visa terms to those we particularly want to attract to the UK, such as scientists and students.

Break-up of the UK: Brexit is a gift to those who favour an independent Scotland. As the SNP never miss an opportunity to remind us, Scotland voted 62% to stay in the EU.[64] Support for independence fell after the 2014 Scottish referendum. It has risen again as Brexit Day approaches, though it is bubbling under the 50% mark. The closer we come to a hard Brexit outcome, the more impetus it gives those who want to take Scotland out of the UK and (back) into the EU. Wales is agitating to strike out on its own too. A recent poll put support for Welsh independence at 41%, the highest in history. And then there's Northern Ireland. Any change in the status of the Irish border could bring renewed calls for reunification. And that would have profound negative consequences for the peace process. Whether such drives for independence represent a benefit or not will depend on your perspective and where you live.

Fading Euroscepticism: Once we are out of the EU, there will be no need to blame the EU for all our ills. Indeed, it would be illogical to do so. Distrust of Europe has poisoned the Tory party for close to half a century. If it survives Brexit, the party may end up looking very different.

The return of duty-free shopping: The Government recently began an ad campaign to promote duty-free shopping after a no deal Brexit. Passengers headed for the EU will be able to buy their personal allowance worth of beer, spirits, wine and tobacco without duty being applied in the UK, much as they can now for non-EU destinations.[65] This would mean less revenue to the Treasury i.e. the Government would in effect be subsidising cheaper booze and cigarettes. (Something health campaigners have expressed concern about.[66])

Greater awareness of the divisions in society: The 2016 referendum was a vote to leave the EU. But it was also a cry for help from many who felt left behind. The Tory austerity project has bitten deep over the last decade. Wages have stagnated in the public sector. There's less funding for the police, schools, local councils and so many other things. The switch to Universal Credit has affected millions. The referendum shook politicians out of cosy complacency and forced them to sit up and take notice.

Boost to UK manufacturers focused solely on the domestic market: New tariffs and the introduction of non-tariff barriers after a no deal Brexit could favour domestic producers selling exclusively to the home market. As the cost of imported goods rises, firms able to source all raw materials in the UK and manufacture here will benefit because their wares will be cheaper by comparison.

Higher revenue for exporters not subject to tariffs: A falling pound will make UK-produced goods more affordable for foreign buyers. This will benefit British exporters in sectors not subject to tariffs. The pound has already devalued substantially since the referendum. Market watchers expect it could fall to parity with the dollar after a no deal Brexit.

Less red tape for some domestic firms: Domestic companies may have to contend with fewer EU regulations as the UK Government will be able to simplify or eliminate some rules. Note however that Brexit will increase the administrative burden on importers and exporters, and on other firms doing business overseas.

Boost to domestic tourism: The falling pound will make the UK a more attractive destination for foreign holidaymakers. It will also make overseas holidays less affordable for UK consumers (who will also have to contend with the impact of Brexit on travel arrangements when they visit the EU). These twin factors should translate into an increased interest in UK destinations and a boost to the domestic tourism sector. Note: the UK hospitality trade currently depends to a large extent on EU staff (15% of sector workers across the UK and 40% in London hail from the EU). So any new immigration rules will need to take this into consideration.[67]

Decreasing carbon emissions: The rising cost of fuel will cut UK demand for flights. And the projected industrial slowdown will reduce factory emissions. The latter reduction will become permanent if large swathes of manufacturing move abroad. An economic slowdown hurts people yet is good for the planet. People with less money travel less. They buy less too, further reducing their carbon footprint. This is the perfect example of a double-edged sword effect of Brexit.

Potential ban on live animal exports: The UK cannot ban the export of live animals as an EU member. Freedom of movement rules and existing UK legislation prevent us from doing so. The UK Government may choose to introduce new restrictions after Brexit, though there is some doubt over the impact of WTO rules. It is also likely that farmers could see their business damaged as a result of tighter regulations.[68]

Blue passports: Included for completeness as Nigel Farage and others raised the matter as an issue during the referendum campaign.[69] In fact, we could have had blue passports any time we liked. The burgundy colour was an EU recommendation, never a binding rule.

Retain the EU membership fee: We currently send £9 billion net to the EU each year. After Brexit, once we have paid off what we owe the EU, that money will be available to spend on other things.

Note that Brexit is likely to create much more than £9 billion a year in new costs for UK firms and consumers. HMRC projects the burden of new red tape on importers and exporters alone will hit £7.5 billion a year.[70] Many companies will have to duplicate chemical testing, trademark registrations, product safety certifications and countless other administrative tasks.

That said, it won't be the UK Government picking up the tab for all those added costs. So the nation's finances will improve to the tune of up to £9 billion, even though the UK as a whole ends up worse off by more than that. An odd state of affairs that looks suspiciously like a massive stealth tax.

A return to imperial measures: Should we so desire, we will be able to go back to measuring things in pounds, ounces and pints. Of course, if we want to export to the EU after Brexit, we will still need to label certain products in metric units. Their system's not changing just because we're leaving.

End European Court of Justice jurisdiction over the UK: Once we're out of the EU, the ECJ will no longer have a say over issues affecting the UK. The ECJ is the highest court in Europe. It interprets EU law on behalf of national courts and issues binding judgements. It also resolves disputes between EU parties, including member states and institutions. Once out of the ECJ's remit, we will have full control over our own laws. Our Supreme Court will become the highest legal authority. (It already is for matters of domestic law, such as the recent prorogation case.)

Take back control of our waters: After a no deal Brexit, we will be out of the Common Fisheries Policy. We will have jurisdiction over UK waters, and will be able to prevent EU fishermen from fishing there. Of course, UK fishermen will no longer have access to EU waters.

Greater tolerance for immigrants: Surveys since the referendum have recorded a marked improvement in the UK's overall attitude to immigrants.[71] This may be because the focus on EU citizens' rights and the impact of our impeding departure on the supply of workers have given many a greater appreciation of the contribution of immigrants to our society. (There has also been a rise in hate crime. A tiny minority, emboldened by the referendum result, have stepped up their vile attacks.)

Other effects of Brexit

The examples below are harder to describe as benefits. They are nevertheless worth recording since they also result from our decision to leave the EU.

Increased business for the insurance industry: We will lose access to the European Health Insurance Card scheme after Brexit.[72] Travellers to the EU will have to buy comprehensive insurance to cover their medical needs. (Those requiring oxygen provision or kidney dialysis will be the most affected as the EHIC scheme covers both procedures.)

Happy hedge funds: Hedge funds and vulture capitalists are gearing up to profit from Brexit chaos. They have placed bets against the UK to the tune of billions of pounds. These bets or "shorts" will pay out if the British economy collapses. One key player is Crispin Odey, who boasted of having made £220 million on the night of the 2016 referendum.[73] He has reportedly upped his position to £300 million ahead of Brexit Day.[74]

The decline of the Brexit Party: Once Brexit is over, interest in the Brexit Party is likely to fade. Although it is not a single issue party, Brexit is its main reason for existing. The clue's in the name. So nobody should be surprised if support for the BP dwindles once we are out of the EU. The BP, along with its UKIP precursor, will have had a greater impact on the UK than any other party in modern times. Give Nigel Farage his due. He can ride off into the sunset knowing he was responsible for affecting the way of life of everyone in Britain for generations to come.

Boom time for lawyers: Law firms have seen a significant uptick in business as a direct result of Brexit. Rearranging corporate relationships is a complex, expensive process. For instance, they have profited from the take-up of Part VII asset transfers in the insurance industry. Firms have sought assistance to move head offices or establish subsidiaries in the EU. They are having to secure intellectual property all over again, recertify products and duplicate other legal work. Family lawyers are keeping busy too. The changing status of EU citizens in the UK and UK citizens in the EU has thrown up many edge cases. Some people are having to engage legal counsel at a cost of thousands of pounds.

Loss of European Court of Justice jurisdiction over the UK: UK citizens will lose access to the European Commission's free complaints procedure. (It allows them to report the UK Government for breaching EU law, e.g. if it fails its environmental obligations.) UK individuals and companies in the EU will find themselves with fewer rights. They will no longer be able to take matters to the ECJ if things go wrong.

Future ECJ rulings will no longer apply to us, though we may opt to transcribe them into domestic law. This will give us more flexibility, but may come at the cost of the protections afforded workers. (The ECJ has found many times for workers, including laws to guarantee equal pay for work of equal value, to prohibit discrimination on the grounds of pregnancy or maternity leave, and to require companies to log work hours accurately to enforce a maximum 48 hour working week.)

Foreign firms pounce on juicy British targets: As the value of the pound drops further, we can expect overseas players to bargain-shop promising UK companies.[75] Boris Johnson's government appears set to facilitate this trend by adopting a more liberal view of overseas mergers.[76]

Removal of a thorn in the EU's side: It's fair to say that the EU is genuinely sorry to see us go. But we must also acknowledge our long-standing role as troublemakers. Brexit MEPs in Brussels persist in disrupting proceedings, as did UKIP ones before them. It is hard to believe that Nigel Farage will be missed given his outbursts in the European Parliament. The UK has often stood in the way of initiatives meant to bring EU members closer together. We have also demanded (and been granted) more concessions and special treatment than most other EU members have.

End of two-party politics: The rise of the Brexit Party and the resurgence of the LibDems have changed the political landscape. The Tories and Labour can no longer count on taking the majority of seats in a General Election. Some suggest it will be very hard for any party to secure a majority under first past the post now that the vote is being split four ways. The European elections in May 2019 signposted this change. The Brexit Party and LibDems made huge gains. Labour and the Conservatives got pushed into third and fifth place respectively. We may see renewed calls for electoral reform, such as a move towards proportional representation. If that happens, politics as usual will be dead and buried.

A renewed intellectualism: The last few years have seen a turning away from experts. Their warnings have been derided or ignored. Ministers have claimed to know more than captains of industry about the latter's businesses. Should the worst or even moderate fears of Remainers come true, the backlash could be swift. The electorate will realise the duplicity of those who understood little or nothing of what they preached. The pendulum may swing away from empty rhetoric, gut instinct and fighting talk, and back to paying attention to those with real-world knowledge.

The EU's Customs Union and Single Market in brief

Since we seem about to turn our backs on the customs union and the single market in pursuit of Brexit, it is important to understand what it is we will be giving up.

What is the Customs Union?

The customs union lets EU members trade goods with each other without restrictions:

- No taxes on imports and exports to worry about, i.e. no tariffs.
- No limits on the amount of goods that can be traded, i.e. no quotas.
- No complicated paperwork, because there are no internal customs checks. Load up a lorry and get going. (Within the Schengen Area, which covers almost the whole of the continental EU, trucks don't even slow as they whizz past borders.)

The customs union imposes a common external tariff (CET) on imports from non-member countries. Under the CET system, individual EU states don't set their own tariffs and quotas. Instead, they all share the same ones. This means EU countries don't have to worry about undercutting each other. There's no incentive to import goods through one or other country since the same tariff is payable anywhere in the EU. This helps to keep economic relations between member states harmonious.

Firms importing goods from outside the EU must pay the correct tariffs, based on country of origin and any free trade agreements in place. Once the goods have legally entered the EU, they can be moved anywhere else in the EU without hindrance. Why? Because every EU country knows the right tariff has already been collected on them. This does away with the need to recheck anything. You can think of the CET system like an amusement park with an entry fee, but no fee for the individual rides. You can enter via any ticket gate (EU country) and once inside you can go anywhere in the park without paying more.

While this arrangement simplifies trade between EU members, it also means that they cannot conduct their own trade negotiations. Since all tariffs and other trade barriers are set at EU level, there's nothing for individual states to negotiate.

A related consideration: rules of origin

Rules of origin specify which country produced certain goods i.e. what their "economic nationality" is. This matters because trade agreements and other arrangements are often limited to a given country.[77]

The EU's trade deals with third party countries treat the whole of the EU as a black box for origin purposes. That means that EU manufacturers can mix and match parts from anywhere in the EU. A British car firm is free to build vehicles with locally produced chassis, German wheels, Portuguese electronics etc. Cars rolling off the end of the production line are "Made in the EU" for trade purposes, even if the stickers on them say "Made in the UK". If they're exported to Canada, the Canadians don't care how much of each car came from the UK. The important thing is that it was made within the EU as a whole.

But once we've left the EU, we will no longer count as an EU member for origin purposes. Imagine that the EU's trade deal with South Korea requires goods to be at least 75% made in the EU. EU firms would be unable to incorporate more than 25% of parts from UK manufacturers without breaching its terms.

This is another consideration UK businesses never had to worry about before Brexit. It won't be enough to be a cheaper producer or a better quality one. If the EU partners you're selling to can never source more than a certain percentage of their parts from you, that is bound to limit your business.

Equally, after Brexit, our independent trade deals will also incorporate rules of origin requirements. But if the UK signs its own trade deal with, say, a 75% rule of origin requirement, UK firms manufacturing for export to that market cannot then incorporate more than 25% of parts from outside the UK. That's fine if sources of local parts already exist at competitive prices. But in many cases we rely on the competences of other EU states. It is cheaper to buy from specialised producers elsewhere in the EU than develop the same expertise at home. Especially since up until Brexit at least, there's no paperwork or customs fees. UK manufacturers are used to treating the EU as one big market when shopping for components. Changing rules of origin requirements after Brexit may force them to shift upstream manufacturing to the UK if they can afford it, driving up their total production cost. Or they may even have to stop making certain products altogether.

What is the Single Market?

The single market represents a deeper kind of integration than the customs union. It reduces or gets rid of non-tariff barriers to trade. These barriers can be things like product safety rules, environmental standards and the like. To make the EU single market work, all EU countries must meet or exceed the same rules, regulations and standards. As a result, a toy made in Germany will meet the same safety standards as one made in the UK. So there's no need to inspect it at EU borders with other EU states, because the countries on both sides already know it's up to scratch. That leaves EU manufacturers free to sell to any EU country without extra checks or paperwork.

You need both the EU's customs union and single market together to make trade fully frictionless. The customs union eliminates tariffs and customs checks. The single market takes care of non-tariff issues. With all these impediments out of the way, companies can treat the EU like one giant playground.

But the EU single market goes much further. It's about a lot more than goods and trade. It includes the free movement of services, capital and people. Financial passporting allows financial firms based in the City to sell investments anywhere in the EU. Banks can take on clients from all over the EU. Insurance firms can protect customers across the EU. Individuals and companies can transfer money and assets all over the EU. Thanks to rules on the mutual recognition of diplomas, professional workers such as architects can ply their trade in any EU state. EU citizens (including British nationals) can live and work anywhere.

These so-called four freedoms (goods, services, capital and people) are a fundamental part of the EU. They're as embedded as a heart in a body – and as essential. That explains why the EU's most rigid red line in Brexit negotiations is that it won't split up these four freedoms under any circumstances. For the UK to benefit from one or other of them, we will have to accept all four. There has been zero sign of movement on this point. Given how core they are to the concept of the EU, you should not expect any.

Could we be in the customs union but not the single market, or vice-versa?

The short answer is yes. We could choose a future relationship with the EU in which we only participate in one or the other. Other countries do exactly that, so we could follow their lead if we so desired.

Customs union only: The UK could be in the customs union without being in the single market. This would leave us on a par with Turkey. (Turkey has a bespoke customs union with the EU that doesn't cover every aspect of trade.) We would no longer have to abide by the EU's four freedoms, meaning we could restrict immigration. We would not have to pay into the EU budget, or follow EU rules and standards. But UK firms and individuals would also lose the benefits of the four freedoms. Our products would be subject to compliance checks at EU borders because our standards could diverge from the EU's. You only have to look at the long queues at the Turkish border to see the effect the change would bring.

Single market only: The UK could be in the single market without being in the customs union. Norway and Iceland are part of the single market but not the customs union. So they respect the same four freedoms, pay into the EU budget, follow the EU rules, but have more flexibility on matters such as setting external tariffs. They don't have a say in the running of the EU or input on shaping EU law because they're not members. Out of the customs union, we would be free to negotiate our own independent trade policy. But we would be subject to the same tariffs and quotas as other non-EU countries. Customs checks would become mandatory. Again, we would have to expect queues at the border where none exist at present.

Important: if we opt to stay in the single market, we must accept all aspects of single market participation. As already discussed, there's no chance that the EU will split the four freedoms for us.

Understanding the Irish border, and the backstop

One of the biggest Brexit stumbling blocks is the Irish border and associated backstop. But what's the problem?

The UK and Ireland both joined the European Economic Community at the same time, in 1973. Their current relationship depends on the fact they're both EU members. Goods, services and people flow freely between Northern Ireland and the Irish Republic thanks to EU freedom of movement rules.[78]

The Irish border stretches for over 300 miles. It straddles farms and villages, and counts hundreds of crossing points. Some roads criss-cross it several times in the space of a few miles.[79] Commuters traverse it daily on their way to work in Northern Ireland or the Republic of Ireland. NI farmers send their milk to cheese and butter producers south of the border. In the course of a year, millions of commercial consignments cross the border. With the dismantling of the last armoured watchtower in NI in 2007, it has become little more than a line on a map.[80]

Things used to be very different. The 1998 Good Friday Agreement brought to an end a thirty year period of sectarian conflict. The Troubles saw over 3,600 people killed. Hardened border posts manned by military personnel were obvious flashpoints, often targeted by militants. Some of the worst outbreaks of violence occurred in the towns and villages near the border.

Nobody wants a return to those dark times, yet a no deal Brexit would jeopardise the peace agreement. The Irish border would become the only land border between the UK and the EU, i.e. between a non-member and a member state. That means different rules would apply either side of the border for the first time in over 40 years. After Brexit, the UK will seek to diverge trade arrangements and tariffs, product standards and other issues from those applicable to EU members. That introduces the need for customs and regulatory checks on goods crossing the border.

Such checks will require physical crossing points, staffed by customs officials and police. But that risks undoing all the good work of the last two decades. A hard border could revive suppressed social, religious and cultural divides. It would end the flexible arrangements many industries both sides of the border rely on.

A remarkable confidential study by the UK Government revealed that Brexit will impact no less than 142 aspects of life in Northern Ireland. Drawn up in September 2017, it finally came to light in June 2019.[81]

Let's look at a few of the unresolved issues that arise from a hard border in more detail:

- One component of the GFA is the EU funded PEACE programme. It supports peace and reconciliation, and promotes economic and social progress in NI and the border region of Ireland. From 1995 to 2013, three consecutive PEACE programmes contributed 1.3 billion euro of funding. PEACE IV, running from 2014 to 2020, comes with a further 270 million euros in funding. The future of the PEACE initiative beyond 2020 and Brexit remains unresolved.[82]

- Another consideration is the Common Travel Area arrangement, which predates the EU. Under the CTA, British and Irish citizens do not have to show their passports when they cross the Irish border (even though the UK is not in Schengen). In practice, nobody's passports get checked. Indeed, there is no infrastructure in place to do so. The assumption is that passports will be checked elsewhere, upon entry to Ireland or Northern Ireland. But after Brexit, Ireland will retain freedom of movement with the rest of the EU. That means EU citizens could enter Ireland under FOM and then cross into NI without being subject to further checks.

- NI and Ireland share a market in electricity. The UK Government has admitted there's a risk to electricity supply in NI without an agreement to preserve this market.[83] It has floated a plan as part of wider contingency preparations to install thousands of generators on barges to try and maintain supply.[84]

Many parties to the discussions on the Irish border issue insist that they will not reintroduce a hard border. The UK government has been adamant on that point. So has Arlene Foster of the DUP.[85] But the underlying problem won't go away just because people are ignoring it. The EU will still need to preserve the integrity of the Single Market and the Customs Union. And that means policing its border with a third country. While it has come around to the admission very late, the Irish government has begun to talk about the need for infrastructure at or near the border.

Brexiters often place the blame in the wrong place, complaining that Ireland is not trying hard enough to solve the issue. But the border works well, and has done for over twenty years. If the UK hadn't been pursuing Brexit, there wouldn't be any problem. It is true that Ireland also needs the border to be as smooth as possible. But the onus must be on us to find a cooperative solution that works for both parties.

Brexit and the Irish border: a (c)analogy

Imagine the border between Northern Ireland and the Republic as a rope strung high across a canal flowing through both countries. The rope marks the boundary between them but does not impede the free passage of boats.

The level of the water in the canal represents the various elements of EU membership: freedom of movement, regulatory environment, product safety standards etc. Since NI and Ireland are currently both in the EU, the water level is the same on either side of the rope.

Once the UK leaves the EU, its situation will start to diverge from that of the EU. That means NI will diverge from Ireland. The water level in the canal will no longer be the same in both countries.

Differing water levels will require something to keep the waterway open. Ireland is bound by EU rules. It cannot vary its water level to track the changing water level in NI. That makes the problem ours to solve.

One day, sufficiently advanced technology (cf. Arthur C. Clarke) might allow the water levels to be equalised without physical infrastructure. But no such technology exists at present. That leaves two options:

A) Build a lock, ship lift or other infrastructure. (You might say that you hate the idea of a lock, even refuse to build one. Physics doesn't care. The problem will remain.)

B) Equalise the water level in NI to that of Ireland's section of the canal, and keep adjusting it to stay equal.

Option A puts at risk the Irish peace process and the Good Friday Agreement. Any such installations would become flashpoints for trouble.

Since "do nothing" isn't an option, that only leaves option B.

That's the role of the Irish backstop, an agreement that says (in analogy terms): "We promise that we will keep the water flowing by doing whatever's necessary to keep the water levels the same."

The Irish backstop

The Irish backstop is an insurance policy designed to avoid reintroducing a hard border, and to preserve the peace of the Good Friday Agreement in all political circumstances. It takes the form of a protocol within the Withdrawal Agreement that Theresa May negotiated with the EU, but failed to get through the House of Commons.

Plugs come with fuses. Baths have overflow pipes. Sky-jumpers carry backup parachutes. The backstop is the legal equivalent of such precautionary measures.

The Withdrawal Agreement negotiated by Theresa May included a transition period, effectively a standstill during which EU rules would still apply to the UK after Brexit even though we would already have left. The backstop would only come into effect after the transition period ended, and only if we failed to negotiate a suitable alternative arrangement with the EU before then.

The version of the backstop agreed by Theresa May would keep the whole of the UK in the Customs Union, and Northern Ireland in many aspects of the Single Market.

Because the UK would stay in the CU, there would be no tariffs, quotas, rules of origin checks or customs processes on UK-EU trade. But we would not be able to sign our own independent trade deals. We would also have to obey EU regulations on matters such as agriculture, fisheries and food standards.

With NI still in the Single Market, EU product standards would apply to goods made there. So consignments would not need checking at the Irish border.

Brexiters deride the backstop arrangement because it would make the UK a rule-taker. They're right. We would have to obey EU rules with no say in shaping them since we'd be out of the EU's decision-making process. But the introduction of a hard border cannot be the alternative because of the intense risk to the peace process.

The other problem with the backstop is that it is potentially indefinite. The UK cannot exit from it unilaterally, nor can the EU kick the UK out of it. Both sides have to agree it's no longer needed before it can be dismantled. But that makes sense. An insurance policy cannot guarantee no return to a hard border if it has loopholes in it.

So how might the backstop get replaced? It will no longer be necessary once suitable alternative arrangements are available. These could combine technology solutions with checks away from the border and trusted trader schemes.

Brexiters claim alternative arrangements already exist that could render the Irish border frictionless. (Despite the fact that no convincing examples of such arrangements can be found on any border anywhere in the world.) Yet they remain unwilling to sign up to a Withdrawal Agreement that makes it clear the backstop will never be implemented at all if alternatives are in place. This logical contradiction suggests they lack the courage of their convictions.

Boris Johnson has indicated he wants to tear up the backstop. But as of early October 2019, the EU have not proven receptive to the idea. Neither side appears willing to budge further, a recipe for deadlock and frustration.

Slaying Brexit Unicorns

It's time to get to grips with the Brexit unicorns: the lies, half-truths and fantasies peppering the wider debate. Many have taken on the status of popular wisdom through constant repetition. But a falsehood remains false no matter how often it is brought up.

1. We have been fed a diet of lies, spanning decades...

The EU is unfamiliar, over there, and something to do with foreigners. That makes it a handy bogeyman for politicians wanting to pass unpopular legislation, justify controversial decisions, or exploit it for their own political benefit by stoking anti-European fervour. Large parts of our media demonise the EU too. They provoke fear and outrage to deliver clicks, comments and shares. The greater the emotional response, the wider the story circulates.

The UK press puts out so many nonsensical stories about the EU that the European Commission has a blog dedicated to debunking them.[86] Between 1992 and 2017, this Euromyths blog busted 682 whoppers: tall tales about rules, regulations, the way the EU passes laws, the functioning of EU institutions etc.

For instance, the Sun claimed that the EU wanted to ban crayons and colouring pencils.[87] It blamed meddling "eurocrats" (a recurring pejorative) and decried a "clampdown from Brussels". (In tabloid-speak, "Brussels" is shorthand for an overbearing administration.) The story included a quote from a pliant MEP bemoaning the limiting of kids' creativity. But as the Euromyths blog explained, the EU was not aiming at pencils and paints.[88] Rather, it had introduced measures to limit lead levels in all toys.[89]

Newspapers also paint the EU in a poor light by conflating proposals it makes with ones it receives. The Daily Telegraph got worked up in 2013 about EU plans to regulate the media (in the context of Leveson).[90] Its fury focused on an independent report submitted to the EU. But the EU had not responded to the report's findings.[91] That's like someone claiming you're vulgar because you *received* a rude letter.

Many of the stories the EU confronts are outright lies. Others start with a kernel of truth but go on to blame the EU for problems of our own making. In 2004, the Daily Mail ran a poison piece about fields filled with discarded refrigerators. It fingered the EU for a "great mountain of metal slowly turning to rust". It was true that some old fridges had fallen foul of a tightened environmental standard. But the UK, in common with other member states, had signed off on the new law in 2000. In other words, our Government had at least 4 years to prepare to recycle older appliances. But as so often happens, it didn't put in the necessary effort.[92] Cue Daily Mail rage. The EU punchbag let our politicians off the hook – again.

Following the Brexit referendum, the propaganda machine dialled up to 11. The Euromyths blog gave up trying to stem the avalanche of absurdity in late 2017. It returned for a brief encore in November 2018 to address a Daily Mail story. Allegedly, EU privacy regulations were stopping German children from sending wish-lists to Santa.[93] You can guess how much truth there was to the report.

Why does our media persist in this sort of behaviour? Two simple, sad reasons: controversy grabs attention, and they know they can get away with it. Indeed, there's zero comeback no matter what they print. Millions read the papers, but only a handful of people will ever see the Euromyths blog. So the press barons know nobody with a big enough soapbox will call them out.

When you've endured a diet of lies for decades, they can be hard to spot. Especially since each lie builds on and reinforces prejudices established by previous ones. It's easy to believe the EU is "banning" our beaches.[94] After all, they banned curvy bananas, didn't they?[95] Ban, ban, ban, that's all they ever do. That might certainly appear to be the case, going by the parade of negative headlines. Reality begs to differ. Our beaches remain accessible, though they may get called out for failing to meet water quality standards. And our bananas can be bendy or straight.

2. "No deal" would be the worst possible deal

A no deal Brexit refers to the situation should the EU and the UK fail to conclude a deal by 31 October 2019. We will leave the EU, but there won't be anything in place to smooth our departure.

The way the expression "no deal" is used in the context of Brexit may seem counter-intuitive. If you don't reach agreement during a normal negotiation, nothing changes. You want to sell your car. The dealer doesn't offer you a price you're happy with. You say "sorry, no deal" and shake hands. Then you drive off in your vehicle. But a no deal Brexit represents peak upheaval. Everything will change from one second to the next. One moment we'll be in the EU, and subject to its treaties and trade agreements. The next we'll be out, and they won't apply to us any more. It will be like jumping from a moving plane to the ground without a parachute. (Gravity always wins, no matter how optimistic you are.)

A Brexit deal with a transition period (such as the one agreed between Theresa May and the EU) is like an amicable separation. You agree to divorce, but you're allowed to keep sleeping in the spare bedroom until you find your feet. A no deal Brexit is like running out of the house in the middle of the night with nothing but the pyjamas you're wearing. Both are disruptive compared to your old life with your partner. But one is much, much more disruptive than the other.

Consider the situation for drivers. At present, you can drive anywhere in the EU on a UK driving license. Not by magic, but thanks to the power of international law. Somewhere in a dusty filing cabinet, there's an agreement on the portability of EU driving licenses. After we leave, that agreement will no longer apply to us. Driving in the EU on a UK license alone will no longer be legal. That's why drivers will need international driving permits (IDPs) to drive in the EU after a no deal Brexit.[96] In fact, they may need 3 different IDPs because each EU country has different rules for non-EU drivers. IDPs will cost £5.50 from a Post Office. But that's only half the story. After a no deal Brexit, they will also need a green card to prove their UK car insurance is valid in Europe. (It should be valid by default, but the document will still be needed as evidence.) Green cards can take up to a month to get from the insurer; some may charge fees for issuing them.[97]

This is one example of the effects of no deal, based on the loss of a couple of agreements. But there are thousands of agreements baked into EU membership. Once we move from the "EU member" column to the "non-EU member" column, none will apply to us. You can see why a no deal Brexit will be so disruptive.

Of course, we can replace any of the agreements if we can persuade the EU to agree alternatives. But we will have to renegotiate each one individually.

There is no option worse than no deal, just like there's nothing colder than absolute zero. In a no deal Brexit, we will have given up all our EU agreements with nothing to replace them. How could we top that? Push shipping containers overboard? Brick up the Channel Tunnel? It is impossible to concoct a Brexit scenario worse than no deal. That's why Theresa May's "no deal is better than a bad deal" mantra was always nonsense.

In August 2018, the UK Government put out the first of over one hundred no deal preparedness notices. These explain what individuals and businesses will have to do to get ready for a no deal Brexit. Individual government departments soon joined in, adding their own advice to the tottering pile. The whole system is a mess. Some notices have never been updated. Others are evolving all the time. Advice valid last week may be out of date today. There is no way of knowing without going back to check again and again. There is also no single repository for this mountain of information. Departmental notices and ones from central Government are listed on different websites. Some are easy to find. Others are buried among news releases and other documents. Pity the hundreds of thousands of firms that trade with the EU. They're supposed to figure out how to adapt their business models on the basis of this shifting morass of information.

But this confusing blizzard of documents does have one huge benefit from the Government's point of view. It provides absolution. After Brexit, firms will line up to complain about the problems they're experiencing. Ministers will be able to wave obscure preparedness notices and say: "It's your own fault. Everything you needed to know was in here. Don't blame us if you didn't read it." A cover-your-posterior exercise par excellence.

So why does the government not rule out a no deal Brexit?

Some in government have a known allergy to experts. Perhaps they don't believe their advisers about the negative consequences of no deal. But one would hope that doesn't apply across the board. The real reason for their apparent disregard for the consequences of no deal emerges when you hear hardliners talking about failing to deliver Brexit. For example:

- Boris Johnson: "I and all ministers in this government are committed to leaving on this date [31 October], whatever the circumstances. To do otherwise would cause a catastrophic loss of confidence in our political system."[98]
- Boris Johnson: "Our job is to engage with everybody and just to point out the real existential threat that faces both parties [Labour and Tory] if we fail to get this done."[99]

- Boris Johnson: "And I think that MPs on both sides of the House also understand that they will face mortal retribution from the electorate unless we get on and do it."[100]
- Dominic Raab: "The Tory party will be toast unless we're out by the end of October."[101]
- Liam Fox: "I think no deal would damage our economy, I've been frank about that, but I think it's survivable. I think no Brexit, politically, is a disaster from which we might not recover."[102]
- Sajid Javid: "And anyone who promised this [no deal] would risk driving us to a pre-Brexit general election this year: a disaster first and foremost for our country and public trust in democracy; but also for our party."[103] (A prescient comment. Boris Johnson's drive for no deal is indeed pushing the UK closer to a GE.)

From these comments, it is clear the push to deliver on Brexit is above all about the survival of the Tory party. Outflanked by the Brexit party, it was obliterated in the European elections. It polled less than 10% for the first time ever, and won just 4 seats (a loss of 15).[104] Boris Johnson's premiership has brought a revival in the polls. His punchy rhetoric is attracting voters back from the Brexit Party. But the Tories are still running scared. If it becomes clear they cannot deliver Brexit, Nigel Farage will snaffle up their votes again. That's why Boris Johnson has vowed to take the UK out of the EU on 31 October "do or die, come what may."[105] That includes a no deal Brexit scenario.

In other words, the prospect of electoral damage outweighs concerns about actual damage. All the chaos and disruption of a no deal scenario will be worth it if the Tory party can regain its lost mojo. Delivering Brexit, even if the negotiations that follow continue for years, will remove the Brexit Party's main reason for existing. And where will most of their voters go? Back to the Tory party.

Delving into the logical contradictions of no deal

The arguments surrounding no deal raise far more questions than they answer. And that should set alarm bells ringing.

Boris Johnson and other Brexiters insist the threat of no deal is essential to persuade the EU to give us a good Brexit deal. But what happens if this bluff doesn't work? What if the EU doesn't offer this mythical better deal? Do we really go ahead and leave the EU without a deal?

We will have to replace all our trade and other arrangements after we're out. But what would our leverage be during this second much tougher phase of negotiations? We can't play the no deal ace, because we're already out. So what is the alternative? And what is our fallback position if we don't like what the EU ends up offering us? Is it to continue to endure the damage of a no deal Brexit?

Since we are going to have to agree a deal at some point, we might as well do it before experiencing the nightmare of no deal. Even if that means delaying Brexit to allow the talks to continue.

Also, how do we reconcile the following positions advanced by Brexit advocates:

- No deal will be so damaging to the EU that it will give us what we want.
- Warnings about the potential damage of no deal to the UK are nothing but Project Fear.

If we accept the assertion that the UK can weather no deal with no more than a few bumps in the road, why can't the EU? They're over seven times our size. Not to mention that although we're leaving, the other EU members are staying together. They will keep all their trade and other arrangements with each other and with the rest of the world.

So the no deal position of some (largely Tory) MPs clearly has little to do with negotiation and everything to do with positioning in advance of a general election. They fear that a failure to deliver Brexit will cost them dear at the polls. And they are choosing to gamble our futures in pursuit of a boost at the polls.

3. What trading on WTO terms will mean in practice

Because we are in the EU Single Market and Customs Union, almost half our trade is totally frictionless. As EU members, we also get to piggyback on the huge pile of trade deals the EU has agreed with other countries. Taken together, these factors mean that a full two thirds of all our current trade faces no or reduced tariffs. This will remain true right up to the final second before the Brexit deadline.

But once the deadline passes, we will be out of the EU and its treaties. With no trade agreements, we will face tariffs, and extra red tape for importers and exporters.

We will have to replace the lost trade deals with custom agreements tailored to the UK's needs. Each will have to be negotiated individually, a process that is likely to take years. That's the only way to get back to tariff-free trade, short of rejoining the EU.

What happens in the meantime? Until we can get new trade deals in place, we will fall back on trading on WTO terms.

The World Trade Organisation (WTO) is a club that the UK and 163 other countries belong to. Its purpose is to make trade between its members easier than it otherwise would be. WTO terms provide a basic framework for trading. They're a complex system of tariffs, quotas and rules designed to make trade a little bit smoother and less painful. But they are meant to be a last resort, not a substitute for a proper trade deal, which is why countries are always chasing new trade deals. Almost all countries with significant economies are WTO members. (The largest countries that aren't members are Iran and Algeria.[106]) WTO members carry out between 95% and 98% of all global trade, depending on how the figure is measured. But very little of that trade takes place on WTO terms. Instead, it happens on the basis of free trade agreements between WTO members.

Pascal Lamy, the former head of the WTO, summed up the difference in terms of football: "The [EU Single Market] is the top league. The WTO is the bottom."[107] In other words, WTO participation is better than a kick around the park using jerseys as goalposts, but it's not a very high standard. It's also all we will have to rely on, if we leave the EU with no deal. Remember, we will start our new life after Brexit without any trade deals, having waved goodbye to the product of over 40 years of intense negotiations. Our trade will continue. But it will be more complicated and more costly than it is at present.

Let's talk about tariffs. Under the WTO, each country sets its own tariffs on every product under the sun. WTO tariff schedules run into thousands of categories. For example, cars made in the UK will be subject to a 10% tariff when exported to the EU on WTO terms. That applies no matter if they're destined for France, Germany or anywhere else within the EU. Fuel will incur a 4.7% tariff.[108] Pork exports will incur tariffs of between 27% and 44%, depending on the specific product type.[109]

Note that the importer pays the tariff, not the exporter. So in theory, someone in the EU will be responsible for the extra costs imposed on what the UK exports. But of course they will turn around and pass the increase straight on to their customers. That's if they even keep buying what we make. More likely, they will look for an alternative source for the product, one not subject to tariffs. Firms in the EU have a huge range of options. They can switch to importing products from any other EU or EEA state. Or they can buy them from countries with which the EU already has trade deals.

At present, UK manufacturers can sell their cars to the EU tariff-free. But after Brexit, once we're trading on WTO terms, UK-made cars will become 10% more expensive for EU consumers overnight. "The exact same vehicles only pricier" is not a brilliant marketing slogan. The story gets worse. All the major UK car firms already have production sites elsewhere in the EU. So once we leave, they'll have a huge incentive to switch to making cars on the Continent. That way, they will be able to avoid the new tariffs and keep selling what they produce to the EU tariff-free.

What if the EU wanted to help us out and drop its tariff on cars to 0%? Unfortunately, that plan would fall foul of the WTO's "Most Favoured Nation" principle. Most favoured nation can be a confusing concept because it's the opposite of what it sounds like. WTO members are not allowed to favour a particular state in their dealings. They must treat them all the same, without discriminating. So if the EU tried to do us a favour by dropping its tariff on cars to 0%, it would have to give the same 0% rate to all WTO members. But that would leave the EU domestic market unprotected. Vehicles would flood in from cheap producers, hurting EU car manufacturers. So we can be sure the EU won't cooperate in this way. They'd be daft to. Of course, if we were to reach a trade agreement with the EU, that would be a different matter. But in that case, we wouldn't be relying on WTO terms in our trade with them.

The EU is not planning to impose tariffs and other conditions on us as a punishment, or to scare us into staying. After Brexit, we will be a non-EU country without a trade agreement with the EU. So the EU must act to fulfil its WTO obligations. If it failed to do so, it would be breaking the most favoured nation rule.

We've already seen how tariffs will make many of the UK's exports uncompetitive. But what will happen to the things we import from the EU and elsewhere?

Once we're out of the EU, we will be able to set our own tariffs on everything we import. We can even decide to make them zero if we want to. For instance, if we get desperate for cabbages (the UK imports half of all its food) we could set the cabbage tariff to zero. But most favoured nation still applies, so the tariff would have to be zero on cabbages from any WTO member. Cue a deluge of cheap cabbages. Great if you're trying to plug gaps in the food supply. But terrible if you're a British cabbage farmer.

You can't have it both ways. Either you shelter behind tariffs to protect domestic producers, or you lower them or cut them to zero to encourage cheap imports. But the latter approach could well destroy your local industry. The rules of the WTO will force us to confront this trade-off for every product sector.

The most favoured nation rule applies to all conditions of trade, not only to tariffs. So we could decide to scrap border checks on EU goods to keep traffic flowing at the ports. But we would have to do the same for goods coming from other WTO member states too. Many WTO members have lower standards of food hygiene and product safety than the EU does. By throwing the doors open to EU products, we'd have no defence against inferior goods from the rest of the world because we wouldn't be checking any consignments.

The UK Government published its draft post-Brexit tariff regime on 13 March 2019. It stated that the proposed tariffs were temporary, for up to 12 months. Its intent was to replace them with a permanent list of tariffs after a consultation. As outlined, 87% of imports to the UK by value would be tariff-free. The UK would apply tariffs to certain categories of goods including meat, finished vehicles and ceramics.[110] Some items that now incur quite significant tariffs will have no tariffs levied on them after Brexit. For instance, jams and marmalades (24% tariff now), televisions (14%) and peas (8%).[111] Good news for consumers of such products, but bad news for UK domestic producers. (It is possible the Boris Johnson government will revise these planned tariffs.)

But we have no control over the tariffs other WTO members will impose on our exports. We are at their mercy. Switching to trading on WTO terms is like a predictable disaster. If we study the various tariff tables, we can see the damage that Brexit will inflict on us in every trading situation, and calculate exactly how much more expensive everything will become.

Some producers may be able to cut their costs to offset the tariffs. Most will collapse in short order. For instance, farmers have already made it clear that the EU's tariffs on lamb would put an end to their livelihoods. There has been talk of the need to cull millions of sheep.

At the same time, the UK government will find itself playing the role of judge, jury and executioner for domestic producers. It will have to choose which to protect, product by product and industry by industry. And it will have to decide which to throw to the wolves by lowering or eliminating the tariffs on what we import.

Is there a way of avoiding tariffs? Yes, and the WTO offers an explicit mechanism for doing so. Under WTO rules, free trade deals supersede WTO terms. So all we would have to do is conclude a comprehensive free trade arrangement with the EU. It would need to cover every product category we don't want tariffs on. Once it was ratified, it would override the EU's WTO tariff schedule. But determining our post-Brexit relationship with the EU is the hardest task on the Brexit to-do list. The matter has already led to three years of political wrangling, with no end in sight. So this is like saying: "Fly? Sure. All we have to do is evolve wings, and we're all set."

Another important aspect of the WTO is tariff quotas. These allow members to import specific quantities of goods at a lower tariff, or duty free. The normal tariff only kicks in once the quota is exhausted for the year. The UK will need to have its own quotas after we leave the EU. If we don't, everything we import will be subject to tariffs.

Because the process of agreeing quotas is immensely complex, and requires the agreement of all WTO members, the EU and UK have suggested using historic data to split up the EU's quotas based on how much of the quota ended up in the UK in recent years. In other words, we would get a share of the EU's quotas and it would have a little less. While this seems like a fair approach on the surface, some WTO members have expressed their displeasure. The issue is that splitting the EU's quotas reduces flexibility. Take the EU's quota on New Zealand lamb. At the moment, NZ farmers can sell their lamb anywhere in the EU and still benefit from the agreed quota. This lets them target the most valuable markets. But after Brexit, they will be forced to sell a certain amount to the UK if they want to keep selling the same total quantity as before without tariffs.

Unfortunately, there are no existing tariff quotas for trade between the UK and the EU so there's nothing we can split with them. That makes sense. Quotas have never been needed, because there are no tariffs within the EU single market. But that means on day one after Brexit, UK lamb farmers will face the full tariffs on everything they export to the EU. Their lamb will become much more expensive as a result. Yet the EU will continue to be able to buy significant quantities of NZ lamb tariff free, thanks to their share of the existing quota agreed with NZ.

What about the lamb the UK imports from the EU? Well, we will either have to impose high tariffs too, driving the price up for UK consumers. Or we will have to reduce our own tariffs on lamb. But under most favoured nation, we will have to offer our lower tariff to every producer, including New Zealand. Cue a flood of NZ lamb muscling out domestic producers.

What happens under WTO if things go wrong? Relying on our WTO membership could prove tricky when there's a problem. The WTO does have a system to deal with disputes (the Dispute Settlement Understanding, or DSU). So the UK could file a trade dispute against Canada, for instance. The DSU lacks teeth. It can't levy fines or order other forms of compensation. It also cannot compel WTO members to take corrective actions. It is limited to making recommendations. If the WTO member found to be in breach amends its behaviour, that's the end of the matter. If it ignores the DSU's recommendations, the DSU may then allow the complainant to retaliate. Such retaliation could take the form of a higher or punitive tariff against the troublesome state. At no point is the wronged party compensated for the original damage suffered.

Currently, companies and individuals can take their disputes to the Court of Justice of the European Union (CJEU). That will no longer be possible after Brexit because we will have left its jurisdiction. But the

DSU is reserved for the use of member states, not private parties. So their only recourse will be to persuade the UK government to take action at the WTO level on their behalf. Complicated and messy, like using a sledgehammer to crack a nut. But since they will no longer have access to the nutcracker, they will have no other choice.[112]

If all the above sounds grim, that's because it is. There are no countries in the world that trade on WTO terms alone. We would be the first.

So if someone tries to convince you that the UK will be fine trading on WTO terms, they either don't know what they are talking about, or they're trying to mislead you.

For example, even Patrick Minford of Economists for Brexit is on record as stating that relying on the WTO would destroy the UK car industry. Speaking to a parliamentary committee, he said: "I think it's perfectly true that if you remove protections of the sort that have been given particularly to the car industry and to other manufacturing industries inside the protective wall, you're going to have a change in the situation facing that industry. And you are going to have to run it down. It will be in your interest to do it, just in the same way as we ran down the coal industry and the steel industry. These things happen."[113]

In other words, Brexiters chasing no deal see UK manufacturers as collateral damage, cannon fodder in the pursuit of Brexit. Perhaps you're less sanguine? Maybe you'd quite like the UK to keep manufacturing things?

4. Why isn't my MP doing what the referendum instructed them to do?

We live in a representative democracy. Every few years, voters go to the polls to elect their local MP i.e. the person who will represent them at Westminster. The election itself may be winner takes all, but an MP represents their whole community, not only those who voted for them or share their politics.

The Code of Conduct for Members of Parliament states that MPs have a duty to act in the interest of the nation.[114] They also have a special duty to their constituents. They must take decisions on merit, and act at all times according to the public trust vested in them.

The public trust. That's your trust, and mine. It's the trust of everyone who voted Leave or Remain, who sat out the referendum, or who was not entitled to take part in it. We trust MPs to act in our best interests. But the right thing to do isn't always what's popular. Decisions made on merit may be very different from ones based on emotion. Head, not heart.

MPs are not slaves to the electorate. Nor are they delegates following instructions. As Sir Winston Churchill put it: "The first duty of a member of Parliament is to do what he thinks in his faithful and disinterested judgement is right and necessary for the honour and safety of Great Britain. His second duty is to his constituents, of whom he is the representative but not the delegate."[115] Their allegiance to their party should come a distant third.

The referendum result wasn't an order, an edict from on high. MPs know the stance they take on Brexit will affect the UK, not for a brief election cycle, but for decades to come. They see the 2016 poll for what it was: a snapshot of public opinion at a specific moment in time. It can and should inform their thinking, but it does not bind them legally no matter how much energy is poured into trying to suggest the contrary. If after weighing all the evidence, MPs conclude that Brexit – especially a no deal Brexit – would be harmful to the country and to their constituents, that is their absolute prerogative. If we don't like their actions, our recourse is to vote them out of office at the next election.

It is important to distinguish between Parliament and the Government. Unlike Parliament, the Government isn't itself elected by the people. As the recent Supreme Court case on prorogation underlined: "The Government exists because it has the confidence of the House of Commons. It has no democratic legitimacy other than that."[116] The Government's own stated Brexit position is of no consequence if it can't muster a majority in Parliament. MPs have no obligation to do what the Government wants. The Government doesn't get to implement their programme because they're the Government. They get to implement it because they can persuade a majority of MPs to vote for it.

It is legitimate to complain that Brexit hasn't happened. But it is wrong to claim that's because MPs are not respecting what the people told them to do. The people *never* had the power to boss them around like that. (It suits the "betrayal" narrative of some Brexiters to pretend they did.) It's like griping that footballers don't pick up the ball and run with it. Those aren't the rules.

In any case, MPs *are* trying to get Brexit done. Parliament took a referendum that was advisory, and decided to implement it anyway. That was obvious when the vote to trigger Article 50 passed with a huge majority.

Ever since, MPs have focused their energy on Brexit. The normal legislative agenda has suffered as a result. But the sticking point has always been the form of Brexit. As many MPs have been at pains to point out, they weren't elected to make their constituents poorer. Nor to leave the country in a precarious state. Theresa May's deal was a step in the right direction, but it contained too many flaws. The one thing most MPs agree on is that no deal is not a responsible option. But an appropriate Brexit arrangement still eludes them. (A minority of MPs want to stop Brexit. If they were in the majority, you can be certain Brexit would already be dead.)

Brexit itself is to blame for the lack of progress. Unpicking a 40 year relationship defined by hundreds of treaties and thousands of laws is a monster undertaking. Over ten thousand civil servants have been working on the project full-time. The Government has spent over £6 billion trying to make Brexit happen. The fact that it hasn't yet is testament to the complexity of our relationship with the EU.

If anyone is neglecting their obligations, it is the MPs pursuing no deal in the face of all the evidence. They may be furthering vested interests or a narrow party agenda. One thing's for certain: they're not acting for the good of the country or of their constituents.

5. We'll have a trade agreement by teatime

Trade agreements are hugely complex. They are about far more than headline-grabbing tariff reductions. They also seek to reduce or do away with a vast range of non-tariff barriers that inhibit free trade. Measures relating to matters such as product safety rules and other regulatory standards, intellectual property, environmental issues, plant and animal health regulations, restrictions on post-sales services etc.

For instance, will trademark holders in one country receive protection in the other country that's party to the agreement? And if so, how will conflicts with existing trademarks get resolved? Can both parties agree a common or equivalent product safety testing regime? (Products certified by agencies in either country are deemed safe in the other.) And so on, and so forth.

A modern trade agreement will cover hundreds or thousands of such issues. Each will need to be codified in minute detail. These are binding legal commitments, not something dashed off on the back of a napkin.

Trade agreements rarely cover all products across the board (let alone services). Instead, they're a long series of trade-offs. One country wants to boost its agricultural sector and shoe industry. The other wants to sell more cheese and computer parts. Each will push for favourable terms that benefit its key industries. ("Let's say we reduce our tariff on the food you sell us from 20% to 2%. What can you offer on the electronics we manufacture? Would you be willing to accept the environmental standards our factories operate to?")

When it comes to our own trade agreements after Brexit, major players such as the USA and China may insist on always getting the best terms. This would be implemented through most favoured nation (MFN) clauses in their trade agreements. If we offer a better deal to any other country in future, we would have to give the same terms to them too. This is far from hypothetical. The EU's recent trade deals with Canada and Japan incorporate such clauses.[117] If we refuse, we may not get a trade agreement at all. But if we accept, it ties our hands in future negotiations. Say, heaven forbid, we made concessions to the USA on food hygiene. If we had MFN free trade agreements with China or other trade partners, we'd have to allow them the same lowered standards too. How much chlorinated chicken can one country consume?

We're the world's sixth largest economy (we used to be the fifth prior to the referendum).[118] This gives us real clout going into negotiations. But it also means we can't dash off a quick trade deal with major players like the one we did with the Faroe Islands, which was almost entirely about fish.[119] No, each one will have to take into account the needs of hundreds of sectors and millions of firms. The EU's free trade agreement with Singapore ran to several thousand pages. Printed out, it was over a foot thick and looked like a comedy film prop. But Singapore's economy is only about an eighth of the size of ours. So you can imagine the forest of dead trees it will take to produce hard copies of our own major trade agreements. And how long it will take negotiators and international legal experts to draft them.

Because of this complexity, trade negotiations involve large teams and many rounds of negotiation. The EU has over 500 staff it can bring in to work on deals. Until very recently the UK didn't have *any*. We haven't needed them because our external trade policy has been delegated to the EU for over forty years. Unfortunately, experienced trade negotiators are like gold dust: expensive and in high demand. As of November 2018, we had only managed to recruit 90 expert level staff.[120]

A typical trade agreement takes years to complete. Looking at some of the largest players, the USA takes an average of 3 years 9 months to reach a trade agreement, Australia 5 years 1 month, China 5 years 9 months and India 6 years 11 months.[121] Those figures are for just one new trade agreement. We will have over 40 that will need to be concluded in parallel to replace the ones we will lose when we leave the EU. 40+ trade agreements and 90 staff. That's like trying to spread a pea-size blob of margarine across an entire loaf of bread.

At the highest political levels, people may say we can reach trade deals soon after Brexit. Trump can wave his hands and claim we'll get a "yuge deal" overnight. But the reality of the processes involved makes that impractical. We will be able to start negotiating immediately after Brexit with any willing counterparts. And we may get a few quick wins, limited deals involving a handful of sectors. But anything comprehensive will take time. There's no way around it. It would be wildly arrogant to assume that our negotiators can achieve what no others in history ever have. The larger the trading partner, the harder it will be to reach a deal. And with so many deals, we will have to prioritise. If the US sends fifty negotiators, we can't very well have a couple of our team sitting across the table. No, we will have to make a substantial investment in time and human capital. But that will mean slowing or abandoning other negotiations.

Of course, in some cases there will be existing EU trade agreements we can use as a starting point. These can adopted as is, or tailored. Indeed, some countries have rolled over existing EU agreements by striking continuity deals replicating their terms. But many are holding out for more concessions on our part. They know that our position will be weaker once we have left the EU, so they're in no hurry. And since half our trade is with the EU, that's the deal that matters more than any other. Yet if anything we're further away from agreement than we were six months ago.

The Red Queen's race... for trade agreements

The EU is evolving all the time.

Since the 2016 referendum, it has seen notable success on the trade front. It has finalised deals with Singapore, Canada, Japan, Vietnam and the South American Mercosur trade bloc.[122] Together, these encompass new markets totalling over half a billion people. And the EU shows no signs of stopping. It has accelerated negotiations with Australia, New Zealand and China.

We will benefit from these new arrangements for so long as we remain EU members. But with every trade deal the EU reaches, the opportunity for us to improve our lot after we strike out on our own diminishes. We are running out of countries that the EU hasn't already partnered with.

The UK faces the same problem Alice did in Lewis Carroll's *Through the Looking-Glass*. She got involved in an odd race organised by the Red Queen. After Alice complained about her own lack of progress, the Queen informed her: "Now, here, you see, it takes all the running you can do, to keep in the same place. If you want to get somewhere else, you must run at least twice as fast as that!"[123]

After Brexit, we will not only have to replicate our situation as it was at the time of the referendum. But we will also need to negotiate comparable trade deals with all the new partners the EU has brought on board since the 2016 vote. Each such deal could take years to complete (the EU has been working on them for a long, long time).

In other words, we are going to have to run twice as fast too. An already difficult task is growing harder with every passing day. And the consequences of leaving are becoming ever more severe.

6. The truth about Brexit and immigration

Immigration is the most controversial and myth-riddled aspect of Brexit. Undue fear of immigration has been with us pretty much forever. It's a hot-button topic, stirred up by the tabloids and exploited by the far right. Hurtful tropes abound, such as "immigrants are stealing our jobs" or "they're only here for the benefits".

The Leave campaigns exploited these fears during the referendum, raising them to stratospheric levels. Dire warnings of immigration out of control. Grim mutterings that our EU membership would render us helpless against the tide of humanity threatening to batter our borders.

Many scare stories suggested Turkey was about to join the EU. (It wasn't. The remaining steps in the complicated ascension process would have taken a decade or more. Not to mention that the UK and other EU member states have a veto on new entrants.) Michael Gove raised concerns over Turkey several times during the campaign (he went on to distance himself from his previous attitude in a 2018 book).[124] Boris Johnson is on record as having done so too. He would later falsely claim he'd never mentioned the subject. ("Since I made no remarks, I can't disown them."[125])

Poison like this was not so much drip-fed to the electorate as sprayed with a fire hose. The flood of disinformation peaked when Nigel Farage unveiled his "Breaking Point" poster (paralleling Nazi propaganda imagery) the same day poor Jo Cox was murdered.[126]

These tactics were nothing if not effective. Two months prior to the referendum, 47% of likely Leave voters cited immigration as a major concern.[127] But a week before the vote, the figure had risen to 52%.[128] That 5% is a key change, given that it's bigger than the final margin.

The hangover from this vile exercise lingers on in the form of a significant rise in hate crime that can be tied directly back to Brexit.[129]

It's high time to cut through the noise and nonsense, and focus on reality.

Immigration and the economy

A major report by the Migration Advice Committee studied the impacts of immigration on the UK.[130] The MAC collected over 400 pieces of evidence, more than for any other report it has ever produced. The report concluded that immigration has had no substantial impact on overall employment opportunities for UK-born workers, or on wages. That's because immigrants create jobs as well as taking them. Their consumption drives up the demand for goods and services in their local area, leading to higher employment. Immigrants also occupy roles that British people are unwilling or unable to do, such as providing the seasonal workforce that our farmers depend on to get the crops in.

65,000 NHS staff in England are from the EU and, across the NHS as a whole, 13.1% of staff are non-British.[131] EU workers fill 5.4% of roles in the care sector, and another 5% of positions are occupied by staff from outside the EU. Despite this, firms face severe difficulties finding and retaining employees.[132] An estimated 442,000 EU migrants work in hotels and restaurants, including almost a quarter of all chefs.[133]

On average, immigrants from the EEA cost the UK far less than British citizens do. It's easy to understand why. Most come here to work as adults, with schooling and university costs behind them. After contributing to our economy for years or decades, they return home when they reach retirement age. That means the burden of caring for them in old age doesn't fall on UK taxpayers.

The MAC report found that, far from being a drain on resources, EEA immigrants pay more in taxes than they receive in benefits. The average EEA immigrant contributes £2,300 a year more to public finances than an average UK adult does. (It should be noted that migrants from outside the EEA cost £840 per person per year on average because they are more likely to be accompanied by non-working adults and dependent children.)

Is immigration outside of the UK's control?

There's a two-part answer to this question. When it comes to non-EEA immigration, we have complete control over who we let into the UK. The Government has free rein to set immigration policy. It can specify minimum salary or education levels, and any other requirements it likes. It can reserve visas for specific categories of workers, such as technology specialists. The recent decision to relax the rules on international students by introducing a 2-year post study visa illustrates this freedom.[134]

But we could also do more to control immigration from the EEA if we chose to. Freedom of movement is not unlimited. We could enforce an EU regulation that would apply to EU citizens wishing to stay for more than 3 months. They would have to work, study, or have enough money to support themselves independently. Successive UK Governments have opted not to impose this rule. Not only did they not enforce it, they barely made any effort to track who was here. The UK is one of the few EU countries not to have a national registration system and ID cards. Instead, our immigration data relies on passenger surveys at airports and other points of entry.[135] Again, this is a choice we made, not something imposed on us.

So it is incorrect to say that our EU membership prevents us from controlling immigration. It is our desire to be welcoming which has kept our borders open (up until now, anyway).

Immigration post-Brexit

The stance the Government has adopted since the referendum represents a complete sea change. The welcome mat is gone. Instead of celebrating the huge contribution of immigrants to our workforce and wider society, it has rushed to reassure the electorate that a clampdown is coming. EU citizens will have to apply for permission to stay in the UK after Brexit. This is of course something they have never had to worry about before. Millions are having to get to grips with the EU Settlement System, aspects of which work only on Android phones.

The UK Government could have taken a simple, inclusive approach. It could have granted every EU citizen living here the automatic right to stay. It has opted for a hard line instead. People who have lived in the UK for years or decades are being asked to provide proof of continuous residency. But since this is the first time EU citizens have needed permission to stay here, many won't have kept hold of such detailed documentation. This introduces a wholly unnecessary level of uncertainty to the process. We're hardly covering ourselves in glory, and other EU countries are watching. In the event of a no deal Brexit, we will depend on their kindness to treat the over one million UK citizens living in the EU well.

Looking ahead, the Government intends to bring in harsh new

immigration rules to curtail migration. It is going to impose new salary requirements on all non-UK staff. One recent iteration of this plan suggests the minimum salary will be set at £30,000 a year. Visas will only be granted to employees whose contracts guarantee their earnings will exceed the threshold. (90% of nurses and half of secondary school teachers earn less than that.[136])

The Indian restaurant sector is among many that the new rule will hurt.[137] Priti Patel had spearheaded an appeal to "save our curry houses" during the referendum. The industry took her at her word, and swung behind the Leave campaign.[138] But far from saving them, it looks like Brexit will close them at a record rate. The new salary threshold is higher than many chefs command, and the owners of smaller restaurants are not in a position to pay them more to make up the difference. (There are not enough local chefs to fill all the positions.)

Looking to the bigger picture, is this really the image of the UK we want to show the world? An insular, standoffish nation – its doors slammed tightly shut – courtesy of a policy that was built on a stack of lies?

The tragedy is that these draconian measures are completely unnecessary. A recent survey found that as soon as the existing EU immigration system was properly explained to them, voters across the political spectrum lost their fears. 64% of voters and 58% of Leave supporters felt the 3-month rule would provide an adequate level of control over immigration.[139] So we are rushing down a dark path we do not have to take. All we have to do is better implement the existing options we have as EU members.

EU immigration and its relationship to freedom of movement

Freedom of movement and EU immigration are two ways of looking at a single picture. We call UK citizens living and working in the EU expats. We tend to consider EU citizens in the UK immigrants. But our expats are other EU countries' immigrants, and vice-versa.

Our gutter press never misses an opportunity to demonise immigrants. Whenever some problem – real or, more often, imagined – can be pinned on them, the i-word screams from the headlines. If it's not immigrants, it's "migrants", a shorthand imbued with even more negative connotations, and designed to emphasize a transient relationship with the UK. The Daily Mail and others have pushed this "expats = good, immigrants = bad" narrative for decades. Their attitude is toxic, and spreads hate. And yet both words represent the same thing. Only the vantage point differs.

7. Why the EU is not punishing us for leaving

Some Brexiters like to claim that the EU is going out of its way to inflict problems on us as punishment for leaving. They complain about a wide range of expected post-Brexit issues, such as the imposition of extra checks on trucks at the ports. For them, the EU's refusal to give us a fabulous deal as non-EU members is somehow sinister.

This view twists reality. In truth, there's nothing untoward going on. The impacts of Brexit are nothing more than the consequence of our loss of EU membership. The EU applies certain rules to EU member countries and different ones in its dealings with non-members. On Brexit Day, we will become a non-member state. The rules that apply to the UK will change to reflect our new status. But the EU won't treat us any worse than it does any other non-EU country.

If you quit your local gym, you wouldn't expect to be able to keep on using its fitness equipment and weights. Your waistline might expand as a result. But you wouldn't turn around and say "The gym's punishing me for leaving by making me fat." That would be absurd. The weight gain is a consequence of losing your gym membership, not something imposed on you by the gym. The same logic applies to Brexit.

Some in the Leave camp have called on the EU to dismantle its rules and let us pick and choose which bits apply to us. They'd be happy with freedom of movement of goods and services, but not of people.

But the EU's so-called "4 freedoms" are the most fundamental aspect of membership, and have been since the very beginning. Its refusal to countenance such an absurd proposal is pragmatic, not malicious. If the EU allowed us to cherry pick, it would have other EU members demanding to cherry pick too.

Imagine going to your boss and explaining that you would like to resign from your job:

Boss: "We will be sorry to see you go, but we respect your decision. And if you want to reconsider before your notice ends, we'd love you to stay."

You: "Can I take my desk with me when I leave?"

Boss: "No, of course not."

You: "What about my laptop?"

Boss: "No, it's company property."

You: "Why are you making my departure so tough on me? This is a disgrace..."

The UK is not a victim of some EU plot. We decided to leave. The EU aren't forcing us out. Indeed, even at this late hour, they would still prefer us to stay. The EU is not punishing us. We are punishing ourselves. The self-inflicted loss of all the benefits of EU membership *is* the punishment.

True, the EU are not going out of their way to make our departure easy. They are negotiating with vigour, backed by the unity demonstrated by 27 countries. Why shouldn't they when they are in a so much stronger position than us? There's no reason to expect them to roll over and grant us special concessions. But not making something easier is not the same as making something harder. They are not sabotaging our exit. They are looking out for the interests of their members, nothing more. Right now, that includes us too. After Brexit, it won't.

8. The myth and reality of sovereignty

Our Parliament is sovereign. It can create or abolish any law. This means that no Parliament can pass laws that a future Parliament cannot change. Parliament is also, in principle, the highest legal authority.

Over the years, Parliament has chosen to delegate some aspects of its sovereignty. It devolved powers to the Scottish Parliament and to the Welsh Assembly. It effectively said: "We will give you agency over this, this and this. What you say goes when it comes to those issues." The Supreme Court, established in 2009, is now the final court of appeal. It can override Parliament's decisions because Parliament granted it permission to do so. This new court shapes our laws with its rulings, such as in the recent case where it declared the prorogation of Parliament void.

The UK also made a sovereign decision to cede some of its power when we entered the European Union in 1973. For example, we no longer control our external trade policy, and the European Court of Justice sits as a higher tier of legal authority above the Supreme Court on certain matters. Yes, Parliament has less independent authority because we're in the EU. But that's by choice. Our sovereignty was never taken from us. We traded a slice of it willingly for the benefits of EU membership, as did the other 27 EU member states. It is wrong to portray the EU as a bully that reached out and imposed its own sovereignty on us.

We can remove the EU's sovereignty over us any time we like by leaving the EU, as we are in the process of doing. We are not trapped within the EU, even though it may feel like that sometimes because we are so deeply integrated with our neighbours. The only thing hindering us is the practical consequences of our departure.

The EU is like a club with a smart dress code. We opted to join the club for the benefits it offers, so we have to dress well. But that's not the same as saying that the club reached out and imposed its dress code on us. So long as we stay in the club, we have to keep wearing smart attire. (Crucially, we sit on the board of the club and have a say in the dress code and all the other rules.) But when we give up our club membership, we can dust off the jeans and t-shirts at the back of the wardrobe.

Let's imagine the UK has left the EU. That we have reclaimed the sovereignty we relinquished. Would that mean we no longer had anyone telling us what to do? Certainly not. The UK is a member of the UN, NATO, the WTO, and dozens of other bodies. Each of these institutions has rules we must follow if we want to stay in them. In other words, we must surrender a certain measure of our sovereignty to them. Each represents a trade-off, exactly like our EU membership. Once we sign our own trade deals, we'll be forced to abide by even more rules.

The issue isn't whether leaving the EU will give us back our sovereignty. It won't. We can never have complete sovereignty as part of a global community of nations. (North Korea manages it by turning its back on the world.)

But if one of the main reasons for leaving the EU is to reclaim sovereignty, do we get enough back to offset all the upheaval? If we want to make our own trade deals, we will have to give up our existing ones. If we want to restrict immigration from the EU, we must accept that the EU will curtail the rights of UK citizens. If we want to be able to change our environmental laws, we are granting a future UK government the power to do so for the worse. And so on, and so forth. In the final analysis, is the price of greater sovereignty worth paying?

The real problem most Brexiters have with the EU when it comes to sovereignty is that it won't let us pick and choose. EU membership requires delegating our own sovereignty over a specific list of competences. To be members, we have to agree to the entire list. There may be things on there that are frustrating or awkward, but they're part of the package. The EU, like any club, doesn't have an a la carte menu of rules.

One important aspect of EU sovereignty that can get overlooked is that of oversight. EU rules mean the UK Government can't go hog wild doing whatever it likes to please big industry donors. For instance, it can't tear up environmental standards or workers' rights. Our EU membership prevents a bonfire of regulations. Granted, some of those regulations will be burdensome. Others will seem unnecessary. But as a whole, they provide a level of protection that domestic legislation cannot replicate. (Remember, UK law can be unmade any time.)

Take a long look at those sitting around Boris Johnson's Cabinet table. They may be your dream team or your worst nightmare. Either way, once we're out of the EU, they will have total control over hundreds of issues from animal welfare to food hygiene and human rights. Are you comfortable with them having that level of power, power that no UK politicians have wielded in full since the early 1970s? Would your answer be the same if it were Jeremy Corbyn or Nigel Farage in office?

Our EU membership does not and must not prevent us from fixing our own problems. The electoral route is the conventional way to effect change if we don't like what the Government is doing. But as the experience of the last few years has shown, there is huge potential for damage between elections. Given the current divisions in the country, the extra oversight the EU offers may prove valuable.

The EU's strength is that it protects the long-term interests of 28 countries rather than the short-term interests of one. It operates on a scale of decades, not the scant few years between elections. It doesn't have to do foolish things to win votes.

What if things go badly wrong with the EU itself? We will always be able to leave. It is not possible for an international treaty to bind us so tight that we can never get out of it.

Brexiters prefer ripping the EU rulebook up to working within its restrictions. Achieving this goal would be easier with public opinion on their side. That's why they spun a yarn about the EU coercing the UK, and seizing sovereignty from us. Look what it did to a once proud country, etc. It's fine to want to take back control. But it's not fine to stir up populist sentiment by inventing a tale about how that control was lost.

You will have £100 less if you go down to the bank and deposit five £20 notes. You will also have £100 less if the bank sends someone to pick your pocket and take the money. If the only evidence you present is your empty wallet, it's hard to know what really happened.

The effect of Parliament having volunteered to give up some sovereignty is the same as if it had been snatched away. But the process is completely different, and the distinction matters because it colours the wider debate. The EU are only the enemy if we set out to make them so.

There is an alternative. The EU doesn't rule over us, or monitor us at arm's length. We are part of it. We can build alliances to change EU rules we don't like, as we have in the past. We have the power to veto many changes to the EU's structure. We also have hard opt-outs from aspects of EU membership such as the euro, and the policy of ever closer union. So we can tear up the rules and leave i.e. persevere on the course we have embarked on. Or we can accept the rules, work with them and improve them.

9. Nationalisation, public sector ownership and state aid

Another aspect of the sovereignty debate is the ability of the state to own and nationalise businesses. But does our EU membership stop us nationalising the railways, utilities or other firms? What is its attitude to public sector ownership or state aid? The answers come with more shades of grey than an E L James novel. Given how vocal Labour has been about its interventionist agenda, they could have particular relevance to a possible Corbyn government.

Nationalisation and public sector ownership

Bottom line: nationalisation is legal under EU rules. Indeed, the UK has pursued various successful nationalisations while an EU member. For example, the takeover of Railtrack by Network Rail in 2002 under a Labour government.

But that doesn't mean that the UK Government has free rein to nationalise and own whatever it likes. One key aspect of the EU's approach is that the state cannot prop up companies that would otherwise fail. In other words, nationalisation isn't a Get Out of Jail Free card for morbidly unprofitable firms. The EU puts a lot of effort into maintaining a level playing field within and between its component member states. This includes ensuring that state-run firms don't have an unfair advantage over the private sector and vice-versa.

As a result, the EU vets and approves all nationalisation plans to satisfy itself that the nationalisation of the asset in question won't distort the market. For instance, steel is in over supply across the EU. So it would be hard to persuade the EU to allow British Steel to be brought into state ownership, rather than letting it fail.

In short, nationalisation is definitely possible. The EU isn't inherently opposed to it. However, the UK government cannot bank on obtaining blanket approval for any and all plans. It has to make and win its case each time.

Labour's stated approach to nationalisation risks falling foul of a different law. (The party has indicated it may nationalise utilities and other firms at below market value.[140]) The European Convention on Human Rights enshrines the right of every natural or legal person to the "peaceful enjoyment of his possessions". But that definition encompasses companies too. They cannot be deprived of assets arbitrarily, without fair compensation.

So whether the EU hinders nationalisation or not depends on your perspective. Its rules aren't a burden if you accept that state-run firms shouldn't crowd out the private sector by running at a loss, and that assets should be acquired at market rates. But if you want free rein to nationalise anything anytime, at whatever price you like, the strictures of EU membership will get in the way.

State aid

EU rules do not block state aid per se. Indeed many EU members, including France and Germany, already spend a great deal more on state aid than the UK does as a percentage of GDP. That said, the EU does impose restrictions on the type and extent of such aid.

The EU approves state aid plans on a case by case basis. Such approval can come very quickly in extremis. During the financial crisis, bank bailout plans were greenlit in hours or days.

When applying for projects, governments must identify the purpose of the state aid, and provide an estimate of its effectiveness. (Bluntly, the EU will not allow money to be thrown down a bottomless pit.) State intervention may not distort the market by distorting competition or trade between member states, or by giving particular firms an unfair advantage. Nor can one-off tax exemptions be used to lure multinationals to a particular EU member state.

The railways

It is worth focusing on the railways in more detail because this is the sector Labour seems most keen to nationalise. Most EU countries already have nationalised railways, so it's obvious the EU doesn't prevent state railway ownership. The local state-run service is either the sole provider in each national market, or a major player. Many state firms also compete effectively in other EU markets. State railways can also be subsidised, subject to certain restrictions. This is why rail travel is very cheap in much of Europe, and will even be free in Luxembourg from 2020.[141]

However, the rules surrounding railway ownership will change from 2023 under a major new EU agreement, the Fourth Railway Package.[142] The FRP will have several consequences:

- It will continue to allow state-owned railways while opening the market to private firms.

- Routes may have to be put out to competitive tender rather than be awarded outright to a single firm.[143]
- State firms will be able to join in the bidding process alongside private ones.
- State-run companies will lose their route monopolies if they fail to meet punctuality and satisfaction targets. In such cases, the routes will be opened to the private sector too.
- State firms can still own both infrastructure and train operating companies, but only as legally separate entities.

Clearly under both the EU's existing and planned rules, it would be possible to partially nationalise the UK's railways. But the state cannot simply take over the whole shebang and shut private firms out.[144] It will have to leave them a way to participate. Nevertheless, a well run and efficient state company could out-compete the private sector for tenders, ending up with a large part of the network. And if it turned out to be neither as efficient nor as well run as private firms, then consumers will benefit from the latter's presence in the market.

State Aid: the bottom line

The EU isn't an implacable opponent of nationalisation or of state aid. Many EU members already practice much greater state intervention than the UK does. But the EU's approach is nuanced. It will not allow the state to trample in hobnail boots all over the private sector. EU rules are intended to keep both state and private firms operating in harmony. So if your industrial strategy is dependent on the State being able to operate without restraints, EU membership becomes an obstacle.

Would leaving the EU free us of restrictions? The short answer is no. Outside the EU, certain State actions might be easier without the need to seek approval. But the EU has no intention of damaging its well-honed system by letting the UK sit offshore, subsidising its industries so that they can dump products below cost into the EU market. It has indicated that state aid will be a red line in future negotiations. So if we have any interest in reaching a free trade deal post-Brexit, we will have to forego our wilder impulses. (State aid restrictions are written into the EU's agreements with Turkey and the Ukraine, for instance, so the precedent is established.)[145]

But the WTO has rules on state aid too. WTO members can impose punitive tariffs on countries deemed to be subsidising domestic industry. Yet another layer of the regulatory onion surrounding us, and the stark reality of trade in a global world.

Another consideration is the large number of bilateral investment treaties that the UK is a signatory to, over a hundred in all. These will survive Brexit. Many such treaties contain provisions dictating the limited circumstances under which investments made by foreign investors may be nationalised. They also contain stipulations about receiving fair market value in return, i.e. equitable compensation.[146]

The only way to pursue a truly unrestricted interventionist agenda would be to rip the UK completely out of the global legal framework. Not just out of the EU, but out of the WTO and out of all our other international arrangements. That would give the State the freedom to go as wild as it liked – but at a cost so great as to be unconscionable.

10. Brexit for tax purposes

There have been suggestions that Brexit is secretly about tax avoidance. The narrative goes that it will let the UK dodge new EU tax rules due to come into effect in 2020. This would allegedly benefit unspecified shadowy financial interests.

There are various flaws with this theory:

- The UK's anti-avoidance rules already meet or exceed most of the requirements of the new EU directive.[147]

- Legislation (already drafted) will bring the rest of the requirements into UK law before the end of 2019.

- The UK has been one of the main countries pushing to tighten anti-avoidance measures. Its involvement in initiatives to that effect go back decades. The latest push came after the global financial crash.[148]

- The other EU members are not leaving. So the EU's anti-tax avoidance directive will apply to them even if it doesn't to us. That means any tax mitigation arrangements involving EU countries will fall under the directive.

- Several of the changes the EU is proposing closely mirror aspects of existing UK law.

- Many tax initiatives result from our OECD membership, which we will retain after Brexit. Key amongst these is the Action Plan on Base Erosion and Profit Shifting, aimed at making multinational firms pay taxes in the same jurisdiction they earn their profits in.[149] The UK was a major contributor to this measure.

- The EU relaxes certain aspects of tax law more than the UK would like. In a dispute between Cadbury Schweppes and the Inland Revenue, the EU's Advocate General stated: "the establishment by a parent company of a subsidiary in another Member State for the purpose of enjoying the more favourable tax regime in that other State does not constitute, in itself, an abuse of freedom of establishment".[150] (The UK was seeking to apply its legislation on "controlled foreign companies" more narrowly.)

- The UK showed clear willingness in the past to adjust its tax laws when they appeared to clash with EU rules.[151]

One aspect of taxation that gets raised frequently in the context of Brexit is the matter of tax havens. The UK's overseas territories, places like the British Virgin Islands and the Cayman Islands, are notorious tax havens. So much so, the UK would leap from twenty-third to top of the Financial Secrecy Index were all such territories included.[152]

The EU operates a tax haven blacklist or "list of non-cooperative tax jurisdictions".[153] All EU countries share and reference this aggregate list. The EU denies blacklisted countries certain types of funding. It imposes strict, binding reporting requirements on tax and financial dealings involving listed countries. Individual EU member states also apply their own sanctions. But the EU's blacklist doesn't contain any EU countries or overseas territories.[154] Critics argue that the EU appears to allow them more leeway than non-EU countries get.[155] So if anything, our decision to leave the EU would increase the likelihood of the UK's overseas territories winding up on the blacklist.

Not only is Brexit not about trying to sideline tax avoidance measures, but our leaving the EU might well result in more such measures applying to the UK.

That said, once it leaves the EU, the UK will certainly have more control over its tax affairs. There are aspects of domestic direct taxation it might choose to tinker with once EU oversight is out of the picture. However, taken together, these would not appear to justify a project as drastic as Brexit.[156]

11. The £39 billion financial settlement

Our financial settlement with the EU is one of the most contentious aspects of leaving. The "divorce settlement" (in media parlance) represents what we still owe the EU for expenses we incurred while a member, including pension liabilities for UK staff. It also covers future funding commitments we have already signed off on. For instance, in 2013 we agreed to join in the infrastructure funding round through 2020.[157] Finally, it takes into account certain things the EU owes us. We will get back the capital we paid in over the years into the European Investment Bank and the European Central Bank, along with some other refunds.[158]

The UK and the EU agreed a net figure of £39 billion after a negotiation that spanned more than a year. (Note what was actually agreed was a complex formula to calculate what we owe, not a specific amount of money. There is no legal document that says "the UK owes the EU £39 billion." That sum is the estimate which emerged from the formula.[159])

£39 billion was the total owing as of March 2019. The amount is lower now because we delayed Brexit, and so we have already paid off some of our obligations as part of daily EU business. By the time we get to 31 October 2019, the bill should be down to £33 billion.[160]

Brexiters often misinterpret what the money's for. They claim we can walk away without paying in the event of no deal. As Boris Johnson put it: The EU can "go whistle".[161] The right-wing press is happy to play along. Articles confect outrage that the EU would dare to demand payment without giving us a deal in return.[162] But we are not buying a deal. We are settling what we owe. We can no more walk away from our commitments than you could cancel a mobile phone contract without paying off the handset in full.

Brexiters back up their mistaken assertion by referring to a House of Lords report from March 2017, "Brexit and the EU Budget". It stated: "Although there are competing interpretations, we conclude that if agreement is not reached, all EU law – including provisions concerning ongoing financial contributions and machinery for adjudication – will cease to apply, and the UK would be subject to no enforceable obligation to make any financial contribution at all."[163] The key word Brexiters gloss over is "enforceable". We would still have a financial obligation but the EU might not be able to collect on it, just as you might be able to dodge debt collectors by running away to Brazil.

Threats of non-payment have been made at the highest level. Boris Johnson said: "I think our friends and partners need to understand that the money is going to be retained until such time as we have greater clarity about the way forward."[164] His sentiment was mirrored by Donald Trump, our ever reliable friend across the Pond: "If I were them I wouldn't pay $50 billion. That is me. I would not pay, that is a tremendous number."

The idea behind these threats seems to be that the EU will roll over and let us tickle its tummy if we pay up. The story goes that they are so concerned about not getting paid, they will capitulate to the UK's demands rather than risk losing the money.

There are four problems with this notion.

1. We're not talking about a lump sum. The money is due to flow to the EU on a decreasing schedule well into the middle of the century. (With life expectancy what it is, the pension component of our commitments may continue into the 2060s or even beyond.) And the agreement includes a commitment that the UK doesn't have to pay more in any given year than it would have as an EU member. That caps our payments at about £9 billion a year. So the EU will never face a single gaping hole in its budget.

2. The full EU budget is about £125 billion a year. Even our maximum possible payment of £9 billion a year is only 7.2% of that. That's an uncomfortable amount to be out, but not something that will tip the EU into recession or even cause it serious difficulty. And when you consider the wider EU economy at £11 trillion a year, our £9 billion would be like a pinprick to an elephant. (That doesn't mean they won't want their money. Pinpricks still hurt. But any plan that relies on the pain of withholding it is doomed to fail.)

3. The financial settlement may not be directly linked to a deal, but withholding it will ruin the UK's reputation. Whatever happened to the British sense of fair play? If we want a decent trade deal with the EU, we are going to have to pay what we owe.

4. If we flat out refuse to pay, we can expect the EU to pursue legal action to recoup what it is owed. We live in a world where bailiffs

> will kick down a door and take the TV over a debt of a few hundred pounds. It's hubristic to imagine the EU will let the matter slide. ("You know what, we had some fun times. We're not going to hassle you over the money. Have a great life.")

Brexiters are also making lofty promises about spending the £39 billion in the UK in short order instead of giving it to the EU as international law requires. Firstly, that's no longer the correct amount, but what's £6 billion between friends? Secondly, this betrays another misunderstanding. They talk as if the money's sitting in a bank vault; on Brexit Day, a fleet of trucks will load it all onto planes ready to be flown to Brussels. But there isn't a single lump sum, nor does there need to be. So their accelerated spending plans do not hold water.

It is worth noting that if Boris Johnson manages to resurrect and pass a Withdrawal Agreement that includes a transition period, we will likely have to pay a similar amount per year during the transition period as we currently do for EU membership. That will come off the total we owe the EU, so the remaining sum will fall quickly. But it would push off the point at which we might start to see savings from having left the EU until 2021 or later.

In summary, the financial settlement is an important part of our leaving preparations. It demonstrates we are a responsible country that pays its debts. That should stand us in good stead in the post-Brexit negotiations. But in the bigger picture, it's a non-issue. We've negotiated it. We should settle our bill like good global citizens. And that should be the end of the matter.

12. Our "worthless" EU membership

As Oscar Wilde's character Lord Darlington observed, a cynic is "a man who knows the price of everything and the value of nothing."[165] He could have been talking about some Brexiters. Witness Boris Johnson's oft-repeated accusation that every month we stay in the EU costs the UK £1 billion.[166] As well as overstating the real cost, his complaint assigns a zero value to everything we gain from EU membership.

Peace? Worthless. Vast amounts of frictionless trade? Worthless. Just-in-time manufacturing? Worthless. Freedom to work and live anywhere in the EU? Worthless. Scientific and technological collaboration? Worthless. Security and defence cooperation? Worthless. And so on and so forth, ad nauseam. Nothing has value in Boris Johnson's book.

His attitude is like saying you could save on your mortgage and utilities by sleeping in a cardboard box on the streets. Or suggesting that Wetherspoon boss Tim Martin should stop wasting money and give up paying rent on his pubs.

You pay for your home because it gives you comfort, security and stability. Tim Martin accepts the cost of rent because the company gets more back in return.

Because some on the Leave side ascribe no value to our EU membership, it's easy for them to claim that since other countries manage fine outside the EU, we will too. To them the loss of our EU membership doesn't enter the equation. Why should it, when it's not worth anything? Once you realise how alien their world view is, it's like a lightbulb coming on.

Brexiters seem happy to rely on nebulous concepts that support their side of the Brexit debate. How much is greater sovereignty worth? What about the freedom to make our own laws? Nobody insists on quantifying these in pounds and pence terms. It would be as absurd as trying to herd mist. Yet they shouldn't be dismissed just because we can't slap a price tag on them.

But the same goes for our membership of the EU. You can't dismiss its benefits just because you can't quantify them. Any evaluation that consists exclusively of a "cost" column is biased, plain and simple.

13. We can take back control of our rules and regulations

One motivation cited for leaving the EU is that we will be able to control our own regulations once more. Why should some supranational body dictate our approach to product safety or to the environment, or tell us how long staff are allowed to work each week?

The notion is appealing. Nobody likes being told what to do. But those making the case leave out a crucial detail: the EU's regulations are a floor not a ceiling.

We can't strip away worker protections established by EU rules, but we can give employees even more rights. We have to make sure our air is at least as clean as EU standards require, but nothing stops us legislating to make it even more minty fresh. (As Defra puts it: "Action to manage and improve air quality is largely driven by European (EU) legislation."[167]) And so on.

Theresa May herself misrepresented the situation. In a key speech in Grimsby on 8 March 2019, she said: "But we will not tie ourselves in automatically to follow EU changes without Parliament having its say. That would mean weakening workers' rights if the EU ever chose to do so."[168] But right now that's not the case. We have to track EU regulations when they tighten, but we can always maintain ours at the previous level if the EU weakens theirs.

Small wonder the average person may be confused.

What might be behind this drive for deregulation? It is true some EU regulations may be ill-suited to the way we work. For instance those applicable to the number of hours commercial drivers can spend behind the wheel.[169] There will inevitably be examples of frustrating red tape if we look hard enough. But we can negotiate exemptions (as we did in the case of the drivers' hours rules). And of course we have a say in the rule-making process itself courtesy of our EU membership.

Another motivation appears more sinister. If you want the power to deregulate, but the existing system already gives you the flexibility to make your own regulations stricter than you're required to, there's only one direction of travel left...

This concern is more than theoretical. Brexiters have placed on record their desire to erode EU standards on numerous occasions. For example:

- In December 2016, Michael Gove and John Whittingdale suggested to the CBI that its member companies could draw up a list of the regulations they would like abolished or reformed after Brexit.[170]

- Also in December 2016, Jacob Rees-Mogg told a Treasury Select Committee hearing: "We could take [deregulation] a very long way. American emission standards are fine – probably in some cases higher. […] I accept that we're not going to allow dangerous toys to come in from China, we don't want to see those kind of risks. But there's a very long way you can go."[171] (Note the "in some cases" part.)

- In March 2017, Gove floated the notion of getting rid of EU regulations on clinical trials and on protecting wildlife habitats.[172]

- In October 2018, Rees-Mogg expressed an interest in getting rid of the MiFID II regulations which came into force in the EU earlier that year.[173] These were intended to improve transparency and reporting standards in financial transactions. (Rees-Mogg co-founded a fund management company, Somerset Capital Management, in 2007. He stepped down from his advisory role at the firm in July 2019, on joining Boris Johnson's Cabinet.[174])

- In August 2019, Boris Johnson made his intent to diverge from EU standards explicit in a letter to Donald Tusk, the EU Council President. It read: "Although we will remain committed to world-class environment, product and labour standards, the laws and regulations to deliver them will potentially diverge from those of the EU. That is the point of our exit and our ability to enable this is central to our future democracy."[175]

- In October 2019, aerospace firms expressed alarm at Boris Johnson's plan to drop Theresa May's commitment that the UK would continue to participate in certain EU regulatory institutions. The BBC reported that ADS, the aerospace industry body, had stated that "continued membership of the European Aviation Safety Agency (EASA) and alignment with EU chemicals regulations" were vital to the sector, and that regulatory divergence would result in "huge new costs and disruptions to many of our member companies".[176]

It is undeniable that deregulation might open up new trade opportunities. For instance, the US has already made it clear it would like to see a deal that includes agriculture. But that would mean opening the door to chlorinated chicken, hormone-fed beef and other dubious products.

US standards of food hygiene have been demonstrated statistically to be much lower than ours. In the UK, salmonella affects just 0.015% of people a year. In the US it affects a whopping 0.37% of the population – 25 times worse! In the case of campylobacter, the US sees an infection rate of 0.4% compared to only 0.096% in the UK.[177]

The fact that someone wants to sell something to us shouldn't be reason enough to hold our noses and accept it. Yet Liz Truss, the Secretary of State for International Trade, has stated that the UK diverging from the EU's level playing field standards after Brexit is "vital for giving us the freedom and flexibility to strike new trade deals and become more competitive".[178]

Our Government has stated its intent to transcribe into UK law what used to be in EU law. But it will then be free to amend our copy at any time, or scrunch it up and throw it in the bin. Politicians love to flex their legislative muscles. Once they have the power to meddle in regulation, some will be overcome with desire to do so. At first, the proposed changes may seem relatively harmless. A small tweak to workers' rights to allow truckers to work longer hours. A minor relaxation of standards on wood coatings. But the slope is slippery, and it is steep. Can we trust those doing the cutting to distinguish between the national interest and what their friends in industry would like? Even when the latter are showering them with money and favours? The pressure to slip with the saw will be immense.

Boris Johnson made a speech at JCB headquarters on 18 January 2019 in which he praised the company several times. He spoke at a podium emblazoned with the JCB logo. JCB diggers provided a backdrop.[179] Three days before the speech, JCB had paid him £10,000.[180] Nothing about this was untoward, but it does make you think. If the line between political and corporate interests can blur so much, where does it lie? And as we saw during the MP expense scandal, not all our politicians are equally ethical.

Some erosion of domestic standards has already begun. For instance, a study by the University of Sussex found that the UK Government weakened the EU rules surrounding pesticides in transcribing them into domestic law. Instead of requiring independent scientific advice on the safety of new pesticides, our version of the law merely obliges ministers to make their own risk assessment. It will be at their discretion whether to consider scientific evidence or not.[181]

If you're of a certain age, you may remember a time when Britain's beaches were little more than open sewers, and a floater wasn't someone on an inflatable unicorn seeking that perfect Instagram moment. But in the mid 1970s, the EU got involved in monitoring and enforcing pollution standards. Through a series of ever more draconian regulations, it forced a step change in the UK's attitude to our beaches. We eventually cleaned up our act, though the UK Government fought the measures at every turn. (Imagine being the person in Westminster arguing to be allowed to keep dumping raw sewage into the sea. What a job!) The UK was the "dirty man of Europe" no longer.[182] Could we have achieved that improvement without the EU? In theory, yes. Nothing ever stopped us imposing our own clean water laws. But would we have done so? The fact that our own Government battled hard to stop the changes suggests not.

Something else is missing from this picture. When you want to trade freely with other countries, your products must conform to their standards at a minimum. We don't accept chlorinated chicken from the USA because it doesn't meet EU food hygiene standards. But by the same token, the EU isn't going to welcome UK products after Brexit that don't meet the EU's own safety and other standards. So even if a future Government did deregulate our standards, manufacturers wanting to sell into the EU will have to keep up with and adhere to EU ones. As a consequence, we could end up with two distinct classes of products after Brexit. Cheaper ones for domestic consumption, produced to laxer standards. (Lower animal welfare meat, less safe toys, less reliable electrical goods, and so on.) And more expensive higher quality goods made for export to the EU, conforming to its standards. Parallel production would make manufacturing more complicated. But firms might still find it worthwhile if lower domestic standards let them cut costs far enough.

Price-sensitive consumers might choose cheap products made to low domestic standards. (Those on limited budgets may not have the luxury of choice.) People with deeper pockets will demand products made to EU standards. The net effect of this sort of deregulation will be to create a whole new culture of haves and have nots within the UK. Those who can afford them will buy good quality food and products. The poor will be forced to make do with high intensity farmed food, and inferior goods too shoddy to sell into the EU.

It's too simplistic to say that EU standards are *always* good, and that there is no case for deregulation. But there is an abundance of reasons to be cautious of a precipitate push towards the latter.

14. Brexit won't end on Brexit Day

Many Brexiters repeat the statement that we need to "get Brexit done" every chance they get. They go on to claim that the UK needs to focus on domestic issues. They're right that the latter have been sorely neglected. But they are being very misleading in suggesting that Brexit will end on Brexit Day. Brexit is a process, not a one-time event.

It is true that we will leave the EU on Brexit Day. Our EU membership will end. We will have fulfilled the referendum promise to leave, no ifs or buts. If Brexit were nothing more than a checkbox on a to-do list, we could tick it and move on.

But the situation is not that simple. As we breathe in the sweet smell of freedom, the hardest work will still lie ahead. Brexit Day is the first day of the Brexit process proper, not the last day of Brexit. It's not like some fairytale wedding, followed by happily ever after.

It's as if we are setting out to run a marathon. Everything so far has been warm-up and preparation. On Brexit Day, we will line up at the starting line and the real race will get under way. A race to secure the new relationships we need with the EU and with other parties. What do we do about the Irish border? Security cooperation? Gibraltar? The rights of EU and UK citizens? And of course our crucial trading arrangements with the EU. There will be a thousand and one issues to resolve.

The two part nature of the deal that Theresa May brought back from Brussels reflected this reality. It included the Withdrawal Agreement setting out the terms on which we leave. And the Political Declaration, a wish list of what our future relationship with the EU might look like. If it ever gets ratified, the terms of the Withdrawal Agreement will be legally binding. The Political Declaration by contrast won't be. It is a statement of intent, but nothing obliges either side to abide by a specific outcome.

All the arguments that have raged over the last three years about the shape of Brexit will continue once we've left the EU. Do we want a close relationship with the EU, like the one Norway has? The political declaration allows for that. Or would we prefer a much looser arrangement like Canada's, on the basis of a comprehensive free trade deal? One that leaves us with greater control over our own affairs, at a cost of more trade friction and red tape. The political declaration supports that too. It's like a menu in a restaurant. A plethora of dishes are on offer, but we still have to choose one. And if the last three years has taught us anything, it's that we're a picky group of diners who never see eye to eye.

So the fights will still go on between those who want a hard Brexit and those who want to keep close ties with the EU. Between those seeking the freedom to set our own trade policy, and those who want tight integration with the largest trading bloc on the planet.

One thing will change: the push to Remain will end. (We have no chance of staying in the EU at that point, because we will already be out.) In its place will come a drive to replicate as much of our former EU relationship as possible to minimise the impact of leaving. And we will no doubt also see the first stirrings of a movement to rejoin. For many, EU membership is too important and too desirable to spurn for long.

The balance of power will change during this second, more difficult negotiating phase. We will be out, so the real or imagined threat of no deal will no longer be available. It would be like threatening to divorce your ex-wife. The EU will watch the impact of Brexit unfold. It will witness the harm Brexit causes our industries, and the administrative burden it imposes on UK firms. It may pity the hard times a good friend is enduring: the chaos and privations, the queues at the ports. But Brexit doesn't affect the EU's relationship with the rest of the world, only with us. From its perspective, the only companies and people impacted will be those dealing with the UK in some way. We will be the ones in a hurry, with a laundry list of outstanding issues to resolve.

The EU's options will be wide open. It will still have 27 members, and one of the largest markets in the world. It will have free trade deals with over 50 countries, and thousands of other treaties to make business and life easier for its 440 million citizens. We will have… nothing.

Boris Johnson may yet bring Theresa May's deal back to Parliament, either as-is or slightly tweaked. It seems unlikely that he will. But if he does and it passes at the fourth time of asking, it will secure us a transition period. That would give us a year or so of relative calm before the Brexit storm hits us. It will be a strange sort of purgatory. We will be legally out of the EU, so the notion of "Remain" falls away. But the transition period will protect us from the ravages of Brexit. Day to day life won't change much. That's a good thing, of course. But the lack of change may breed complacency. The general public may conclude, incorrectly, that Brexit was not damaging. That there was nothing to worry about after all. "Huh. Was that what all the fuss was about?" (Parallels with Y2K, as explained later in this book.) The tabloids will reinforce this mistaken view with an endless stream of gloating "it was all Project Fear" headlines because to publish anything else would be to admit that they were previously complicit in disseminating false information.

But the transition period only postpones the Brexit damage. It's like walking the plank over a sea teeming with sharks. So long as you linger at the end of it, the sharks can't hurt you. But after a year or so of watching fins popping in and out of the waves, we will have the plank removed from under us. So we only have limited time to arrange a boat.

Firms will still face uncertainty during transition. The act of having left will resolve the question of whether we are leaving the EU or not. But they won't know how much Brexit will affect their business until they know what our post-transition arrangements will be. But we won't be able to resolve that until our politicians come to agreement. The heat death of the universe may come first, judging by recent events.

The uncertainty will also end if there's no transition period and we exit without a deal on 31 October (or whenever). It will give way to a chilling clarity: the knowledge that we shredded our relationship with the EU without anything to replace it.

Either way, our departure will push companies to activate their remaining contingency plans. Firms are reluctant to spend money if they don't have to. Many will have held off on major moves as long as possible because of the question mark hanging over Brexit. But the door to remaining in the EU will slam shut when we leave. With our fate clear, they will speed up moving production out of the EU, reconfiguring supply lines and taking other mitigating actions.

The only way to "get Brexit done" in the sense of "finished quickly" would be to revoke Article 50 and stay in the EU. Brexit would be over and our EU membership would carry on as normal. Doesn't that sound more appealing than years or decades more negotiation and uncertainty?

15. Brexit scepticism and "Project Fear"

The dangers posed by Brexit can feel unreal because we have little experience of the overnight upending of the normal. The UK rarely faces natural disasters. We do not have to cope with volcanoes, tidal waves or earthquakes (fracking tremors aside). Nor do we endure hurricanes like those that ravage the Atlantic and Pacific basins each year. The Great Storm of 1987 earned its capital letters because it was a freak black swan event. Our domestic misfortunes are much more limited in scope. Train crashes, rivers bursting their banks, the occasional shipwreck etc. Most impact a small area or group of people, leaving the rest of the country unaffected. There's always someone in a position to lend a hand. The closest we get to all being in it together is when an Arctic blast blankets us in white. Cue transport chaos, and minor shortages in the shops.

The generation that lived through the Second World War aside, few have experienced upheaval on a major scale. Nor have we endured catastrophes that have lasted for any length of time. This otherwise fortunate gap in our experience disadvantages us when it comes to analysing Brexit objectively.

It's hard to internalise the idea of food shortages when you're confronted by bulging shelves. It's difficult to believe the government could force pharmacies to ration medicines. "There must be some mistake," we shrug, before getting on with our lives. Even if we grasp Brexit warnings on an intellectual level, they don't hit us viscerally.

But our inability to appreciate the true level of danger does not lessen it. If anything, it amplifies the problem. Until Brexit "gets real" we will continue to dither and dodge, rather than face the issue square on.

What applies at the personal level applies to businesses too. An August 2019 survey showed only one in ten firms in Northern Ireland have prepared for no deal. Barely one in three larger firms have made any effort.[183] This despite the fact that Brexit, and especially a no deal Brexit, will have a greater impact on Northern Ireland than on almost any other part of the UK.[184] Across the UK as a whole, only 741 companies have applied for the grants set aside by the Government to help them learn how to handle new customs processes. That's 741 out of close to a quarter of a million firms that trade with the EU.[185]

To be fair, it's also hard to prepare when you don't know what kind of Brexit we're getting. And a lot of companies don't have the resources or competencies to invest in preparing for all the eventualities, including those that may never happen.

In short, we are not nearly ready enough. To some extent, that is because Brexit mitigation measures can only go so far. They cannot replicate the situation we currently enjoy as EU members. But it's also because we don't appreciate the need to prepare. We cannot get over our disbelief because the scenarios seem too far-fetched.

The more that politicians, industry figures and experts try to raise the alarm, the more their efforts are dismissed as Project Fear. Brexiters exploit our innate scepticism. "Well, they would claim that," they say, waving away the latest prediction.

Many people accept this Project Fear "explanation" and move on. What they should be doing instead is questioning the motives of both sides in the debate. Why are those making predictions saying what they do? How does a senior doctor, a haulage industry insider or an international trade specialist benefit from making things up? What's the merit in them doing so? Is it credible that hundreds or thousands of experts have gone public with identical conclusions just to frighten people?

If you believe they are trying to overturn the referendum result, why? What do they stand to gain from stopping Brexit? The simplest explanation is the most believable: they want to prevent the situation they warned about because *they will experience it alongside the rest of us.* They also want to give us the best chance to prepare. Forewarned is forearmed.

The motivation of the Brexiters is obvious. If people swallow their Project Fear brushoff, they won't have to admit to the problems that Brexit will cause.

An example of this came when Michael Gove appeared on the Andrew Marr Show on 1 September 2019. Gove claimed there would be "no shortages of fresh food".[186] The British Retail Consortium responded immediately, saying: "The retail industry has been crystal clear in its communications with government over the past 36 months that the availability of fresh foods will be impacted as a result of checks and delays at the border."[187]

A second example of the phenomenon came the very next day, in the form of an exchange between Jacob Rees-Mogg and Doctor David Nicholl on LBC Radio.[188] The doctor had called in to ask "what mortality rate are you willing to accept in the light of a no deal Brexit?" JRM responded by saying he didn't think there was any reason to suspect an increased mortality rate, calling it "the worst excess of Project Fear". He went on to attack the credibility of the doctor at some length. This, even though the doctor had already explained he had been involved in drafting Operation Yellowhammer, the no deal Brexit mitigation document commissioned by the UK Government.

Our Prime Minister is not immune to knowing-better-than-experts disease. Boris Johnson dismissed the Brexit concerns of Jaguar Land Rover chief executive Ralf Speth in January 2019. When the host of a radio show put it to him that Mr Speth knew more about car manufacturing than he did, Johnson replied: "I'm not certain he does."[189]

Speaking of Operation Yellowhammer, how can the Government's confidential Brexit planning document constitute Project Fear, as a parade of ministers have claimed ever since it was leaked?[190] What would be the point of falsifying a major document drawn up with the input of hundreds of subject matter experts? One that was never even meant to see the light of day?

There is no quick cure for doubts about Brexit's true impacts. But a big step in the right direction is to treat any mention of "Project Fear" as a signal to lean in and pay more attention, not less. Above all, be honest with yourself. If you're nodding along to the Project Fear label, is that because of your enthusiasm for Brexit? Or do you have first-hand knowledge that warrants your scepticism? Keenness is no substitute for facts.

16. Are we really leading the charge to exit the EU?

Some Brexiters like to claim that the UK is at the front of a queue of countries waiting to leave the EU; other nations are sure to follow us out the door.

Recent data doesn't support their view. 25 out of 28 EU countries profess to be predominantly happy with how the EU is run – even places where support for anti-EU hardliners has been on the rise, such as Italy and Poland. In France and the UK, somewhat less than half the population are satisfied with the way the EU works. Greece is the only country that has an overwhelmingly negative view of how it operates. Greece also happens to be the only country (apart from the UK) in which less than 50% of people are optimistic about the EU's future.[191]

Why is that important? Because it's all too easy to project our own feelings about the European project onto our neighbours. In doing so, we lose sight that others may not feel as we do.

This is reflected in the muted interest in Frexit, Grexit and other coinages derived from Brexit. Calls to leave the EU have dampened down considerably since our own decision to quit the block.[192]

Put plainly, we are not in the vanguard of a horde of rebel nations that are just waiting for our signal to throw off their own chains. If anything, we are an object lesson on the dangers of doing so.

17. In my day, a pound was worth a pound...

The pound plunged against other currencies in the immediate aftermath of the referendum. One pound was worth US$1.46 the day before the referendum and US$1.37 a couple of days after, a fall of 6.1%. It was worth US$1.25 on 24 July 2019 (the day Boris Johnson became Prime Minister) and just US$1.22 as of 9 October i.e. 17.9% less than at referendum time. The pound-euro exchange rate picture is no prettier. A pound was worth 1.30 euro before the vote, and 1.22 euro immediately afterwards (6.1% less). It was worth 1.12 euro on 24 July and just 1.11 euro as of 9 October (15.8% less).[193]

Those claiming that the pound's depreciation has nothing to do with Brexit point out that currencies fluctuate all the time. True, they do, but it is important to distinguish daily changes from long-term trends. Glance at any currency chart going back a decade or more and the disconnect at the exact moment of the referendum will leap out at you. The vote for Leave set the pound plunging like a roller-coaster. Having fallen, it started trading in a new, lower band. One way to think of what happened might be to imagine the pound as a rubber ball bouncing around one storey of an office block. Off the floor, off the ceiling, off the floor again, always within certain boundaries. Bounce, bounce, bounce... The referendum was like taking the lift to a lower floor, then setting the ball bouncing again.

Boris Johnson appears to have had a similar effect to the referendum, in miniature. The pound fell as he took office and has bumped along its new lows ever since. From a certain point of view, having him as Prime Minister has literally made the UK poorer.

Companies that trade overseas endure currency fluctuations as a cost of doing business. Larger firms hedge their long-term exposure by locking in a given exchange rate six months or a year ahead. But it has become clear that the effects of the referendum were far greater than firms had planned for. Many, many companies lined up to issue profit warnings in the aftermath of the 2016 vote. Some were able to delay doing so because of hedging arrangements, but eventually pound shock caught up with them too. The amounts in question were substantial, losses of tens or even hundreds of millions of pounds per firm. And as we've already seen, the situation has not improved since.

Who benefits from a falling pound?

In theory, British exporters should gain from a weaker pound. After all, their products will be more affordable for buyers abroad. But many firms rely on imported raw materials, especially from the EU. So their input, transport and other costs will have gone up, dampening this positive effect.

One sector that has been a clear beneficiary is inbound tourism, i.e. foreign tourists coming to the UK.[194] We have become a bargain destination, a shopper's paradise (compared to pre-referendum prices anyway).

Some Brexit supporters like to claim that the performance of the FTSE100 discredits the negative narrative around the pound and Brexit. This notion is based on a fallacy, since firms quoted on the FTSE100 are huge multinationals that conduct most of their business outside the UK. The lower pound makes their overseas earnings worth more when repatriated to the UK, boosting their bottom line. In that respect, the FTSE100 cannot be considered a reflection of the wider economy. Most firms don't have the luxury of overseas subsidiaries funnelling foreign revenue home.

Who gets hurt by a falling pound?

UK tourists heading abroad find their pounds don't go very far these days. Airport bureaux de change (notorious for their rip-off rates) are offering holidaymakers much less than 1 euro per pound. And although online forex firms offer better rates, overseas holidays remain significantly more expensive than a few years ago.

The devalued pound has driven up costs for firms reliant on imports. These went up 6% as soon as the referendum result came in, and now they're having to pay 16%-18% more for the same products and services compared with before the referendum. (That's before inflation.) Some firms have managed to absorb all or part of the increase. But many, especially in the food and drink sector, have taken drastic measures to make up the difference. Shrinkflation is rampant. We've all experienced it: you pick up something at the supermarket and find it's smaller or lighter than expected, yet no cheaper. Perhaps the most notorious example is the Toblerone bar, which lost its traditional look, becoming rake-like as it shrank from 170g to 150g. Manufacturer Mondelez later reversed its stance after significant criticism and restored the chocolate bar to its original shape, but positioned it at a much higher price.[195]

The falling pound has also negatively impacted the UK's GDP relative to other countries. (GDP tends to be measured and compared in dollar terms.) This is one of the reasons why our economy, the fifth largest in the world before the referendum, has sunk to sixth place since it was held.

UK companies have become juicy takeover targets because of the cheap pound. Recent examples include the July 2019 sale of Cobham for £4 billion to a US private equity firm[196] and the acquisition of Greene King by Li Ka-shin (Hong Kong's wealthiest man) in August 2019.[197] If the pound weakens further when Brexit proper happens, as most market observers expect, we could suffer a feeding frenzy as our most desirable assets get snapped up for a song. Conversely, UK firms will find foreign assets more and more expensive to acquire, limiting their global competitiveness.

The devalued pound makes the UK a less attractive destination for foreign workers. Migrant workers, only over here for a few weeks or months, are the worst affected. The money they save to send or take home is worth a lot less than it used to be. This affects recruitment in sectors such as hospitality and agriculture. The latter is particularly dependent on migrant labour; tens of thousands of people come to help with the harvest.[198] Farmers have been forced to let huge quantities of fruit and vegetables rot because the seasonal EU workforce they depend on has dried up. One, based outside St Andrews, said enough broccoli to feed 15,000 people was wasted.[199] On a farm in Ledbury, 87,000 punnets of raspberries went to waste for want of 100 pickers.[200]

18. Other countries do just fine outside the EU

Since countries such as Japan and Canada thrive outside the EU, why are we so afraid to join them?

The logical flaw in this question is that the countries being held up as examples of successful non-EU states have never been in the EU. They've had years and years to build up their relationships with other countries, layer after layer, like geological sediment: bilateral free trade deals, participation in regional trade associations, industry partnerships, knowledge transfers and so on. It is these complex networks of arrangements which have allowed them to thrive without the EU.

We can, too, provided we have the kind of agreements in place that they already do – the real issue to focus on is the need to develop those agreements, which will take decades.

So yes, we can eventually end up with the same kind of trade agreements etc. as other non-EU countries. But we're starting 40 years behind them, so we will have to endure an intervening period of poor trading conditions and all the other chaos that comes with Brexit until we get into a reasonable position. We'll all be running the same race, but the EU will be miles ahead and the other countries will all have massive head starts on us.

Someone born blind can live a full life, albeit with minor restrictions. But a person struck by sudden blindness in old age will find it almost impossible to adapt, and may never recover their autonomy.

If we were a new country taking our first steps in the world, we might decide that EU membership was not for us. But we're not. We have that relationship already. It's no good pretending it doesn't exist.

19. Things were fine before we joined the EU

Some Brexiters have their gaze locked on the rear-view mirror. We were fine before we joined the EU, so why not again?

Put plainly, the world now is not what it used to be. For instance:

- Globalisation happened. Communication improvements shrank distance and cheap air travel brought everyone closer.
- Industries which once employed millions – coal mining, shipbuilding, steel etc. – withered and died, even as the service sector grew like a weed.
- The internet has made it possible to check the prices of a supplier in Manchester as easily as one in Madrid or Munich. Thanks to the EU's single market and customs union, all of them compete for business on a level playing field.
- We no longer have the resources of an Empire to draw on (most people would say that's a very good thing).
- Our natural resources were never plentiful; now North Sea oil is running out.
- Instead of building up a sovereign wealth fund over the decades, successive UK governments chose to spend surplus oil taxes and other revenue on keeping non-oil taxes as low as possible.[201] This naked populism has left us without anything stashed away as a nation to weather any prolonged downturn. Contrast this with Norway's prudent stewardship, for instance: today, the Norwegians are sitting on over a trillion dollars of state investments.[202]

Brexit will not reverse any of the above trends. Indeed, it cannot.

But change wasn't confined to the UK. Back in the early 1970s, before we joined the Common Market, China was still a largely agrarian economy, the Soviet Union languished behind the Iron Curtain, and "Made in Japan" meant shoddy goods rather than the badge of quality it is today. We now face potent competitors that weren't on anyone's radar screen forty years ago.

The EU will always be a hop and a skip away across the Channel. Geography precludes us from ever having a closer trading partner. There is also the not inconsequential matter of our existing EU membership. We have been members for so long – two generations – that we have dismantled dozens of institutions whose functions we now delegate to the EU. Re-establishing them, as we must after Brexit, will be an involved and costly process.

Wallowing in backward-looking isolation won't be splendid, only lonely. We can never recapture the good old days. And if we take off the rose-tinted spectacles for a more honest look, we will see those days were never that good to start with.

20. They need us more than we need them

Since the EU exports more to us than we do to them, they supposedly have more to lose from Brexit than we do. This is the origin of the myth that the German auto industry will come galloping over the hill to save us. As David Davis put it in February 2016: "Within minutes of a vote for Brexit the chief executives of Mercedes, BMW, VW and Audi will be knocking down Chancellor Merkel's door demanding that there be no barriers to German access to the British market."[203]

The reality is very different.

The EU is by far our largest trade partner. We export £289 billion in goods and services there, and import £345 billion. So our trade deficit is £64 billion. At first glance, the EU would indeed appear to have more to lose than us if new trade barriers make trading harder.[204]

But we ignore the relative sizes of both economies at our peril. The potential loss of up to £289 billion of export trade is a huge blow for a single country (the UK). The potential loss of up to £345 billion in exports is a lesser blow when spread across 27 countries (the EU). If you take a pint of blood from a Chihuahua, it will die. Draw the same amount from a human, and they'll earn a cup of tea and a biscuit for being a good citizen.

We need proper context. The UK population is 66.6 million, the EU's is 513.5 million.[205] Our economy is worth £2.2 trillion, theirs £14.6 trillion. It is obvious they are in a position to spread the pain of Brexit much more than we are.[206]

All the other EU countries will still be EU members after Brexit. They will continue to enjoy frictionless free trade with other EU27 states. In other words, EU firms will be able to tap into a market 6.7 times the size of ours in their attempt to make up any post-Brexit loss of UK trade. We will have to resort to scrabbling for business in our much smaller domestic market.

The situation will be even more tilted in the EU's favour. It will still have all its trade deals with the rest of the world (Japan, Canada, South Korea and so on.) So EU companies will find it relatively easier to pivot to new markets than UK firms will. But British companies will face tariffs on their exports to those same non-EU countries, at least until we can get deals in place. As a result, British-made products will become even less competitive.

We can keep watching that hill, waiting for the German car manufacturers. But we will wait forever.

21. Fish tales about Brexit and fishing

"Take back control of our waters" was one of the key messages of the Leave campaign. The week before the referendum, Nigel Farage led a fleet of fishing boats up the Thames to Parliament in a high profile stunt. There it encountered a rival Remain fleet spearheaded by Bob

Geldof. Much shouting ensued.[207] Brexiters have brought up the subject of fishing regularly ever since, making hay from the idea that the UK will be able to break free of the EU's Common Fisheries Policy.

Although fishing is a small industry, it is a dominant source of jobs in some of the most disadvantaged communities. The plight of its workers has caught the public's imagination. There is an undeniable romance to the notion of Britannia ruling the waves again, albeit only in matters piscine. As such, fishing has had an outsize impact on the wider Brexit narrative. But context remains important. As of 2017, the industry employed 11,692 people who landed 724,000 tonnes of fish and shellfish, worth £980 million.[208] (For comparison, the UK auto industry counts over 800,000 workers in its supply chain, and has a turnover of £82 billion.[209])

Many of the biggest problems facing the fishing industry have nothing to do with the EU. Leaving won't solve them, but it may well create new ones.

Each coastal state of the EU has an exclusive economic zone (EEZ) extending 200 nautical miles off its coastline. It nominally has the right to control the fish within its EEZ. But the EU's Common Fisheries Policy pools all these different EEZ into a single EU-wide zone, so in practice that right is not applicable. The EU then distributes catch quotas to individual member states based on historic fishing patterns and other considerations. It decides which vessels can access what parts of the zone, and sets limits on the number of vessels in a fleet and the time they can spend at sea. The UK divides its share of the EU quota between England, Scotland, Wales and Northern Ireland. Each region's quota is subdivided further, into fixed quota allocations (FQA). Industry players can lease or trade these FQA. The UK Government has oversight of this process; the EU's involvement ends with its allocation of quotas to EU member states.

Lax government oversight has allowed a handful of firms to grab the lion's share of the sector. According to a 2018 Unearthed investigation, just 25 firms control two thirds of the UK's fishing quota. Many of the biggest quota holders are foreign entities.[210] Almost four in five UK vessels are under 10m in length, yet well over half the total capacity of the fleet comes from a small number of vessels over 24m long. These so-called supertrawlers are responsible for catching three quarters of all fish.[211]

Smaller firms have suffered from this concentration of quotas and catch capacity. But since this situation was caused entirely by domestic policy decisions, leaving the EU is unlikely to break the grip large players have over the industry.

One Brexit carrot dangled in front of the fishing industry is that we will no longer have to share our waters with EU fishing vessels. But reciprocity is at stake. If we lock EU firms out of our waters, the EU will bar UK firms from its own.

The EU would seem to have more to lose than us as EU fleets catch eight times as much fish in UK waters as UK ones do in EU waters.[212] However, like most things Brexit-related, the situation is more nuanced. We export two thirds of all the fish we catch to the EU. After Brexit, tariffs will apply to fish landed in the EU by UK vessels. In a no deal scenario, UK vessels will lose the automatic right to land their catch in any EU port.[213] They will face extra customs formalities and inspections too. An official vet or local authority environmental health officer will have to supply an Export Health Certificate for fish exported to the EU. Every single batch of exports will have to be checked.[214]

Brexiters tend to focus on the catch disparity, while glossing over the difficulty of maintaining access to crucial EU markets.

Enforcement of our EEZ will also be an issue. We only have 12 patrol vessels to cover an area of sea three times the size of the UK.[215] It's not only a question of ensuring that vessels are fishing in the right places. A leading expert on international fisheries law fears that violence could break out between UK and EU fishermen, fuelled by long-held grudges.[216]

Another problem: fish swim where they want. They don't care about a dotted line on a map marking the limits of an EEZ. So the UK will have to cooperate with other nations to maintain stocks.[217] We will not be as independent as we would like to think.

And then there's Norway. One of our biggest fishing competitors, it is in the EEA but outside the EU. As a consequence, it is subject to tariffs on processed fish. That's why Norwegian fish is often exported for processing, including to Scotland. But after Brexit our own tariff situation will worsen with respect to the EU market. So Norwegian firms will no longer get the same benefits from using Scottish companies to process their catch as they do at present.[218] It would be logical for them to move the work elsewhere, especially since they already outsource to Denmark and Poland.

And it's not just about the fish

The shellfish sector identified severe problems arising from a no deal Brexit scenario. In a report to Government, it explained that new tariffs would cost up to £41 million a year. It noted that while the UK was the dominant supplier for many species, it didn't have a monopoly on any. In other words, the EU would always have alternatives. The report also drew attention to non-tariff barriers, such as lengthy customs formalities. The resultant transport delays would impact freshness and shelf life.[219]

22. The world is big, very big...

Brexiters like to talk up the opportunity to replace our EU trade with trade with the rest of the world. It's almost as if they've never seen a map...

The Continent is nearer

Take a look at a globe. You'll see the UK and France are so close, they're almost touching. With the base of your thumb on Dover, you can stretch it to reach half a dozen EU countries. Transport by road and rail, ship and tunnel is quick and easy. The Continent is but a hop, skip and a jump away.

Farmers can pick lettuces in French fields in the morning, and have them in UK shops by mid-afternoon. Car parts can flow from German factories to UK assembly parts in half a day. British food producers can restock shops in the Netherlands in a few hours.

By contrast, shipments to and from China take 23-25 days to make the long sea crossing. India is 19-29 days away. The USA is 10-30 days away, depending on whether we're talking about the East Coast or the West Coast.[220] Those are only the transit times. Door to door takes much longer because of customs formalities and other processes.

The EU will always come first

Unless we invent the teleporter, there can be no beating geography.

The EU is and will always be our closest market. The character of trade we do with the rest of the world will always be different to that which we do with the EU. Leaving the EU might allow us to grow our trade with non-EU markets faster. But unless we keep trade with our next door neighbours flowing freely, we're going to come unstuck. Car assembly plants can't run if they have to wait 30 days for components to arrive. Fresh food can't survive a three week sea crossing. No amount of wishful thinking will change that.

Economists have a well-established model of trade called the gravity theory. It posits that countries trade more with other countries close to them and with large markets. Far away markets are less desirable unless they're so big that it's worth the extra effort of reaching them.

Our trade with the EU benefits from both these effects. The EU market is huge, and very near. So we do vast amounts of trade with it. We trade less with markets further away, but we make exceptions for big counterparts such as the USA, China and Japan.

No amount of free trade deals can shrink the distance between us and countries outside the EU. At best, they will make such trade modestly more appealing. So we had better be sure we can maintain trade flows with the EU before messing with our existing arrangements. We turn our backs on what we have now at our peril.

Couldn't we just switch to air transport?

It is true that we already conduct about half our trade with countries outside the EU. But most of that takes place by sea. In 2017, the UK transported 486,000,000 tons of freight by sea versus only 2,739,000 tons by air.[221] That's 177 times less than we move by sea. It's such a massive difference, there is no realistic prospect of replacing sea freight with air freight.

At a pinch, we might be able to fly in extra pallets of medicine or supplies of certain fresh foods. But there is no chance whatsoever of switching the bulk of our trade from sea to air. The skies above Britain would have to be black with planes, with flights landing every couple of seconds, to make a dent in the volume of goods travelling by sea. Even if that were feasible, we might as well take a blowtorch to the planet.

23. Could an airlift by our plucky RAF get around post-Brexit shortages?

The RAF airlifts bulky cargo into combat zones and participates in relief efforts. But what if the Government were to ask them to help transport vital supplies to make up for post-Brexit shortages caused by queues at the ports? How much of a difference could they make?

There are 4 main types of plane in the RAF's transport fleet:

- Boeing C-17 Globemaster: Fleet of 8. Max capacity 76,655kg/aircraft.[222]
- Lockheed Martin C-130J Super Hercules (C4): Fleet of 14. Max capacity 33,000kg/aircraft.[223]

- Airbus A400M Atlas: Fleet of 22. Max capacity 37,000kg/aircraft.[224]

- BAE 146 C.Mk 3: Fleet of 2. Max capacity 10,600kg/aircraft.[225]

For simplicity, let's assume the whole fleet could take part in the relief effort. (In practice, some craft would be undergoing maintenance. Others would be operating on missions from which they could not be recalled.) Let's also assume that they're packed to the gills with supplies, i.e. each is loaded to maximum capacity.

All these planes working together could carry 1,910.44 metric tonnes per trip – a fair few packets of aspirin. But divide the tonnage by the UK's 66 million population, and you get 29g per person. Less than the weight of a Mars bar, even in these shrinkflation times.

How does that compare to goods carried by road and sea? Well, the maximum weight capacity of a 40ft shipping container that's legal to transport on UK roads is 26,000kg. So the whole RAF fleet could move the equivalent of 73.5 containers per trip (perhaps one is a 20ft pipsqueak?)

The Pride of Burgundy, one of P&O's smallest ferries on the Dover-Calais route, has capacity for 120 freight vehicles.[226] Eurotunnel's truck shuttles can carry 32 trucks each, and it has 18 of them.[227] So that starts to put the RAF's effort into perspective.

Let's really size things up. All told, the UK's major ports handled 116.7 million tons of freight imported from the rest of the EU in 2017.[228] If the RAF operated its full transport fleet twice a day every day for an entire year, it could carry 1,394,621.20 tonnes of cargo. That's around 21kg per person – the weight of a female British Bulldog.

Although that's a useful amount of extra capacity, one we might be grateful for, it only represents 1.2% of what flows into the UK by sea and rail each year. It's the difference between a wineglass and a bathtub. And remember, this is all based on an over-optimistic scenario in which every plane is flying all the time.

In conclusion, the RAF could certainly make an appreciable dent when it comes to essential items with a short shelf life, such as insulin or medical isotopes. It might even be able to airlift limited quantities of food. But it is incapable of replacing to a meaningful extent the traditional sea and rail freight routes we rely on.

24. Why Brexit is nothing like Y2K

Some people dismiss Brexit concerns by comparing them to Y2K. "There was all that fuss about how planes were going to fall from the sky and civilisation would end. And then nothing happened. Such a swindle." This view is based on a misunderstanding of the Y2K problem and how it was resolved.

Y2K or the millennium bug was a problem affecting old computer systems. They used to use two digits to store the year in dates, "96" for "1996" and so on, rather than four. Programmers wrote software that way because memory and storage were super expensive. A saving of two digits across hundreds or thousands of dates in a database seemed well worth pursuing. And technology was changing so fast, they didn't expect their software to still be in use ten, twenty, even thirty years after they'd coded it. They were wrong. Banks didn't throw out their outdated machines. Neither did power stations, hospitals or thousands of other institutions. Going into the Nineties, two digit years were everywhere.

There's no issue during the 1990s. But what happens when you get to 1 January 2000? The year part of that date will have to be stored as "00". But some programs assumed that the date would always increase. Other software already used the code "00" for other purposes. Still others divided values by the date, which in the case of zero was impossible. In other words, the behaviour of the software would become unpredictable. Not ideal if it's the brains of a nuclear reactor or an air traffic control system.

That's Y2K in a nutshell. An obvious, well-defined risk that could be explained in a couple of minutes to a layperson. (By comparison, Brexit is a nightmare of complex dependencies and competing interests.)

The work to remedy the Y2K problem began years before the fateful date. Programmers and systems specialists (i.e. experts) examined every line of code in hundreds of thousands of programs, looking for legacy date issues. They then patched, upgraded or replaced problematic software and systems.

Governments got involved, providing clear, concise advice and help to businesses. The affected systems were meticulously tested after being repaired. Similar efforts took place all over the world.

At some point the media cottoned onto the problem. Cue lurid stories of an impending apocalypse. Most experts were more sanguine. But the worry was always that someone, somewhere, wouldn't do their job, and dependent systems would fail.

In the event, after hundreds of billions of dollars worth of remedial work and millions of hours of effort, nothing much happened.[229]

Here's where the misunderstanding creeps in. Nothing happened not because there wasn't a problem, but because the problem was so clear and the deadline so obvious that everyone put in enough effort to resolve it.

The deadline for Brexit is also (relatively) obvious: 31 Oct 2019. But that's where the similarities end:

1. The problems caused by Brexit are not clear. We don't even know what kind of Brexit will happen or even if it *will* happen
2. The problems caused by any Brexit scenario are far, far more complex, diverse and unpredictable than the one-issue Y2K bug
3. We can't test Brexit in advance before it happens
4. We've barely begun with finding solutions (see bullet 1)

So evidently Y2K and Brexit are not comparable in any meaningful way.

Other things worth knowing

Brexit will make everything you buy online from the EU more expensive...

Recently, I bought a Star Wars Rebel Alliance money clip from ThinkGeek's closing down sale for the equivalent of about £25 including delivery. (ThinkGeek was an ecommerce firm in the USA.) The Royal Mail put a postcard through my door telling me I would have to pay £13.70 in customs charges and fees before they would release the parcel to me.

Currently, you have to pay VAT and sometimes also customs duty on most goods coming into the UK from outside the EU. You generally don't have to pay anything on consignments valued at up to £15. You pay VAT on goods between £15 and £135, and you pay both customs and VAT on things valued at more than that.[230]

In the case of my trapped parcel, that meant that I had £5.70 to pay in duties. If you're wondering why the difference between that and the £13.70 amount, it's because Royal Mail charge an £8 handling fee.[231] Parcelforce levies a fee too. Lo and behold, theirs is also £8.[232]

The net effect of all these charges was to turn something that seemed reasonable value at £25 into an expensive purchase at £38.70. Had I realised what it would end up costing me, I probably wouldn't have bought it.

But let's pull back from my money clip and look at the bigger picture. That £8 flat fee for processing payments means that low value purchases are disproportionately affected. If you buy something worth £15.01, you'll end up paying probably a penny in VAT, but will be charged £8 for the privilege of doing so. That £15.01 item just became £23.02.

Why is this significant in the context of Brexit? Because if we leave the EU without reaching a deal which includes special dispensations for customs arrangements, this same regime will apply to all parcels from abroad, not just those from outside the EU. Anything you buy on Amazon France, for instance, or from an online retailer in Ireland, would fall under these rules.[233]

That may seem bad enough, but there's a second wrinkle. In the Customs Bill white paper published in October 2017[234], the UK Government set out its plans to change the rules post-Brexit. It made clear its intention to abolish Low Value Consignment Relief, a mouthful of an expression that refers to the VAT dispensation on goods under £15. After Brexit, VAT will be due on goods of *any* value.

Your £5 pair of socks from the EU will cost you £5 (socks), plus £8 (handling fee for your VAT payment) plus £1 approx (VAT) for a total of £14. Quite a magic trick!

These changes slam the door on being able to exploit price differentials across the EU to get hold of goods more cheaply than you can in the UK. And they will also make the things you can't get domestically that much more expensive.

Net effect: far less cross-border ecommerce as UK consumers cut back on or stop their purchases from overseas. Overseas retailers lose their UK customer segment. Brexiters might see this as a win for domestic suppliers.

But think of all the UK businesses selling their products to other EU countries. Absent a suitable agreement (as would be the case in the event of a no deal Brexit) their customers will face the same extra costs. Orders from abroad may dwindle or dry up completely.

Who stands to benefit from these changes?

Domestic suppliers who don't have to source their products from the EU may see an upturn in business from the reduced online competition.

If every single parcel that comes into the UK incurs customs charges after Brexit, all those £8 handling fees will boost the bottom line of companies such as Royal Mail and Parcelforce. That said, they will be forced to dedicate substantially more warehouse space to storing parcels ahead of collection, and they will have to deal with many more complaints from disgruntled customers who won't understand the nuances of the situation, but only that their £5 socks are costing them £14. There will also be increased traffic into Post Offices and collection points from customers unable or unwilling to pay their charges online.

Border Force will have a lot more work to do on behalf of HMRC, since they will have to check every incoming consignment. On the other hand, there is the potential to collect additional VAT and customs duties on shipments that have been exempt to date. It is also likely that there will be more scrutiny of parcels in general, since every single one will attract duties. No more undervaluing that expensive item or pretending it's a gift – not that you would do that, of course.

And who will lose out?

UK and EU consumers lose, as do export businesses.

Consumers, because they are having to pay higher prices when they shop. UK consumers will suffer the most because they will be left with a choice between a limited range of home-produced products and a wider selection of import goods at increased prices. EU consumers will be affected too, but they'll still be able to shop in 26 other countries without incurring customs charges.

Export businesses will take a hit because these effectively higher prices will have a chilling effect on their sales. Remember, none of the extra cost of that £5 pair of socks goes to the original retailer.

A minute's delay at the ports will lead to days of queues...

A no deal Brexit will cause chaos and long tailbacks at the ports. The Operation Yellowhammer planning document describes the possible effects on the Kent ports of our change in situation: "In a reasonable worst case scenario, HGVs could face maximum delays of 1.5-2.5 days before being able to cross the border."[235] The Government's official No-Deal Readiness Report, released in October 2019, explains the circumstances behind these expected delays: "The EU would impose new controls at borders for UK businesses that trade with the EU. These would include new customs procedures and sanitary and phytosanitary (SPS) checks on animals, products of animal origin, plants and food."[236] Inevitably, any extra time spent on the resulting paperwork must lead to extended queues and reduced cross-channel movement of goods. When each vehicle takes slightly longer to process, traffic will soon back up.

The following illustrative example shows how very modest delays can have an outsize impact. To keep things simple, we'll ignore cars and coaches, and focus only on commercial vehicles. (This is an order of magnitude exercise, not an accurate estimate.)

Consider the Port of Dover. It handles around 7,000 trucks on an average day, ie about 300 an hour if we assume they arrive at regular intervals around the clock.[237] That's one truck every 12 seconds. Let's say it takes 60 seconds for one of the checkpoints at the entrance to the port to process a truck. Check the ticket, lift the barrier, wave the driver through. Let's also assume that the port operates at capacity i.e. arriving traffic is busy but free-flowing. It would take 5 checkpoints working in tandem to stop queues building up.

Fast forward to after a no deal Brexit. Imagine that all the new checks and paperwork it will bring add up to an extra minute per truck, so each takes two minutes to process rather than one. That's still less than the length of a song on the radio – hardly seems worth worrying about.

Except… a knock-on effect kicks in almost immediately. The port used to be able to cope with 300 trucks an hour. But with the departure admin now taking twice as long, it can only handle 150 trucks. That leaves an excess of 150 vehicles every hour arriving and joining the end of a lengthening queue.

Truck drivers turning up an hour after Brexit won't only have to contend with an extra minute of processing time. They will first have to wait an hour to get to the front of the queue. And the situation will keep getting worse and worse, an extra hour's worth of waiting traffic for every passing hour, because the port can never catch up. You can see why the Government's reasonable worst case figures are plausible.

You might assume that the problem could be mitigated in various ways, e.g. by building more checkpoints. Unfortunately, the topography of the White Cliffs around Dover limits expansion. There is no way of increasing handling and holding capacity to the extent needed. Calais has more room, and has spent €700m on expanding its facilities, including building new docks. France has also hired an extra 700 customs agents for Calais and other ports.[238] That's not to suggest they won't see problems too, but they are more ready than us.

But the UK Government has not sat idle. It has organised modifications to parts of the M20 and M26, at a cost of £30 million, to set up "Operation Brock".[239] If necessary, sections of both motorways will be usable as HGV queuing areas. Queues will occupy one or more lanes, with restrictions placed on the traffic using the still-flowing lanes. If even this space runs out, Manston Airport will provide overflow parking. All in, this scheme should be able to accommodate several thousand queuing vehicles heading for the ports and the Channel Tunnel.

The police are likely to help by operating a triage system. Drivers without all the right paperwork will be directed out of the queue and diverted to holding areas. This will help to keep the length of the queue manageable on the motorways themselves.

At some point, the queue will find a natural equilibrium. Either there will be no more parking space left at all, and the police will have to turn drivers away. Or it will dwindle at the point beyond which no haulage company is willing to accept the delay. For instance, it may turn out that no firm can absorb the cost of more than 18 hours of waiting time. So the queue will die out 18 hours from the ports. Until Brexit happens, we can't know for sure where it will end.

Note that the Government has already taken all the above remedial steps and more into consideration in preparing its estimates of the scale of the problem for Operation Yellowhammer and the Readiness Report. And yet the documents maintain the potential for days of queues.

A second referendum and other ways to break the Brexit deadlock

Parliament has held what feels like countless Brexit votes. There was no majority for Theresa May's deal or for alternative forms of Brexit such as Common Market 2.0. But there was also no majority for leaving the EU without a deal or for revoking Article 50. Some of the votes were close; all ended in failure. Since MPs have turned down every course of action, we're now stuck. But stasis isn't an end point. We still have to *do something*.

The views of MPs on Brexit seem too diverse for them to ever agree on a single course of action. The only thing they concur on is the need to stop no deal. This takes an element of danger off the table, but doesn't get us any closer to solving Brexit itself. We need to find a different way of breaking the deadlock. The most obvious would be to go back to the people and ask them what to do next via a second referendum.

Of course, organising another referendum (or anything else) will take time. Nothing can happen in the remaining few weeks before the 31 October deadline so we will need to agree another Article 50 extension with the EU first.

The case for a second referendum

We know so much more about Brexit than we did in June 2016. People didn't vote the wrong way back then, but they did vote on the basis of incomplete information. Brexit was presented like an exciting mystery box, a dramatic contrast to the bland status quo. Brexiters made promises they weren't in a position to keep. But now we know what's inside the box. We have seen all the possible Brexit scenarios. We understand what trading on WTO terms would mean. We realise implementing Brexit will be not be cheap, quick or easy. But above all we have seen the effect of Brexit on the cohesion of our country and witnessed its impact on our day to day lives. (Even before Brexit itself happens.)

So let's transfer all this new knowledge into an actionable decision that we can implement without delay. One that will allow us to break the deadlock around Brexit.

That's where a second referendum comes in. It circumvents a stuck Parliament and gives control over Brexit back to the people.

If Brexiters are sincere in their belief the UK still wants Brexit, they should not fear a second referendum. "It could overturn the result of the first one" is a self-defeating argument because it can only do so, by definition, if the public mood *has* changed.

Remainers should also approach a second referendum with open minds. Assuming that the question is well-defined and the conduct of the referendum fair, they should abide by the outcome even if it goes against them. That's not to suggest they should abandon their internationalist outlook. Nothing stops them mounting a campaign to rejoin the EU as soon as we are out. But if the British people's verdict is Leave again, then leave we must, even if it is with supreme reluctance.

Defining the referendum question

The implementation of the first referendum foundered on the vagueness of the "Leave" option. We should not repeat that mistake. If Leave were to win again on a binary "Leave" or "Remain" choice, that would confirm the nation's desire to leave. But it wouldn't get us out of our current impasse.

Although Brexit breaks down at the broadest level into Leave vs Remain, there are in fact 3 distinct positions:

- Remain in the EU i.e. preserve our current membership status
- Leave with a negotiated deal in place
- Leave without a deal (the "no deal" or "get on with it" scenario)

At present, the only deal on offer is Theresa May's thrice-rejected Withdrawal Agreement and Political Declaration package. It might be possible in theory for a different Government to negotiate a different deal, but this would extend the time needed to hold the second referendum further.

The danger with including no deal on a second referendum ballot

No deal, i.e. leaving the EU without a negotiated arrangement in place, isn't a deal at all. It is wrong to think of it as a destination. It is nothing more than a waypoint on the road to an undefined end state. By leaving without a deal, we get to put off deciding how we want to coexist with the EU until after we've left. But we still need to make our minds up. We can't ignore the massive market on our doorstep. Many industries cannot survive long-term without a good trading relationship with the EU. "No deal" ticks the "we're out of the EU box" but doesn't resolve anything.

No deal isn't the end of Brexit. It signals the start of the second, much harder phase of the negotiations. We will still need a deal in the no deal scenario, but we will be negotiating it after we're already out. Our leverage will be at its lowest, because our walk-away position will be to return to the chaos of no deal. (Remaining in the EU will no longer be an option.) Brexit will be with us for years if not decades to come. As the Irish Taoiseach Leo Varadkar put it: "There's no such thing as a clean break, or just getting it done. Rather, we'll just move on to a new phase."[240]

Unfortunately, the pain of Brexit isn't going to hold off until we can sort ourselves out. It will hit us on day one. We will have to endure the Brexit damage even as we cobble together a future relationship with the EU.

So it is clear why no deal is dangerous. It would seem irresponsible of the Government to include it in any second referendum. But hardcore Brexiters have done such a good job of talking up no deal (or "clean Brexit" as they've recently dubbed it) that excluding it could lead to a backlash from a significant portion of the Leave electorate.

Types of second referendum

It is possible to structure a second referendum in many different ways, depending on its purpose, and whether an acceptable Brexit deal has been agreed or not. Each form of second referendum has strengths and weaknesses.

1. A binary "yes/no" confirmatory referendum on a specific deal

The Government has agreed a deal with the EU but can't get it past Parliament. (This is the situation Theresa May found herself in. MPs debated this sort of referendum several times as a way to resolve the impasse over her deal.[241]) So the Government would go back to the people, and explain that the deal on offer was the best it had been able to negotiate. The question would be of the form: "Do you agree with the Brexit deal as negotiated? Y/N".

This approach has the virtue of honesty, an admission that the Government cannot gather sufficient parliamentary support for its deal. (Of course, some might argue that a different Government could have negotiated a better one.)

If a majority of voters approved the deal, it would be enacted using the referendum as validation. If they rejected it, it would be dead. But in that case we still wouldn't have an answer to what to do about Brexit. We would have closed off one door, no more.

This option is as stupid as repeating the first referendum, because it has the same fundamental flaw: "no" means nothing. It also sets a massive precedent by bypassing the explicit will of Parliament using a referendum. This would be a huge shift from representative to direct democracy. What would stop future governments from taking a similar approach with other policies they were having trouble getting through the House of Commons?

2. A binary referendum to pass a deal, or stay in the EU

In this scenario, the Government wants to put Brexit to bed. It has managed to reach a deal, but can't get it past Parliament. At the same time, it doesn't want Brexit to drag on forever. So the question would be "Would you like to leave the EU with this specific deal, or stay in?"

This approach has the advantage of resolving Brexit. Both referendum outcomes are actionable. It also limits campaigning to the achievable. In other words, there would be no point in Leave making claims incompatible with the deal, because these would never materialise.

But it risks alienating those in the Leave camp who wanted neither the deal on offer nor to remain in the EU. Hard right parties would find in it plenty of ammunition to fan fears of an establishment stitch-up.

3. A binary "deal or no deal" referendum to confirm the manner of our departure

In this type of referendum, Remain would not be on the ballot at all. The choice would be between a particular negotiated deal, and leaving without a deal. Presumably the logic would be that we voted to leave, so all we need to determine is how to do so.

While such an arrangement might satisfy those who still wanted to leave and those who believed respecting the outcome of the first referendum trumped the dangers of Brexit, it would outrage Remain. Of all possible referendum arrangements, this would be the most controversial in that it would explicitly offer nothing at all to those on one side of the first referendum. And given that recent polls suggest over half the UK now backs remain, that's a lot of people to annoy. Far from beginning to heal the divisions, this form of second referendum would risk entrenching them forever.

It also has the disadvantage shared by all referendums in which "no deal" appears on the ballot: if no deal wins, nothing gets resolved. We crash out of the EU and suffer the consequences, but we're no nearer understanding our future relationship.

4. A binary referendum of last resort

This would take the form of a shoot-out between "Remain" and "no deal". It would be the final admission that the Government had failed in its quest to reach a deal. The referendum would let the electorate choose between giving up on Brexit and taking our chances outside the EU. But such a simplistic choice would greatly increase the probability of a damaging no deal. Although no responsible Government is likely to want to take that risk, the scenario is included for completeness.

5. A 3-way choice between remain, a deal and leaving with no deal

This scenario would give voters three options: remain, leave with a negotiated deal, or leave without a deal. Something for everyone, in other words. The choice with the highest vote wins. But of course there are the attendant dangers of including no deal on the ballot. It is also quite possible that the winning option would fail to achieve a majority. So we would end up with a form of Brexit (or with Remain) chosen by less than half the electorate. Most voters would face disappointment, just like in a general election situation.

This arrangement looks like a fix because it places a thumb on the scales on the side of Remain by splitting the Leave vote two ways. What happens if Remain wins with fewer votes than the two Leave options combined? The recriminations would never end, and with just cause.

6. A two-stage question, producing a 3-way Brexit outcome

This form of second referendum would comprise two questions:

- Q1. Should we remain in the EU, or leave the EU? (Remain/Leave)
- Q2. If the majority is to leave, what type of Brexit do you want? (Leave with a negotiated deal / Leave without a deal)

All voters would answer both questions. This would give the entire electorate some influence over the final shape of Brexit. The result of Q2 would only take effect if Q1 delivered a majority for leave.

Those favouring a no deal outcome might complain of the impossibility of achieving it. After all, Remain voters would be very unlikely to choose it in Q2. But Q2 is fair, despite this objection. The Brexit we ended up with would represent the wish of over 50% of all voters.

The alternative, of limiting Q2 to those who voted Leave in Q1, could deliver a no deal Brexit that only a minority wanted. (e.g. Q1 Remain 48%, Leave 52%; Q2: Deal 49% No deal 51%. No deal, the "winning" outcome, would be the choice of 51% of 52%, or 26.5% of all voters.) It is also democratically illegitimate in that it would disenfranchise by design a section of the population.

The first question mirrors the original referendum, which could invite criticism that it is a rerun of the 2016 vote. There is also the issue that Leave might appear to dominate the ballot paper, with three references to Remain's one. That might lead to accusations that the playing field wasn't level.

7. A 3-way transferable vote

In this scenario, voters would face 3 options: remain, deal and no deal. They would select their first and second preferences from these options. This might involve numbering their choices, or ticking "first preference" and "second preference" columns.

The votes would get divided into three piles based on each voter's first preference. Were there already to be a majority of first place preference votes for one outcome, it would be the winner. If not, the votes on the smallest pile would get redistributed to the other two. The redistribution would be on the basis of the second preferences expressed by those on the eliminated pile.

For example, "Deal" is the least popular first choice and gets eliminated. Ballot papers marked "1: Deal 2: No deal" end up on the no deal pile. Ones marked "1: Deal 2: Remain" go on the remain pile.

At the end of this redistribution phase, one of the two piles will contain more than 50% of all votes. That outcome is the winner.

This method has the advantage of delivering a result that reflects the first or second choice preference of over half of all voters. But it is not as intuitive as more straightforward voting systems. So it will be harder to convince a suspicious electorate that the outcome is fair. Another problem is that this arrangement seems likely to eliminate the deal option first.[242] So a transferable vote would produce a more "extreme" outcome (from a Leave or Remain perspective). Finally, the most popular first preference option could lose if too few second preference votes support it. Again, this introduces questions of legitimacy.[243]

Conclusion

All the above second referendum options have issues; some would be a disaster. The two-stage question (option 6) and the 3-way transferable vote (option 7) show the most promise. Both offer the potential of returning a straight and fair result, one that would account for the will of the entire electorate, not only the winners. But both options are far from perfect. Perhaps we should explore alternatives for breaking the deadlock?

Alternative ways to break the Brexit deadlock

A blind ballot of MPs

MPs vote on the record. They file through the "Aye" or "No" lobbies of the House of Commons. Tellers tally them, working in pairs to ensure the count is fair. Three clerks in each lobby record the names of those who have voted. The list of votes (and abstentions) gets published soon after each vote.

This strict oversight prevents fraud, but it also reveals the way each MP voted to their party and the whips. This can have a chilling effect. MPs feel pressured to vote along party lines, especially if a three-line whip is in place. We recently saw an extreme demonstration of the consequences of breaking the whip. Boris Johnson expelled 21 senior Conservatives from the Tory Party, including former Chancellor Phillip Hammond, Father of the House Ken Clarke, and Nicholas Soames (Sir Winston Churchill's grandson). Over 350 years of parliamentary experience out the door for the "crime" of having voted the wrong way.

Another consequence of public scrutiny is it allows incentives to be used to influence votes. Key MPs may get offered peerages, Cabinet positions or other perks. All they have to do to collect on what they were promised is vote a particular way.

The system is fair, in that every MP gets an equal vote, and there can be no ballot stuffing or other tricks. But it also stands in the way of MPs voting their conscience. Few dare to take a principled stand since doing so could mark the end of their political career. Most will give in to the "blackmail" of the whips instead.

You could argue that's how things are. And you'd be right. But maybe Brexit merits lateral thinking, given that it is the most divisive issue MPs will ever face. What if they could take part in a blind ballot on a range of Brexit outcomes? Off the record, without their party peering over their shoulder, they would be free to vote in the real national interest and that of their constituents. Such a process might tease out a majority where none existed before.

The practicalities of a blind vote need not be onerous. Suitable safeguards to prevent cheating, and some kind of check to ensure MPs could not "prove" which way they voted (i.e. no phones). If they were able to document their vote, it would lay them open to the lure of incentives.

The psychology of the vote outcome would be more complicated. The result would provide a genuine insight into what each MP thought of the Brexit situation. It might produce a majority for one course of action. White smoke, we're saved! Except that it could be tricky to convince people already suspicious about the delay in implementing the referendum that they should trust the result of an anonymous vote. There's no easy answer to that (persistence will be critical). But that doesn't mean the idea should be dismissed out of hand.

A citizens' assembly

A citizens' assembly would draw together several hundred members of the public. They would spend a couple of weeks or so listening to expert testimony and factual advice about Brexit. After each session, they would deliberate on what they had heard. Impartial facilitators and moderators would be on hand to help smooth the debate. At the end of the process, the CA would make an informed recommendation on the best way to proceed. We could think of it as a very large jury pronouncing its verdict on Brexit.

The composition of the assembly would need to reflect the demographics of the UK, as well as the 52/48 Brexit split of the 2016 referendum. There would need to be an element of randomness, as for jury duty selection. Participants would receive compensation for attendance.

Supporters of the idea point to the success of the "deliberative democracy" exercise in Ireland around the highly charged topics of gay marriage and abortion.[244] In both cases, the recommendations of the citizens' assemblies ultimately became law. Rory Stewart is a high-profile fan of citizens' assemblies and has pushed for one to be held to resolve the Brexit question, with the Archbishop of Canterbury acting as mediator.[245]

But the process is not without its detractors. It is unclear whether the participants can ever be representative of the wider UK population. The major time commitment would exclude those unwilling or unable to dedicate themselves for so long. It would also exclude those disengaged from politics.[246] But if attendees are more politically engaged than the average person, then they will also have stronger inherent views. And what about the safety of participants? Are they at risk if they produce a recommendation reviled in certain quarters? (We have already seen how far Brexit can inflame passions.)

Finally, there is the issue of what to do with the recommendation the assembly produces. Are MPs meant to implement it as-is? Or use it to shape their own thinking? Can the Government ignore the CA's advice if it doesn't like it?

Perhaps the citizens' assembly approach could be used to define the specific "Leave" option for a second referendum. It would pre-empt endless political wrangling by setting out the exact form of Brexit that "Leave" choice represented.

A general election

Boris Johnson has been pushing for a general election to bring clarity to Brexit. (Oddly, he has also stated repeatedly that he doesn't want one.) But would an election resolve the Brexit question?

There are two main issues with a general election scenario when it comes to Brexit.

The first stems from our multiparty, winner takes all electoral system. Because it's first past the post (FPTP), MPs can get elected with less than 50% of the votes cast in their constituency. The percentage of votes they need to win falls as the race becomes more competitive. The Tories, Labour, the Liberal Democrats and the Brexit Party are all expected to poll strongly. It is likely some MPs will win seats with less than a third of the vote.

Let's imagine that the Tories decide to run on a "no deal" platform i.e. they pledge to take the UK out of the EU without a deal. That might encourage the Brexit Party to take a back seat. But that would still leave three parties in real contention.

We could see the Tories end up the largest party despite a national vote share in the low thirties. They would presumably proceed with no deal based on the democratic mandate of the people.

Would that be fair? On the one hand, our electoral system is what it is. It may be unfit for purpose now that the cosy two-party arrangement seems to have broken. But until we replace it with something else, it's all we've got. Under the existing rules, the Tories would indeed have a mandate. They would have the most MPs, after all.

On the other hand, 65%+ of voters would have cast votes for parties with other Brexit positions. The practical effect of FPTP is to impose the views of a minority on the majority. The winning party gets to enact its manifesto. Other parties don't get a look in. But that has consequences when it comes to an issue as divisive as Brexit. Far from bringing the nation together, a Brexit imposed by diktat will divide it further. A general election under FPTP cannot deliver the type of consensus a second referendum might. Especially when in some parts of the UK, parties may achieve a dominance at odds with the wider result (for instance the SNP in Scotland).

There is a second problem with a general election. We've seen what happens if one party gets a majority of MPs. But what if no single party nor combination of two parties can form a government? It feels like we're stuck now. But that's as nothing to the mess we'd be in then.

The influence of the Brexit Party and a strong showing by the Liberal Democrats could make it impossible to form a Government. Other parties will not partner with ones bent on no deal. So the Tories (and maybe the Brexit Party) will have no luck finding coalition partners. But all the opposition parties together might not be able to muster a majority of MPs either. And even if they did have the numbers, their views on Brexit might not be sufficiently compatible. Ours would be a hung Parliament to end all hung Parliaments.

What would happen then? In theory, there would have to be yet another general election. (Sorry, Brenda!) But what's to suggest that would provide resolution? Voters fed up with the parlous state of our politics might stay away in droves. And we could end up just as stuck afterwards, only with trust in our political system at rock bottom.

Right now things are messy. We have a Prime Minister in office but not in power. (As of 9 October 2019, the Government's majority stood at minus 45.) But at least the opposition parties have come together to oppose no deal. Are they going to gamble that sense of shared purpose on the vagaries of a general election? Or will they decide to keep Boris Johnson glued to the hot seat and turn the temperature up? Time will tell.

A Government of National Unity

Opposition MPs and rebel Tories could team up to form a government of national unity (GNU) after winning a successful vote of no confidence (VONC) against the current government. The GNU would likely exist for a short time and a limited purpose. It would ask the EU for an Article 50 extension to postpone the danger of no deal. It would then organise a second referendum followed by a general election, or just a general election. (In theory the GNU could stay together until 2022 since there's no obligation to hold another general election before then. Considering the clashing personalities and politics of those involved, it would be unlikely to survive that long.)

A government majority of -45 indicates a GNU is possible on paper. But would it work in practice?

The biggest problem is Jeremy Corbyn. He has been adamant about wanting to lead a minority Labour government after any VONC. This sentiment is understandable given his position as Leader of the Opposition (LOTO). Unfortunately it does not account sufficiently for political reality.

A Labour government would obviously not be a GNU because it would consist only of Labour MPs. (A GNU draws from all parties.) That would make it much harder for other parties to back it. And Corbyn is a divisive figure. Most rebel Tories have already made it clear they won't back him. Without their support, Corbyn doesn't have the numbers.

The LibDems recognised the challenging political arithmetic early. They have stated they will back a unifying figure capable of commanding cross-party support at the helm of a proper GNU. (For example Ken Clarke or Harriet Harman.)

Jeremy Corbyn's role is pivotal. As LOTO, he is the only opposition MP able to call a VONC that will secure debate time. (Without the VONC, the horse trading to form the GNU cannot start.) So Corbyn needs to kick the first pebble down the hill. But he has said he will only hold a VONC he can definitely win. That will not be possible if he insists on becoming the next prime minister. Catch 22.

But Jeremy Corbyn could go from roadblock to hero if he were willing to set his PM ambitions aside temporarily. He would stay LOTO. He could take on a senior role in a GNU led by someone less controversial. And he could go into the general election with his head high, having demonstrated his willingness to put the national interest ahead of personal ambition.

A more radical scenario would see the GNU stay together for the duration. MPs from all parties would work together to lance the festering boil of Brexit and let the poison drain away. Fix Brexit, fix the country, fix the political system. Unlikely, but not impossible.

What would happen if Brexit were stopped?

There is only one way to stop Brexit: revoke Article 50 and remain in the EU. Extending Article 50 merely pushes Brexit Day into the future. It delays Brexit, but does not stop it.

Let's set aside the thorny question of *how* we arrived at the decision to cancel Brexit. (It could have been a second referendum, a general election or another of the mechanisms we've already seen. Or it could have been via a different route.) Instead, let's focus on the practicalities of what would happen if we did decide to do so.

Legal stuff first. The UK has an absolute right to revoke Article 50 any time. If we cancelled Brexit, we would be able to stay in the EU under our current membership conditions. We would retain our vetoes, the rebate, and all other special dispensations we have. That too is a matter of law.

This is not to say that nothing would change in future. For instance, the current EU budget cycle ends in 2020. If we stayed, we would be committing to the 2021-27 budget process. We would have a say in drawing it up alongside the other 27 EU members. The conclusion of that process might see us paying more in membership dues than we do now. It's impossible to say at this juncture.

But we would still have our opt-out on matters such as membership of the Euro or participation in Eurozone bailouts. They would not apply to us if we did not want them to, no matter the direction of travel of the EU. And because of our veto, we would not have to get involved in attempts at deeper defence integration i.e. what Brexiters refer to as the "European army". (We would also be able to veto the removal of our veto powers, which seems pleasingly circular.)

Staying in is simple, in procedural terms at least. All Boris Johnson has to do is secure the necessary backing from Parliament to revoke Article 50 then notify the EU of our intent. As soon as they accept our request, the Brexit process ends. No more worrying about trying to reach a deal. No more talk of cliff edges and stockpiling. No more firms sprinting for the door. Brexit would be an ex-parrot.

Unfortunately that's the beginning of the story, not the end.

For one thing, we can only rewind the clock so far. The passing of uncertainty should stem the exodus of jobs and assets to the rest of the EU. After all, firms will know their commitment to the UK market is safe.

But many companies have already dedicated significant time, money and effort to getting Brexit-ready. And we won't get back the EU agencies that moved abroad. So the damage caused by our abortive attempt to leave will linger.

This should not trap us in a sunk cost fallacy. Yes, when the dust settles, it will be obvious that Brexit has already cost us dear. But the consequences of an abortive Brexit are nothing compared to what they would be if we went ahead. Desperate gamblers don't know when to stop chasing their losses. "The next bet will see me whole again," they think, just before going broke. That doesn't have to be our fate. We can treat Brexit as an object lesson and move on.

The cracks in our society were present long before Brexit. The referendum merely served to bring them into sharp relief. Britain is broken in so many ways. Since our domestic problems were not caused by the EU, staying in will not be a magic cure for all that ails us. But it's a start. Without the distraction of Brexit, politicians will be able to refocus on domestic issues for the first time since the 2016 referendum.

Cancelling Brexit should bring an immediate economic dividend. The preparation costs are gone, spilled milk we should waste no time crying over. But the Government has set aside tens of billions of pounds as a provision against the disruption of a no-deal Brexit. With Brexit out of the way, that money will be available for key priorities. We can spend it on the NHS, homelessness, mental health issues, schooling and other issues.

But companies have been holding back as well. Brexit has been depressing investment for years. With uncertainty vanquished, the UK will be open for business again. Firms can resume their plans for new products, new factories, new jobs, new markets… Many will benefit from the EU's new trade deals, agreed since the beginning of the Brexit process. Like the one with Japan that came into force in February 2019. The EU's largest ever deal, it is predicted to add £3 billion a year to the UK economy.[247] Another, concluded in June 2019 with the South American trade block MERCOSUR, may prove significant since nearly 5,000 British companies export there.[248] By remaining EU members, we will continue to reap the rewards of such deals indefinitely.

Remember those bulging warehouses full of stockpiled goods? We can expect the revocation of Article 50 to kick off a shopping bonanza the likes of which we have never seen as firms run down inventories. Black Friday every day of the week. A cheery uplift for families worn down by worry over Brexit. The tourism sector will breathe a sigh of relief too. It will be OK to plan a holiday as if life were normal, because it will be. No worries about insurance green cards and international driving permits. No need to fear grounded flights and massive queues at the ports. Those with ongoing medical needs can rest easy in the knowledge that their vital supply of medicines won't get interrupted.

But it's not all going to be roses, and we should not delude ourselves that it will be.

For one thing, despite a huge backlog, a large number of Brexit-related laws have already been passed by Parliament. It will be a job and a half to untangle that mess and put things back to normal. Especially since the EU has also changed since the referendum, so the legislative goalposts have moved. Civil servants will keep as busy as bees on that puzzle. Until the last traces of Brexit can be excised, it will put something of a dampener on the affairs of Government. But it will be nothing like the distraction it is now.

But the difficulties will be most acute on the political side. The ERG will still be with us, as will Nigel Farage, the Brexit Party and their MEPs. The events of the last three years have already shaken up our cosy two party system. Ending Brexit may shatter it. We can expect to see the Conservatives fade as a potent force, even as the Brexit Party surges. A still harder right party may exploit our renunciation of Brexit to gain traction. Meanwhile, Labour has its fair share of problems too. Many former Labour voters who lent their vote to the LibDems or other parties may never return. There is clear room for an enlarged centrist group, made up of MPs who have more in common with each other than traditional party lines suggest.

So the end of Brexit could well mean the de-facto end of majority Government. The votes will split so many ways that no one party will ever gain the upper hand again, even under first past the post.

But that could be a good thing. Most of our continental neighbours are already used to coalitions and consensus building. Might it be time we learned the same spirit of cooperation? MPs working together in the national interest rather than to further party agendas. The politics of confrontation replaced by the politics of compromise. Politicians and the public would gradually get used to this new normal. And when the time came for political reform, it would be less controversial. (The idea of proportional representation is no longer scary if coalitions have been demonstrated to work well.)

If there is a silver lining to Brexit, it's this: attitudes to immigration have shifted in the last few years. Surveys show that we value immigrants more, and are more tolerant of them. We are also more conscious and appreciative of their contributions to our society. This may seem paradoxical when hate crime is rising, the far right stirs up trouble at every opportunity, and the UK Government holds up the end of freedom of movement as a virtue in its own right.

But the poll numbers don't lie. Those who shout the loudest in the face of reality can only grow hoarse. The quiet majority know better.

They understand that immigrants are our friends, colleagues, neighbours and family. They appreciate how they add to the rich vibrancy of daily life, and underpin vital sectors from the NHS to farming. They internalise a fundamental truth: we are all people. Some of us just happen to come from somewhere else.

Finally, we have the million euro question. What do we do about Brexit itself? Cancelling it doesn't shut the door on leaving the EU for all time. However, we are not allowed to treat the Article 50 mechanism like a switch to toggle the Brexit process off and on again. The law obliges us to be sincere in our intention to stay. But circumstances change; if we're able to demonstrate a new and genuine mandate for leaving, nothing precludes us attempting to do so again, though we might find the EU much less cooperative next time.

Logic suggests we should give up Brexit as an unworkable idea, make the most of what we've got right now, and try to reform from within the parts of the EU we don't like. (A light touch approach would be best; we've caused enough trouble as it is.) But Euroscepticism won't go away if Brexit is called off. You can't cure hypochondria by refusing sufferers treatment.

Like the monster in a horror franchise, Brexit may not stay dead. We must be vigilant.

Beyond Brexit

If, after everything that has happened, Brexit ends up being stopped, we can't shrug and call it quits. If nothing else, the turmoil since the referendum has revealed profound fault lines in our politics and our direction as a nation. The status quo is no longer good enough. With that in mind, here are a few pointers for things we might want to change…

Infrastructure, transport and housing

- Establish a cross-party Regional Sifting Committee, responsible for ensuring public expenditure is less London centric. It could include MPs, Lords and business leaders to give it continuity beyond the election cycle. The committee would vet major projects to make sure a fair proportion get allocated outside of London and the South East. It would have the power to delay or veto projects if too many were already clustered in SE England. This way, voters all over the UK would know for certain their region was getting a fair share of investments. Developers, knowing they'd face the RSC, would broaden their planning horizons.
- Kill the HS2 project. Then spend half the money saved to improve the entire rail network. Focus on electrification, selective track dualling, advanced signalling, track upgrades etc. Concentrate on regional rail links. Reserve the rest of the funds to do the same all over again a few years later. The first round

of fixes will reveal new problems which the second pass can mop up.

- Undertake a big bold package of public works – say a symbolic £39 billion worth – targeted at the regions and deprived parts of the UK. We may have to borrow to pay for it. But the economy will be in a much better state with the spectre of Brexit behind us. And the cost of borrowing has never been so low. We can afford it.

- Improve the NHS properly. Not a mere figleaf to patch up the cracks. Make it fighting fit for the modern world. Yes, it will take money. Yes, it's needed. Find a way to make it happen.

- Build houses, lots of houses. Get back to the levels of the 1960s and 1970s, when local authorities and housing associations built hundreds of thousands of homes a year.[249]

- Bring proper superfast broadband to most parts of the UK. Fibre connections should provide 100Mbps or higher speeds, rather than the anaemic 24Mbps target pursued by the UK Government.[250] Many other nations are already rolling out gigabit connectivity. If we're going to invest in a national broadband programme, let's make it as future-proof as possible.

- Require cross-party collaboration on major public works projects. This stricture would apply to any project over a certain value, or lasting more than a given minimum time. Such a change will ensure impartial oversight of how taxpayer funds are being spent.

The economy

- Recognise and celebrate the merits of a booming economy in London and the South East. Then milk the cash cow and spread that delicious cream across the rest of the UK.

- Stop demonising the financial industry. That doesn't mean we should pray twice a week to the patron saint of bankers. But we should at least accept the part the financial sector plays in our nation's finances. It employs 1.1 million people, or 3.1% of the UK's workforce. Yet with all forms of taxation included, it contributes £75 billion to the Treasury. That's 10.9% of total government receipts.[251] Without it, we would have no chance of ever balancing the books.

- Set up a crack team of top taxation professionals to comb domestic statute books looking for loopholes. Pay them well for their superstar expertise. The additional taxes collected will more than compensate for their salaries.

- Beef up the role of the Office of Tax Simplification to reduce the burden of red tape.[252]

- Foster an entrepreneurial mentality that rewards a "British dream" (parallels to the American Dream). Entrepreneurs Relief is a start, but so much more is possible, including business rate breaks for new retail ventures.

Politics and government

- Reform the political system to move towards proportional representation. First past the post is a reasonable approximation with two main parties in contention. It breaks down completely with three or four making a strong showing. Most other EU countries already operate on proportional representation. PR breeds compromise and collaboration, rather than confrontation. It also ends the absolutism of a minority of the electorate stamping their will on the majority.

- Devolve more power to regional assemblies, and shrink the size of the House of Commons and the House of Lords.

- Turn the House of Lords into an elected second chamber. Elect members to the HOL by proportional representation. Stagger HOL elections so that they never coincide with House of Commons ones. The oversight role of the HOL is valuable and worth preserving, but there's no reason to provide it via hereditary peers and party appointees.

- Reconsider the need for a written constitution. Relying on precedent may have been a harmless anachronism so long as Governments were willing to behave. But as recent events such as the court battles over prorogation have shown, our system breaks down when a Prime Minister no longer cares about what has come before.

- Abandon the £4 billion plan to refurbish the Palace of Westminster for continued use.[253] Reduce the scope of the project to conserving the building itself. It is an iconic structure well worth preserving for the nation. But it will never be as fit for purpose as a structure designed from the ground up with the needs of Parliament in mind.

- Establish a purpose-built Parliament fit for the twenty first century. Locate it somewhere with great transport links. Give up the adversarial layout of the debate chamber. Instead, adopt a circular arrangement like in the Scottish and European Parliaments. Be generous with space, including ensuring enough seats for all MPs. As far as safety concerns allow, provide more opportunities for the public to watch MPs at work. (For example, tall bulletproof windows surrounding the circular chamber.)

- Consider a system that assigns seats at random (outside of the front benches). It would juggle the seating arrangements on a daily basis, and fill the chamber uniformly. MPs would be able to request small groups of seats together, say up to 4, subject to availability. But they would sit where the system assigned them that day, rather than in rigid political blocks.

- End the culture of secrecy in Government other than in real cases of national security. Outlaw the use of non-disclosure agreements. Transparency should become the default. Publish as much information and advice as possible, so that the public know as much as our politicians do. Shine a bright light into the darkest corners.
- Smash the links between politics and lobbyists. Clamp down on the right of MPs to hold second jobs (this may involve raising MP salaries). Prohibit them from taking on regular media positions. Strengthen the restrictions on the type of roles MPs can take on once they're no longer in politics.
- Publish transparency reports for all thinktanks whose data MPs rely on for decision-making.
- Impose a bar on all foreign donations to domestic political parties.
- Guarantee to resolve all future political scandals in full, in a timely fashion. No more kicking matters into the long grass. No more whitewashes and cover-ups. Persevere with investigations to the end, long after the scandal has left the headlines. Politicians might act with greater propriety if they knew wrongdoing would never be brushed under the carpet. And such a move will begin to restore shattered trust in politics.
- Make it easier for the public to track not only what MPs said or how they voted, but attendance too. MPs do not have to attend debates and committee meetings, but such data could still be instructive.

- Develop a Parliament app that lets people keep tabs on what their MP is doing, including speeches and debate contributions, votes, bills and proposals, etc.
- Reform or abolish the Honours system.
- Treat the electorate like adults. Be more up front about long term trends that will impact the population in negative ways. Demographic change for instance. Longevity is increasing. The burden of looking after older people will keep rising. It shouldn't be controversial to point this out. Yet politicians of all stripes shy away from the subject as if it's the third rail of politics. The problem isn't going to go away, no matter who's in charge. So why not start a real conversation about it for once, instead of avoiding the topic?
- Enhance civics lessons in schools. The Brexit debate demonstrated that many people don't understand how our political system works or how the EU functions. But it has also driven interest in politics to a record high. Crucial votes in the House of Commons gather audiences of over a million. The time is ripe to teach children more about UK politics, and about the EU and our relationship with it (the known is less scary than the unknown). Parliament already offers more than 40 teacher resources and lesson plans.[254] The EU also has a variety of teaching material, including some tailored to the UK.[255] [256] These resources could be combined with citizenship material from key stages 3 and 4.[257] Possible topics:
    - How representative democracy works
    - What MPs do
    - How laws get made
    - The different roles of the House of Commons and the House of Lords
    - Parliamentary traditions and procedures

- General elections, local elections and European elections
- The judiciary
- Our unwritten constitution
- The Union, regional parliaments, and devolution
- Northern Ireland and Ireland, the peace process, the Good Friday Agreement and the Irish border.
- Brief history of the EU and its precursors
- The politics of the EU
- The merits and consequences of EU membership
- How the EU passes laws
- The interaction between UK and EU law

Immigration

- Unwind the EU settlement scheme, explain what will happen to the data collected from the over a million people who have already registered, and reassure EU nationals that they are all welcome in the UK.

- Reform the way our immigration system applies to those from the EU. Take into account existing EU controls on immigration the UK has ignored, such as the three-month rule.[258] (Such changes should *not* be retroactive.)

- Dismantle the remnants of the hostile immigration environment. Begin with the absolute assumption that immigrants are here legally. That change alone would transform the tone of Home Office communications. Revisit all immigration processes to reduce the burden of proof. Stop using employers and landlords as immigration enforcers. Abandon incentive and bonus schemes predicated on immigration targets. Treat people as human beings, not case numbers.

- Abolish immigration restrictions on top scientists from anywhere in the world. (Something that Boris Johnson recently discussed doing.[259])
- Bring in Boris Johnson's proposed 2-year visa for international students, giving them the right to stay on in the UK after their studies end.[260]
- Clamp down on attempts to demonise immigrants for issues that are nothing to do with them.

Our place in the world

- Reconsider the need for a nuclear deterrent. Replacing our Trident submarines looks set to eat up £40 billion or more. Running costs will come to another £2 billion for every year of operation.[261] If Trident's replacement lasts until the 2060s, at least another £80 billion will get swallowed by the waves. That's an awful lot of hospitals, to take just one alternative use for the money. Besides, the threats we face are evolving. Drones. Cyberwarfare. Economic colonialism. Terrorism and non-state actors. Even with a resurgent Russia, we are a long way from the dark days of the Cold War. Consider the circumstances in which the deterrent might get used. Imagine the submarine commanders actually had cause to open their safes and act on the instructions of the Prime Minister. In such a scenario, it is likely we would already be dead. Posthumous revenge seems both pointless and churlish when the same vast sums could do so much to improve the lives of the living.
- Lay to rest the myth of British exceptionalism. Yes, we used to have an empire, because we beat the rest of the world to big guns and big ships. But it's gone now, and it's not coming back. Leave the nostalgia to the Yesterday channel, and focus on a future in which we are a middle-sized country with a strong

economy, off the coast of a prosperous trading bloc. Let's learn to be comfortable as we are, not wallow in past glories.

- In this new spirit of realism, admit that we're not the best in the world at absolutely everything. That's not to do the UK down. We have truly world-class scientific and tech sectors. But we should not disregard the fact that other countries can be years ahead of us. From smart cities to rapid transit solutions or new types of payment system, we should be borrowing from the best. If the wheel we're looking for already exists, why recreate it as a British wheel when we can buy in the expertise? If something works in Japan or China or South Korea or elsewhere, there's no reason why it can't work here too. Let's put more energy into looking and learning. If a solution fits our needs, we can adopt it wholesale. And if it doesn't, then we can apply our ingenuity to adapting it to the UK market.

A grand reconciliation in the national interest

We can only begin to move beyond Brexit if political parties agree a temporary truce on the subject. An election cycle contested around non-Brexit matters would let the mood of the nation reset, and give the othering "Leave" and "Remain" labels time to fade. Focus on the NHS, education, social care, housing etc. but keep Brexit off the table.

The ceasefire could begin with a cross-party mea culpa from Parliament. This would acknowledge that Brexit had defeated the combined best efforts of 650 MPs: "We tried to implement the referendum result. We failed. We're sorry."

All parties represented at Westminster would follow up this joint apology with a public commitment not to introduce the topic of Brexit in their manifestos or in campaign materials. They would exert best efforts to limit discussion of Brexit at the local level. (It would also be off the agenda at PMQs.)

Of course, it is absurd to imagine the Brexit Party would go along with these restrictions. But it has never been part of the decision-making process in the House of Commons, so its situation is different anyway.

If all other parties were to agree to give the topic of Brexit a break, that would represent a positive first step towards defusing the tensions that have built up since the 2016 vote.

Conclusion

When you dig into it, Brexit is as complicated as a Swiss watch whose every component is itself made up of thousands of Swiss watches. That's a reflection of the magnificent, infernal complexity of the EU itself, and of our relationship with it. Nobody alive understands the consequences of Brexit in their entirety. It would be like trying to grasp the mind of God. As for this book, it has scratched a few epidermal cells at best.

The EU is an amazing legal construct, the result of the most sophisticated integration exercise ever undertaken by any group of countries. It has kept the peace in Europe for over seventy years, and enabled its member nations to prosper and thrive. It has unlocked countless opportunities, be it for students on Erasmus exchange programmes, scientists in collaborative projects, or companies drawing on the resources of an entire continent. If we want to holiday there, we grab a passport and jump on a plane, and most things will work pretty much as they do back home. It has fuelled trade and investment that underpins millions of jobs. The EU multiplies our strength, letting us punch above our weight on the global stage. Through financial passporting, it has allowed London to become the undisputed king of finance. It has also made the world – or at least our little corner of it – feel like a cosier, more welcoming place.

None of this happened by magic. It is a constant process of iteration and refinement, one that we get to share in as an EU member. We should take pride in having a major say in the policies of the largest and strongest trading block in the world. It can be hard to grasp how unique the EU is because it's all around us. We're so used to the freedoms it gives us, we have stopped acknowledging them.

Of course, the EU is not without its flaws. It is overly bureaucratic, though not as much as its detractors claim. The direction of travel towards greater political unity does not suit us. (Although we have opt outs, it is understandably unnerving.) The EU prevents us from striking our own trade deals and places restrictions on everything from state aid to environmental standards. We are far from alone in expressing unhappiness with how it is run. But we are the first member – and, if recent polling is to be believed, the last – to take that unhappiness and gamble everything on leaving.

Perfect is the enemy of good. Focus too closely on the EU's flaws, and we risk losing sight of all its benefits. That would be a crying shame because there will be no undoing Brexit once we're out.

Don't minimise the importance of Brexit. Don't dismiss the experts. You wouldn't do that in any other walk of life, so why start here? By all means keep a pinch of salt handy. But pay attention to what they're saying, even if it's unpalatable. (Told you the salt would come in useful.)

There will always be things wrong with the EU. The question is, do the things that are right about it outweigh them? And do we have enough confidence in ourselves as a nation to believe we can steer its future direction in our favour? For my money, they do, and we jolly well should.

And if anyone threatens to smash up the unfathomable sophistication of our EU relationship with a sledgehammer by leading us to a no deal Brexit, just say no. Then say it again, louder.

- THE END -

Thank you for taking the time to read Slaying Brexit Unicorns. Please turn the page for the appendices, including a long list of examples of the current effects of Brexit, and a glance back at Brexit in the Theresa May years. If you enjoyed this book, please tell your friends or post a short review on Amazon. Word of mouth is an author's best friend and enormously appreciated.

Edwin Hayward

Appendix A: Current effects of Brexit

Brexit is already having a massive impact on the UK, even ahead of our official departure. Jobs are going, investment is drying up, companies are moving assets to EU27 countries or redomiciling. In sector after sector, organisations are being forced to meet the challenges of Brexit head on, and absorb the costs of doing so.

Although we have only experienced the outermost bands of the Brexit hurricane so far, many firms are already re-evaluating their UK presence. Chaos looks set to replace certainty as our trading and regulatory environment changes. Prudent companies plan years ahead, especially when making large-scale capital investments. The lack of clarity around Brexit prevents them doing so.

It may be possible to overlook individual instances of Brexit damage listed below. But collectively they form a crime scene, one spread across such a wide area that nobody has connected all the evidence before.

That ends here. It is time to face the reality of Brexit.

No-deal Brexit Preparations

In the UK

The Government allocated £4.2 billion to Brexit preparations while Theresa May was PM. (Equivalent to £26,250,000 a week since the referendum.) In July 2019, Sajid Javid – the new Chancellor – announced that an extra £2.1 billion would be made available. £434 million of that was to ensure the continuity of vital medicines and medical products.[262]

In December 2018, agreements worth £107.7 million were signed with 3 ferry companies. The Government's stated aim was to provide extra capacity on short routes in the event of a no deal Brexit. The contracts were awarded in haste and were not put out to tender. It soon became clear that one firm, Seaborne Freight, had neither ferries nor industry experience.[263] When Brexit was postponed, the contracts with Brittany Ferries and DFDS were cancelled at a cost to the taxpayer of over £50 million.[264] All this, despite the original plans having been drawn up by external consultants, who pocketed £800,000.[265] The Government also settled legal action by Eurotunnel out of court by paying it £33 million. The firm had complained of being locked out of the contracting process.[266] Subsequently, P&O decided to sue the Government for £33 million over its Eurotunnel settlement. Were the case to proceed, the hearing will take place on 16 November.[267]

DExEU (the Brexit Ministry) has spent over £100 million (estimated) on staff since the referendum. That figure is only for the salaries of the people in the department. It does not cover any other costs.[268]

Portsmouth City Council is facing costs of £4 million to prepare for Brexit, as it battles to put in place measures that would prevent gridlock at the port. Its plans include setting up a lorry park at Tipner, and checkpoints on the A31.[269]

The Government spent £5.5 million on keeping Manston airfield open. It intends to use the space as overflow lorry parking in the event of a no deal Brexit. The system would operate once the motorways leading to the Channel ports ran out of queuing capacity.[270] (Fun fact: the location was the starting point for Chris Grayling's infamous traffic jam simulation. 150 vehicles were requested, but only 89 drivers turned up[271].)

£30 million was earmarked to establish a contraflow queuing system on the M20, and another £5 million was spent on works on the M26 to provide additional holding capacity for lorries.[272] The M26 motorway was completely closed every weekday night between 19 November 2018 and 21 December 2018 to prepare sections of it for conversion into lorry parking in case of Brexit disruption at the ports. The work included installing crossover points in the central reservation to enable traffic to be directed onto the opposite carriageway.[273]

The National Audit Office found the Government paid consultants £97 million between April 2018 and April 2019. They were engaged because the relevant Brexit expertise was supposedly unavailable internally. Six firms received 96% of all the farmed-out work.[274] A second round of contracts, covering a period until April 2020, is worth another £159 million. 20 consultancy companies will share the new spoils.[275] An NAO inquiry reported that government departments had failed to meet the standards of transparency expected of them when publishing the details of contracts. Problems included late disclosure, and the redaction of key information.[276]

Theresa May's EU withdrawal agreement was deemed such a hit at the time, the Brexit department spent £45,637 on printing 1,300 copies of the document, which runs to close to 600 pages. According to the BBC, a large number of the copies remained in the Parliamentary Vote Office months later.[277]

Highways England had to pay food and accommodation costs of £119 per person per day for its 80 staff involved in Operation Brock.[278] The series of measures, imposing traffic flow restrictions on Kent motorways, was in place from 25 March until 12 April 2019.[279]

HMRC blamed Brexit for the worsening level of service it has been providing. Highlighted issues included increased delays answering calls, and returning correspondence. It had 5,400 staff working on building customs, VAT and excise systems in readiness for Brexit, at a cost of £261.7 million. That's close to 10% of its entire personnel.[280]

The Government set up an £8 million fund to train companies and trade intermediaries such as freight forwarders. The application period for funding closed in May 2019, with only 741 companies having applied. But up to 240,000 companies will need to adopt new processes to trade with the EU after Brexit.[281]

Days after he became PM, Boris Johnson announced a £100 million ad campaign to prepare the UK for a no deal Brexit. The ad blitz will be spearheaded by two US firms. It will include TV, radio and online ads, as well as a newspaper campaign.[282]

As of December 2018, there were over 10,000 civil servants working on Brexit, and another 5,000 waiting in the wings.[283] Some were staff transferred from other roles, others were new hires. Defra alone hired 1,300 extra people in 2017-2018.[284] In April 2019, more than 6,000 civil servants who had been working to prepare for Brexit were stood down. The exercise cost the UK Government a reported £1.5 billion.[285] In August 2019, it was revealed that over 2,000 civil servants will be moved into Brexit preparation roles in the run-up to the revised October 31 deadline.[286]

The NHS in Wales has stockpiled 5,000 pallets of supplies, including toilet paper, and 22 tons of baked beans. (The warehouse also contains medical supplies.) It is keeping the exact location of the warehouse confidential, although photos of the interior were released to the press. The director of procurement, Mark Roscow, noted: "[The supply] represents eight weeks, and over eight weeks it would disappear."[287]

England's 343 councils have been allocated £20 million to prepare for no deal Brexit. That's equivalent to just over £58,000 per council.[288]

The Government abruptly cancelled all summer holiday leave for special advisors on 7 August 2019. Staff were informed they would not be allowed to take breaks until after 31 October 2019. Those with holidays already booked would be compensated.[289]

The UK Government had over 700 unfilled Brexit-related posts with just over two months to go until the revised October 31 deadline, include roles in border control.[290]

Wild Water, a specialist cold storage firm in Wales, has run out of warehouse space due to demand for Brexit stockpiling. It is working on building extra capacity.[291]

HMRC has fallen behind on its new Customs Declaration Service, a major new IT system meant to handle customs processes after Brexit. It was due to be ready in 2018, then for 29 March 2019. HMRC missed both deadlines. (Apparently because of staff seconded to other Brexit preparation roles.)[292]

The Department of Health warned hospitals they could face shortages of imported food after a no deal Brexit. It offered guidance to catering firms and procurement services on "actions to take in preparing to use substitute foodstuffs to maintain nutritional balance of patient menu/meal offerings."[293]

Defra is planning to set up a 24/7 emergency crisis call centre in advance of a no deal Brexit. It would operate for a temporary period of three to six months.[294]

The Police Service of Northern Ireland has imposed leave restrictions on its staff. These cover a six-week period in October and November 2019, spanning the revised Brexit deadline.[295]

Elsewhere in the EU

The Irish Government is offering firms up to 60,000 euro each to train staff on filing customs returns. 6,000 euro is on offer per trainee, with a limit of 10 per company. It's expected the number of declarations will rise over tenfold after Brexit.[296]

Dublin Port is spending €30 million on Brexit preparations. This includes €10 million on primary inspection posts, and €20 million on secondary posts for State agencies that will carry out customs clearance checks, as well as food and animal health checks.[297]

The Dutch Finance Ministry set aside 100 million euros to finance Brexit preparations. 900 new customs officers were expected to be hired; as of April 2019, more than half had been hired, but only 300 had completed training.[298][299]

EU Citizens

The Government has decided that all EU, EEA and Swiss citizens must apply to stay in the UK if they want to keep living here after 30 June 2021.[300] If the UK leaves the EU without a deal, the deadline for applications will be brought forward to 31 December 2020.

The Home Office estimates that between 3.5 and 4.1 million people will need to register before the EU Settlement Scheme ends.[301] That implies they will have to handle an average of over 4,000 applications per day, or over 5,400 applications a day if the UK leaves without a deal.

£175 million was spent on developing the system underpinning the EU Settlement Scheme, including an Android app.[302] (As of October 2019, the app is still not available for iPhone.) The registration system was beta tested between 28 August and 17 October 2018. The trial comprised a little over a thousand applications. 66% of straightforward cases were completed within 7 days.[303] A second private beta test took place before a public trial of the system began on 21 January 2019.[304]

The full registration system opened on 30 March 2019, and over 50,000 applications were received during the first weekend.[305] As of October 2019, the Government claimed to have received over two million applications.[306]

Initially, registrations incurred an application fee of £65. The fee was abolished, following protests, before the full system went live. Applicants who had already paid it received refunds[307]. That doesn't mean the process is entirely cost-free. Applicants may incur expenses while assembling the documentation to prove their eligibility to stay here. They may also be forced to travel to a regional processing centre if they cannot use a suitable Android phone. And if their application is rejected and they are obliged to appeal, they may have to pay for legal help.

The rhetoric around the settlement scheme hardened as the revised Brexit deadline approached and the talks foundered. On October 10, media reports indicated that the Government might seek to deport EU citizens who fail to register to stay by the deadline for doing so, unless they can evidence a "good reason" for failing to apply.[308]

Financial Sector

1. National issues

The UK economy contracted in the second quarter of 2019. It was the first quarter of negative growth since 2012. Cited factors included stockpiles being unwound after Brexit was postponed, shutdowns in the car sector, and a weaker construction sector.[309]

The Government boosted its foreign currency reserves from £50 billion to £63 billion over the year to June 2019. £8 billion of the increase came after the original Brexit deadline of 29 March.[310]

Brexit is killing off a crucial source of early stage venture capital funding. Investment from the European Investment Fund (EIF) into the UK fell 91% during 2017, from €708.8m to €61.1m. This drop came at a time when EIF funding to the rest of Europe remained steady.[311]

The Government is injecting £200 million into the British Business Bank, a state-run scheme, ahead of Brexit. The intent is to mitigate the reduction in small- and medium-sized business financing offered by the EIF.[312]

A January 2019 Lords report indicated that Brexit has had a "material effect" on the UK's relationship with the European Investment Bank (EIB). The EIB lent €7bn to 54 projects in 2016, €1.8bn to 12 projects in 2017 and a mere €932m to 10 projects in 2018. The shortfall is expected to impact major infrastructure projects.[313]

Research by recruitment specialists, Morgan McKinley, found that new job openings in the financial services sector declined from over 24,000 a quarter at the start of 2017 to under 8,000 by Q2, 2019. The firm said: "Major banking organisations as well as those from the wider financial services space have refrained from investing in talent due to the lack of clarity."[314]

The European Banking Authority (EBA), the EU's banking regulator, moved its operations from London to Paris. The relocation affected 160 staff. The selection of the new venue was confirmed in a vote by EU27 ministers on 20 November 2017.[315] The EBA closed its Canary Wharf office on 30 May 2019, and re-opened in Paris on 3 June.[316]

A $15 billion hedge fund is gearing up to profit from Brexit chaos. Marathon Asset Management's Bruce Richards told Bloomberg: "The U.K. is fine for now, and there's some value here and there, but I hold back my investments for now because come a year after Brexit, we believe there's a recession waiting."[317]

Hedge funds and City traders reportedly held short positions worth almost £8.3 billion as of September 2019. (Short positions pay out when the market falls. In other words, they are betting against the success of the UK.) They took out the majority of these positions after Boris Johnson became PM. According to the report, many of the firms in question had donated to his leadership bid, to the Tory party, or to the Vote Leave campaign during the referendum.[318]

The hedge fund belonging to Crispin Odey, a pro-Brexit Tory party donor who contributed to Boris Johnson's leadership campaign, has taken short positions against major UK firms. These positions reportedly totalled almost £300 million in early August 2019.[319] Mr Odey, who had given over £800,000 to pro-Brexit campaigns, boasted the morning after the referendum that he had made £220 million overnight by betting that the markets would collapse after a Leave vote. On camera, he said: "I still think tomorrow they are going to take it all away from me. I've lived for too long in the Euro world. You might have been up all night but, you know, I'm feeling fresh as a daisy."[320]

2. Company changes in the UK

Barclays received legal permission in January 2019 to move €190bn (£166bn) of assets from the UK to Dublin in advance of 29 March 2019. This represents about 15% of the bank's total assets. It is doubling its Dublin operation to 300 staff.[321]

HSBC reported in its 2017 annual report that the bank had incurred US$28 million of "costs associated with the UK's exit from the EU".[322] As one part of its Brexit-related preparations, the bank shifted ownership of its Polish and Irish subsidiaries from the UK to its French unit.[323] In April 2019, costs imposed by Brexit were estimated to have risen to US$179 million.[324] In August 2019, it was reported the firm was moving more roles from London to Paris.[325]

RBS has set aside £100 million against possible bad loans resulting from Brexit. CEO Ross McEwan said: "There's a lot more uncertainty in the marketplace until we get agreement, and that's what this is reflecting."[326]

Columbia Threadneedle transferred £6.2 billion of assets from UK domiciled funds to Luxembourg domiciled funds.[327]

Bank of America has spent around US$400 million preparing for Brexit. It set up new subsidiaries in Paris and Dublin, moved some staff, and shifted US$50 billion of assets to Dublin. Vice chairman Anne Finucane said the changes were permanent: "Dublin is our headquarters for our European bank now – full stop. Even if there were no Brexit, that has happened, there isn't a return there. The bridge has been pulled up on that."[328]

Deutsche Bank moved about half of its new euro swaps business away from LCH (UK-based clearing house) and onto Eurex, based in Germany.[329]

BrokerTec is moving its European market for short-term financing from London to Amsterdam. The platform trades over 200 billion euros worth of short-term financing instruments a month. Managing director John Edwards said: "All of our euro-denominated bonds and repo will move to Amsterdam. We saw no benefit in splitting liquidity pools. Our UK business will not be able to provide services to the European clients."[330] In March 2019, regulatory approval was granted by authorities in the Netherlands to establish the necessary legal entity in Amsterdam.[331]

The Financial Conduct Authority (FCA) states in its 2018/19 business plan that they "have identified total EU withdrawal demand [costs] of around £30m", and that part of that will have to be funded by raising the fees they charge firms.[332]

TP ICAP, the world's biggest interdealer broker, said its 2018 full-year earnings would incur about £10 million in costs related to Brexit. It has selected Paris as its post-Brexit EU headquarters.[333]

Canaccord Genuity announced on 31 March 2019 that it was restructuring its capital markets business in the UK. In a press release, the firm said "A prolonged period of political and market uncertainty in the UK has impacted capital raising and related activities in the region resulting in unacceptable returns." It also stated that the plan would result in "a significant reduction in the Company's London-based capital markets staff level". The company recorded a charge of C$12 million in Q4 to cover this move.[334]

In June 2018, MS Amlin received permission from the National Bank of Belgium to redomicile Amlin Insurance SE from the UK to Belgium.[335]

3. Company changes outside the UK

SwissQuote cancelled plans to expand in London. Instead, it bought a bank in Luxembourg to secure access to EU markets. CEO Marc Buerki said: "We anticipate limitations [in London] due to Brexit… It is still a good place to be, but the expansion plans we had two years ago before Brexit happened had to be stopped in favour of this strategic move with Luxembourg."[336]

Standard Chartered secured a full banking license from Germany, and turned its Frankfurt branch into a subsidiary. It doubled the number of employees based in Germany to around 200. Alexander Engel, the chief financial officer of the subsidiary, confirmed the changes wouldn't be rolled back: "The point of no-return has passed, independent of what happens on the political side."[337]

Daiwa Capital Markets established a new subsidiary in Germany to continue to provide a full service to its EU-based clients after Brexit. The subsidiary started operations on 3 September 2018.[338]

Bank ABC secured a banking license to upgrade the status of its Paris branch to an EU subsidiary. The firm noted: "Once established, this new entity (continuing to trade as Bank ABC) will enable the bank to operate much as we do today across the bank's European network."[339]

Marshall Wace, one of the biggest hedge funds in the UK, has obtained a license to run management companies in Ireland. It plans to grow its Dublin presence as a protective measure against Brexit. (Related aside: its chairman donated £100,000 to the Leave campaign during the referendum.)[340]

MarketAxess, a fixed income trading specialist, has been granted approval to operate its trading platform and reporting services in Amsterdam. Christophe Roupie, head of Europe and Asia, said: "Recognising the potential impact of Brexit on European financial markets, we were one of the first movers in establishing an office in the Netherlands."[341]

JPMorgan has spent over US$100 million on Brexit preparations. The firm secured extra office space on the outskirts of Paris.[342] Over 300 employees have allegedly signed new contracts that would see them move to France or Germany in the event of no deal.[343]

Architas, an asset management firm, has been expanding in Ireland by creating 11 new roles there. Their chief executive officer said: "Like all asset managers, we have been reviewing our operations ahead of Brexit."[344]

GoldCore opened Ireland's first institutional-grade gold storage vault in October 2018. The firm did so with the expectation that investors would wish to move gold bars from London to Dublin. It set an initial target of attracting 0.5% of the US$300 billion of gold bars held in London.[345]

XTX Markets, a high frequency trading platform, announced in October 2018 that it will open an office in Paris to trade European stocks. It will be seeking appropriate authorisation from the French regulators. It plans to keep its London presence.[346]

Credit Suisse is expanding its existing EU operations, including offices in Frankfurt, Paris, Madrid, Milan and Amsterdam. It has committed to maintaining a presence in the UK to service non-EU clients. It plans to relocate a number of bankers from London to its continental European offices.[347]

Nomura obtained a securities trading license from the German regulator. It established a new broker-dealer in Frankfurt to maintain EU passporting rights.[348] It started the process of transitioning clients to the new entity in advance of the original 29 March 2019 Brexit deadline.[349]

Investment management firm Man Group upgraded the regulatory permissions of its Irish entity. It also opened a physical office in Dublin, initially with 7 staff. In its 2018 annual report, the firm stated: "This ensures that Man Group will remain able to service its existing European clients and to access new business in the EU."[350] In its interim results for the six months ending 30 June 2019, the company detailed the additional Brexit mitigation steps it had undertaken: "This enhancement to Man Group's European footprint has been further developed in 2019, with EU branches of Man Group's Irish entity established in Italy and the Netherlands."[351]

Soldo has secured a licence from Ireland's Central Bank to protect against Brexit uncertainty. The firm's CEO said: "It's crazy to think we've been forced to work for a year and a half on a hugely complex project, mostly duplicating something that we had already, to prepare our business for something that may or may not happen."[352]

Mitsubishi UFJ Financial Group selected Amsterdam as its new EU base in 2017. The company said: "The new subsidiary in Amsterdam will ensure that the Group can continue to provide these (securities) services to its EU clients, even if the cross-border passport is lost as a result of Brexit."[353] Its Amsterdam office opened in March 2019.[354] In July 2019, the firm implemented a voluntary redundancy programme in London with a view to cutting 50 jobs.[355]

Hermes Investment Management is setting up a new office in Dublin as a post-Brexit base. The firm received the necessary authorisation from the Central Bank of Ireland in December 2018. Their CEO said: "Since the referendum in 2016, we have always planned for a 'hard Brexit'. We recognised early on that we had to make appropriate contingency plans in the absence of certainty, in order to ensure, to the extent possible, that we remain able to manage our clients' assets in line with their expectations of us."[356]

Sumitomo Mitsui Financial Group obtained approval from the ECB to establish a banking subsidiary in Frankfurt as part of its preparations for a no-deal Brexit. It intends the subsidiary to begin operations in 2019.[357]

Insurance Industry

Standard Life reported £12 million of "Brexit related costs" in its 2018 half-year results report.[358]

Lloyd's of London transacts 15% of its business with EU counterparts. It opened its post-Brexit headquarters, Lloyd's Brussels, in November 2018. The new operation has 50 staff, and will service customers across the EU27.[359] Chief executive Inga Beale commented in July 2018: "Lloyd's is to open a subsidiary in Brussels so we will be full steam ahead, and many other banks, insurers and other financial services firms will be moving at pace now."[360]

STM Life plans to transfer the policies of policyholders resident in Gibraltar, the UK, the Isle of Man and the Channel Islands to a sister company in Malta. (Reminder: Gibraltar will leave the EU at the same time as the UK will.)[361]

Royal & Sun Alliance Insurance plc transferred approximately 6% of its insurance and reinsurance business to a new legal entity in Luxembourg. The change became effective on 1 January 2019.[362]

Admiral Group PLC transferred some of its liabilities and contracts to an entity in Spain which it spent 3.5 million euros setting up. The firm also conducted a Brexit stress test to check the resilience of its business.[363]

Aviva is moving £9 billion in client assets from the UK to Ireland. It gained legal approval for the transfer on 19 February 2019, and expected it to be effective on 29 March 2019.[364]

UK insurance and investment group Royal London is facing costs in excess of £21 million to move £1 billion of financial assets from the UK to Ireland in advance of Brexit. Its new Irish office will employ about 20 staff.[365]

Hiscox transferred some assets of their business to Luxembourg, using the Part VII transfer mechanism. The transfer, affecting £421.5 million of liabilities, took effect on 1 January 2019.[366]

Markel International set up a new insurance company in Germany to handle EEA business it used to service from London. The new organisation is licensed, capitalised and already writing risks. The firm also transferred certain existing business to the new entity.[367]

Liberty Specialty Markets decided to situate its post-Brexit headquarters in Luxembourg.[368] The company opted to redomicile its insurance company from the UK to Luxembourg while maintaining its London presence.[369] The firm received the required license from the authorities in December 2018.[370]

Insurer AIG restructured its business over Brexit concerns. It set up a new entity in Luxembourg, and transferred its EEA and Swiss business to it, away from its UK company. It completed this process in December 2018.[371]

Insurer Tokio Marine Group used the "Part VII process" to transfer its portfolio of Continental European policies from two UK-based subsidiaries (Tokio Marine Kiln, and Tokyo Marine HCC International) to a new entity in Luxembourg.[372]

Gambling Sector

Bet365 is transferring the bulk of its Gibraltar operation to Malta. In a statement, the company said this was to "ensure [EU] market access and to maintain and enhance operational efficiencies."[373] It agreed to acquire a significant new property development in Sliema to serve as the firm's operating hub.[374]

Ladbrokes owner GVC is moving some of the servers that host its gambling sites from the UK to Ireland. The firm said: "Under the regulations of some EU countries, the servers hosting our online gambling platform need to be located in an EU member state."[375] Its EU-focused divisions will start to operate under a Maltese online gambling license.[376]

888 Holdings obtained a new gambling license in Malta, and established servers in Ireland to mitigate against Brexit risk.[377]

Health Sector

Legislation was put in place in February 2019 to allow for Serious Shortage Protocols to be imposed on prescription medicines. If the SSP is activated for certain medicines by the Secretary of State, pharmacies would be required to issue equivalent medicines, products of different strengths or formulations, or smaller quantities than called for in the prescription. The Government is making pharmacies responsible for determining what the appropriate course of action is for each patient. They will have to turn them away as a last resort if they decide there are no suitable alternatives for them.[378]

The European Medicine Agency, Europe's medicines regulator, has moved from London to Amsterdam. It employed close to 900 people in London. Around 30% of staff were expected not to relocate.[379] The agency left London on 1 March 2019, and opened for business in Amsterdam on 11 March. Some employees will continue to telework before moving to the Netherlands later in the year.[380]

After Brexit, the NHS faces costs of almost £500 million a year to secure the necessary visas and other documentation for its overseas staff and their dependents. The processes it will have to follow will become more complicated, and more costly. In a typical year, over 25,000 staff from outside the UK (EU & non-EU) join the NHS.[381]

Recardio halted clinical trials of a new heart drug in the UK because of concerns over Brexit, and the drug approval regime.[382]

In its 2018 annual report, GSK outlined its approach to Brexit contingency planning. The firm is having to re-test and certify its medicines in the EU. It will also have to update packaging, secure additional warehouse space, and help affected staff to obtain settled status in the EU and the UK. The report detailed the costs GSK expected to incur: "As a result, we have taken a risk-based approach to planning and mitigation, allocating costs of up to £70 million to implement relevant changes over the next one to two years, while the future relationship between the UK and EU is negotiated." It also highlighted the future costs that Brexit would impose on its business: "We anticipate subsequent and ongoing costs arising from Brexit could include further customs duties and will include the cost of duplicate testing and release of our products. We continue to estimate these potential costs at approximately £50 million per year."[383]

Pfizer stated that its preparations are well advanced towards making the necessary changes to its business to meet EU legal requirements once the UK is no longer a member state. "The one-time costs of making these adaptations are currently estimated at approximately $100 million."[384]

STERIS plc decided to redomicile its operations from the UK to Ireland. Chief executive Walt Rosebrough said: "Along with most of the world, we certainly did not expect Brexit at that time [the company moved to the UK], and the subsequent uncertainties surrounding Brexit. Simply put, significant benefits are at risk if we remain domiciled in a country that is no longer a member of the EU."[385]

Wasdell Group set up a new pharmaceutical facility in Dundalk, Ireland (its first site outside the UK). It invested over 30 million euros into the development. In a statement, the firm said: "The building of the new facility will not only assist with our strategy of growth over the coming years but also provide our solution to a 'hard' Brexit if this becomes a reality."[386] The company's new EU headquarters secured the necessary licenses in July 2019, and opened for business.[387]

AstraZenica has spent £40 million on stockpiling medicines in the UK and Europe. In October 2018, chairman Leif Johansson confirmed that the company's freeze on investments, announced in 2017, would be maintained: "If a transition deal does not make clear what will happen in the future, we will maintain our decision not to invest. A Brexit agreement will need to ensure that Britain does not become an isolated island in the middle of the Atlantic Ocean."[388] The company is duplicating batch testing of UK-tested medicines, changing packaging, and coordinating drug licenses.[389] In February 2019, the firm's CFO described some of the preparations it had made: "To safeguard against shorter-term friction at borders, we have moved stock from the UK to European distribution centre to be as close as possible to customers on Brexit day, and built an additional six weeks of stock for UK supply."[390]

NHS trusts were instructed in a letter dated 22 July 2019 to have their key Brexit teams "in post and ready" by the end of August (giving them less than 6 weeks to prepare). The letter also stated that: "As part of these preparations we expect all providers and commissioners to have full contingency plans in place to ensure safe services for patients can continue to be provided in the event that the UK leaves the EU without a deal."[391]

Boyds, a pharmaceutical and biotech consultancy, opened a new office in Dublin in spring 2019. It did so to ensure that its clients could still benefit from access to the European Medicines Agency after Brexit. Founder Alan Boyd: "We need to ensure we are positioned to continue this vital work with the EMA."[392]

Roche Diabetes Care has prepared for Brexit by stockpiling at least six weeks of stock of all its product lines, a task that involved securing additional storage space. The firm also assessed other import routes other than its usual Calais-Dover link.[393]

Almac Group invested £30 million into a new European campus in Dundalk, Ireland, so that it could continue to conduct clinical trials and drug certifications for EU clients after Brexit. (The company's global HQ is in Northern Ireland.)[394]

Veterinary drugs producer, Dechra Pharmaceuticals, decided to go ahead with its hard Brexit contingency plans in September 2018. These cost the firm £2 million to implement.[395]

The FT reported that Shionogi, a Japanese drugs company, was planning to move its HQ from London to the Netherlands. The move is notable because Boris Johnson feted their choice of London as a base when he was Mayor of London.[396]

Close to 5,000 midwives and nurses from the EU left the NHS between March 2017 and March 2019. That represents 13% of all EU staff working for the NHS. This drop was partially offset by an increase in staff from outside the EU.[397]

Based in London, British Standards Institution (BSI) is the largest certifier of medical devices in Europe by value. It is opening a Dutch subsidiary to give non-EU companies a choice of UK or EU27 certification. Most affected firms are likely to opt for the latter.[398]

Johnson & Johnson expects to spend US$80 million on new customs clearances and conformity assessment processes. The firm anticipates that its Brexit costs in the UK will peak at US$180 million in 2025.[399]

A Sheffield company, B.Braun Medical, spent £3 million on Brexit preparations. Its chief executive said he "can't see anything positive about Brexit", noting it was "dead money" that could have been spent "recruiting, developing and training people."[400]

Food & Drink Sector

Dominos Pizza has spent £7 million stockpiling ingredients to guard against supply disruption. In a statement, the firm said: "A potential no-deal Brexit carries the increased risk of disruption to raw material supplies into the UK and foreign exchange volatility which could increase food costs."[401]

Dairy Crest has been working to reduce its Brexit exposure, including speeding up the purchase of ingredients and packaging materials. The firm said: "There is significant uncertainty around Brexit and the impact of a potentially disorderly exit is hard to predict."[402]

Pub group, Marston's, stockpiled £6 million worth of beer ahead of the original March 2019 Brexit deadline. The firm noted: "We continue to closely monitor the Brexit situation and are well placed to implement any necessary contingency plans."[403]

In August 2019, the Food and Drink Federation asked for some aspects of competition law to be set aside in the event of no deal. It said firms would be obliged to work together to prioritise shipments and tackle shortages. It is seeking a "letter of comfort" from the Government to provide legal reassurance.[404]

Quality Meat Scotland set aside £150,000 (5% of its annual budget) for Brexit contingency planning. Their chief executive said: "We are working with all our key industry partners to try to be ready in the event of a no-deal Brexit."[405]

Bewleys, the Irish coffee group, incurred €11.9 million in costs preparing for a hard Brexit, including increasing its warehouse facilities, and expanding its roasting capacity in the UK.[406]

C&C Group, the Irish drinks group, decided to delist from Euronext Dublin and move its entire listing onto the FTSE. Stephen Glancey, the firm's boss, said that the 40% of shareholders in the UK would find a sole London listing easier once the UK leaves the EU.[407]

Premium Wines of Romania pulled out of the London Wine Fair 2019 in May. The Romanian department of agriculture has decided to stop funding activities in the UK until the outcome of Brexit becomes clear.[408]

Pirate Grog's Rum is moving production of its non-UK stock from London to Amsterdam. The firm said: "We see it as the right time to do this for the business. Brexit is something that the company has to take into account."[409]

Clifton Quality Meats shut down in August 2018, affecting around 80 jobs. The firm cited the fall in the value of the pound as one of the factors in its closure, as well as uncertainty in the sector following the collapse of a rival supplier.[410] Its most recent full accounts showed a turnover of over £11 million a year.[411]

KellyBronze Free Range Turkeys is moving 10% of its breeding stock to the Netherlands and Germany. The firm faced a shortage of seasonal workers, who would normally return year after year. The firm's managing director said: "Without the guarantee that we will remain in the customs union and have access to EU labour, we can't risk keeping all our production in the UK."[412]

Nestlé has been stockpiling key product lines ahead of Brexit, both in the UK and in continental Europe.[413] The firm's chief executive said:

"We've been running extra levels of stocks, to be sure that even if there are some distributions and customs interruptions, we are not running our supply chain dry."[414] The company admitted that the depreciation of the pound since the Brexit vote forced it to put up prices, something it had been reluctant to do.[415]

Apetito, a firm which supplies hot meals to care homes and hospitals, spent £100,000 on frozen storage space for 1,700 pallets, and £5 million on stockpiling raw materials and finished meals.[416]

Premier Foods (makers of Bisto, Oxo & Mr Kipling) estimate their working capital will be depleted by £10 million as a result of the need to stockpile raw materials as a contingency before Brexit.[417]

Lidl's Irish unit is planning to enforce contract provisions binding UK suppliers to paying all import tariffs that may arise after a no-deal Brexit. In other words, the firms will be prevented from passing the increased costs along.[418]

Bread prices will go up in Ireland under a no deal Brexit because the flour used for commercial baking is milled in Northern Ireland (Ireland has no bulk mills) and will be subject to tariffs of €172 a tonne.[419] But problems breed opportunity. A family of crop farmers is working on a €25 million project to open Ireland's first flour mill for 50 years.[420]

Law and Order

Scotland Yard has been obliged to set up a "no deal safety net unit" at a cost of over £2.4 million. This included £250,000 to rent an office near parliament to accommodate the substantial team.[421]

A confidential plan is apparently being drawn up to give civilian Traffic Officers new powers if no deal Brexit goes ahead, including demanding and checking the documentation of drivers. They will also be able to impose fines of up to £300 on hauliers who try to get around queueing restrictions.[422]

Police Scotland announced that around 300 officers would be on standby to deal with Brexit issues. They are to be deployed from late August, in advance of the new October Brexit deadline. Their remit includes handling protests, and dealing with disruption at the ports.[423] The force has already spent over £7 million on Brexit preparations.[424]

Police Scotland's dedicated Brexit unit was stood down in May 2019 after an 8-week programme that racked up costs of up to £2.5 million. (The UK Government refused to refund the costs, stating they should come from Holyrood's existing Brexit budget.)[425]

The operational HQ for "Operation Atalanta" was relocated from the UK to bases in Spain and France. OA is a EU maritime mission that combats piracy off the Somalian coast. The move took place on 29 March 2019, affecting around 100 staff. Command of the programme passed from the UK to the Spanish Navy.[426]

Transport

CldN, a short-sea ferry operator, has brought in 2 new ships, including the so-called "Brexit Buster" Celine. With a 600 truck capacity, it's the world's largest short sea roll-on roll-off ferry. Dublin Port had to be upgraded to accommodate it. The idea is to bypass the UK, and transport goods directly to Belgium and the Netherlands. The firm's CEO said: "Let me take one [headache] away from you. In terms of maritime success to and from Ireland, we have got this."[427] The first ship started operating in April 2018. On 29 March 2019 (the original Brexit day) it was joined by a second massive ship, the Laureline.[428]

Dozens of firms have reflagged ships from UK flags to flags of other EU countries in recent years. Since the beginning of 2019 alone, 234 vessels were reflagged from the UK. (For context, there were 1,306 vessels in the UK registered merchant fleet at the end of 2018.[429]) A spokesperson for one company, CMA CGM, said: "[In] light of Brexit, and to avoid uncertainty with our fleet and despite a strong relationship with the UK Ship Register, we have decided to transfer our UK-flagged fleet to other EU countries." P&O Ferries commented that their decision to reflag ships would mean "significantly more favourable" tonnage tax arrangements by keeping them flagged in an EU member state.[430] But what's good for them is bad for the UK, because HMRC will no longer collect the tonnage tax on those vessels.

The port of Cork in Ireland is doubling the size of its customs building ahead of Brexit. The port is used by lorries on ferry routes connecting to France and Spain, and more traffic is expected along those routes in the event of a hard Brexit.[431]

The port of Waterford in Ireland opened a new freight shipping route to Rotterdam in July 2019. The container-based service, operated in partnership by BG Freight Line and Maersk, will run on a weekly schedule.[432]

Brexit-that-never-was smashed the car industry in April 2019. Most firms had contingency plant shutdowns planned that they were unable to cancel last minute when the Brexit deadline moved. For example, Jaguar Land Rover shut down its plants at several locations across the UK for a week in early April 2019. These shutdowns were arranged to be contiguous with the plants' Easter closure the following week.[433] Across the industry, production fell to 70,971 vehicles from 127,970 in the same period a year earlier.[434]

Jaguar Land Rover has opened a new plant in Slovakia (expected capacity of 100,000 cars/year by 2020). It stands ready to shift car production away from the UK, depending on the outcome of Brexit.[435]

UK car manufacturers spent a combined £330 million on no-deal Brexit preparations up to July 2019. At the same time, production in the UK fell 20.1% in the first six months compared to 2018.[436]

BMW said in July 2019 that its UK plant would no longer manufacture engines destined for South Africa. Production was switched to Germany instead. The firm made the switch because of concerns over tariffs post-Brexit.[437]

In September 2019, Pandragon announced it was closing 22 of its 34 Car Store used car dealerships with a loss of 300 jobs. The firm said it had resorted to heavy discounting and trade auctions to offset "weak consumer confidence related to Brexit uncertainty".[438]

William Wright, the founder of Wrightbus was the first major business figure in Northern Ireland to back Brexit. He did so, he said, because of the immigrant crisis.[439] The firm cut close to 200 positions in February and June 2018. At the time, its chairman blamed "continuing uncertainty" in the UK market, which was causing customers to delay or postpone orders.[440] The company entered administration in September 2019, with a loss of 1,200 jobs.[441]

Ferrovial, Heathrow airport's operator, is moving its international headquarters from the UK to Amsterdam. A spokesperson said: "The reason for the move is to maintain the group's international companies under the umbrella of [EU] legislation."[442] In June 2016, it was announced that Heathrow SP Ltd, which owns the airport, had reduced its Brexit contingency allowance from £114 million to just £35 million.[443]

Over 600 UK aerospace firms have asked to be regulated in Europe as third-country parties. In a no deal scenario, the CAA can no longer grant regulatory approval for parts made in the UK to be used across the EU. British manufacturers will need authorisation from a European aviation authority to sell parts into Europe.[444]

EasyJet spent approx. £4 million on Brexit preparations during the 6 months ending 31 March 2018. These involved setting up an AOC in Austria; most of the costs were incurred in the re-registration of aircraft.[445]

Dart Group stated in its 2019 annual report that it had received approval from EASA to be given third country approval status for Jet2.com so that it can continue to operate aircraft in Europe after Brexit.[446]

Flybmi went bankrupt in February 2019, with the loss of 376 jobs. The regional airline cited a variety of factors in a statement, including: "Current trading and future prospects have also been seriously affected by the uncertainty created by the Brexit process, which has led to our inability to secure valuable flying contracts in Europe and lack of confidence around bmi's ability to continue flying between destinations in Europe."[447]

Rolls-Royce shifted design approval work on its large aerospace engines from Derby to Germany.[448] It built up additional inventory, and relocated some inventory to mainland Europe.[449] In August 2019, the firm said its Brexit preparations had cost it almost £100 million.[450]

Once we leave the EU, we'll also be out of the "Connecting Europe Facility" pan-EU transport strategy. EU maps will be redrawn (from a policy perspective, not literally) so that the UK doesn't figure on them any more. This means we will no longer be able to tap into a pool of tens of billions of euro in grants and other funding aimed at building new transport infrastructure in Europe, or rehabilitating and upgrading existing transport links.[451] From 2014 to 2019, UK beneficiaries participated in 51 projects, and received €341.1 million in co-funding, facilitating projects worth €901.8 million.[452]

Space

The Government will conduct an 18 month study, at the cost of £92 million, to look for a home brewed alternative to the Galileo GPS satellite system.[453] (After Brexit, the UK will no longer have access to Galileo's encrypted military signals on security grounds.) All the funding is allocated to planning. It doesn't cover manufacturing satellites, or conducting space launches. Early estimates peg the cost of replicating the actual system at between £3 billion and £5 billion.[454] That's a hefty chunk of change to get back to the status quo we would have enjoyed had we stayed in the EU.

In September 2018, the new work order for the "Galileo Control Segment" (ground infrastructure intended to monitor the Galileo satellite constellation) was awarded to GMV Aerospace and Defence of Spain. Previously, GCS had been provided by Airbus in Portsmouth.[455]

Retail

Halfords Group plc stated in its interim results for Financial Year 2019: "The weaker pound since the Brexit vote has increased our cost of sales by a cumulative circa £40m by the end of FY18 compared to FY16."[456]

Art dealer David Zwirner will open an outlet in Paris in the autumn of 2019, his first in mainland Europe. He commented: "Brexit changes the game. After October, my London gallery will be a British gallery, not a European one. I am European, and I would like a European gallery, too."[457]

The Body Shop opened a new European distribution centre in Frankfurt, and cut around 20 UK roles. A spokesperson said: "The continued uncertainty about the impact of Brexit requires us to be proactive in managing every aspect of our business to meet our customers' needs."[458]

Panasonic is moving its European HQ from the UK to Amsterdam. The legal aspects of the move were completed in October 2018, as the £200 million capitalised UK company was absorbed by Panasonic's Dutch entity. The move was prompted by concerns that Japan might see the UK as a tax haven post-Brexit, which could lead to a higher tax burden being imposed back in Japan.[459]

Sony is merging Sony Europe into a new Amsterdam subsidiary in order to move its legal headquarters from the UK to the Netherlands. The firm aims to avoid disruptions to shipping and customs procedures. No UK staff are expected to be affected.[460]

In December 2018, the owner of an online retail sports company, FreestyleXtreme, described what the firm was doing to prepare for Brexit. He said it had opened an office in Romania, and was also planning to set up a warehouse in Germany. Explaining that 15 jobs in the UK had already been lost, he warned: "For our business and thousands of others across the country, the options available to us in the event of a no-deal are to relocate if possible, downsize significantly if possible or go bankrupt."[461] Sadly prescient words. The firm emailed its customer base in August 2019 to inform them it had ceased trading.[462]

Unilever is stockpiling several weeks' worth of Ben and Jerry's ice cream and Magnum bars in the UK, and deodorant in the EU, in case of supply chain problems due to Brexit.[463]

John Lewis saw profits drop 99% from £83m to £1.2m in the 6 months to 28 July 2018. Chairman Sir Charlie Mayfield cited a number of factors. He said: "[we decided] not to pass on to our customers all cost price inflation from a weaker exchange rate."[464] The company bolstered its financial position ahead of Brexit, building up record liquidity of £1.5 billion by March 2019.[465] In September 2019, the firm unveiled its first loss in its 155 year history. It warned explicitly of the dangers of a no deal Brexit to its business.[466]

The Swiss watch industry saw a massive 58% increase in shipments to the UK in February 2019, as retailers stockpiled ahead of Brexit.[467] Even some brands that normally do not keep inventory in the UK resorted to warehousing stock here.[468]

Online retailer AO World spent £15 million on stockpiling in the run-up to the original Brexit deadline. Founder, John Roberts, said: "We feel very ready and have spent a lot of money. I'd class that as wasted a lot of money. We could have invested that money on much (more) positive things."[469] Prescient words, as the original Brexit deadline was of course moved. In June 2019, he said: "That was a huge process and cost that the business took on to manage that, then it all became a non-event so we're unwinding that process as we work through."[470]

Pets at Home stated in November 2018 that it had stockpiled pet food and products worth "a couple of million pounds" in advance of Brexit, and warned that 17% of the goods it supplied came from outside the UK.[471] In May 2019, the firm said that its Brexit stockpile (estimated at £4 million) had been run down, and would have to be rebuilt.[472]

It was announced in August 2019 that a Wall Street investment fund would buy Majestic Wine's 200 physical stores. MW will become an online-only retailer. However, £5 million of the £100 million sale price is contingent on the post-Brexit regulatory landscape. This payment will be deferred for 2 years until Brexit is resolved.[473]

Bisto and Mr Kipling owner, Premier Foods, saw its international sales fall 18% in the 13 weeks ending 29 June. In a statement to investors, the firm said: "This was due to the unwind of Brexit-related stock in Irish customers' supply chains."[474]

DPD has set up a bonded warehouse the size of 10 football pitches to handle the backlog of parcels expected to accumulate under a no deal Brexit. Goods from the EU would incur duties and taxes, so packages would be held there until the recipients paid. The parcels would then be released for final delivery.[475]

Mondelēz (maker of Cadbury products) is preparing for a no-deal Brexit by stockpiling chocolate. The company's European president warns that the UK is "not self-sufficient in terms of food ingredients".[476]

Fashion retailer, New Look, decided to close 25 more stores that originally planned, 85 in total. The firm cited "significant headwinds and uncertainties, including Brexit."[477]

Tech Sector

In its 2019 annual report, Elektron Technology plc stated it had invested £600,000 into increasing short-term inventory to mitigate the risk of a no deal Brexit.[478]

In October 2018, Scisys sought shareholder approval to redomicile its holding company from the UK to Ireland in order to: "protect shareholder value & mitigate the possible negative effects of Brexit on the Group's space business".[479] The change was clearly beneficial, since the firm picked up new work on the EU's Galileo satellite programme within months.[480]

Apple reseller, Solutions Inc., closed several stores and called in the receiver in February 2019.[481] In its accounts for the year ended 30 June

2017, the firm stated: "In November of this financial year [2016] Apple increased the pricing on their products due to the fall in the value of sterling. This also had a negative effect on sales."[482]

Manufacturing Sector

Manufacturers will have to shell out millions of pounds on retesting and recertifying the safety of their products post-Brexit. The EU's CE mark will no longer apply in the UK; instead, a new UKCA mark is being introduced. But the effect of this is to force companies to test products twice, once for the UK and once for the EU market.[483]

The government estimates that it will cost the chemicals industry £450 million to re-register chemicals under a post-Brexit regime. This is because the UK will no longer be a participant in the pan-EU REACH database. Firms will have to pay to duplicate their existing registrations (this restores the status quo, but does not confer any meaningful benefit).[484]

Mahle Powertrain closed a factory in Wellingborough in April 2018, with the loss of 110 jobs. Plant Manager Anthony Green said: "There is nothing we could have done about it, it's all through the uncertainty of the diesel engine and automotive market. Brexit may have something to do with it too."[485]

Eurocell plc is a manufacturer, distributor and recycler of window, door and roofline PVC products. Its h2 2019 report stated that it had invested in stock building to guard against interruptions in the supply of raw materials. It added approx. £3 million to finished goods for key product lines.[486]

Vision Gelpack, a polyethylene products manufacturer, entered administration in March 2019. Around 50 jobs were lost. A company spokesperson said: "The decision to put the company in administration mirrors harsh realities to do with future prospects that have been affected by the uncertainty surrounding the Brexit process."[487]

The Philips Avent factory in Suffolk is to close, with the loss of around 500 jobs. The closure, scheduled for 2020, is said to be partially Brexit related. Operations are moving to the Netherlands and Indonesia.[488]

Dmack, a tyre manufacturer, announced that a plan to build a £200 million factory in Carlisle had been derailed by Brexit. The firm's founder said: "We were in partnership with Super Deal tyres but the Brexit deal ruined that. They are a US company. Once Brexit was announced, they pulled away from the deal." The company set up production in Italy instead.[489] Dmack's UK operation filed for bankruptcy protection in August 2019.[490]

Waterloo Air Products made a number of changes to its business model to guard against Brexit disruption. It built up stock levels, brought some manufacturing processes in house, and changed the source of some materials from the EU to the UK.[491]

Aztec Oils bought a manufacturer in the Netherlands, and plans to produce its lubricants there as a contingency against Brexit interrupting the supply of its products. It also increased its stockpile of raw materials in the UK. Mark Lord, the firm's managing director, noted: "We are as prepared as we can be for a very uncertain future."[492]

GWP Group opened a third warehouse, increasing its overall storage capacity by 20%. The firm intends to use it for distribution in the South West, and as a contingency plan against Brexit. Ruth Cook, the managing director, said: "One of the steps we are taking is to increase our buffer stock of raw material and finished product, and the additional space provided by the new warehouse will be a great help with managing this."[493]

Pressmark Pressings Ltd, a company making auto parts, borrowed £200,000 so that it could double its reserves of steel to 15 days in advance of Brexit.[494]

Rovop, an underwater robotics firm, opened a new centre in Rotterdam in May 2019. There were no UK job losses. Director Steven Gray said: "as a result of the restrictions which will be put in place, whether we have May's Brexit or a hard Brexit [...] any future recruitment will be there and not in Aberdeen."[495]

Ingredients manufacturer, Ulrick & Short, is building a new plant in the Netherlands to diversify its supply chain and guard against Brexit disruption. The firm is also stockpiling its main products in the UK. It noted: "The lack of clarity is probably the worst thing for manufacturers as it means they have to prepare for all eventualities, and can't prepare for a specific outcome."[496]

Alloy Wire International, a specialist wire provider, took on extra warehouse space. It built up over $5 million worth of additional inventory. The firm said it was "the biggest investment we've ever made in stock".[497]

In April 2019, Calsonic Kansei, a Japanese car parts manufacturer, said it would cut 95 of the 400 staff at its Llanelli plant. The company said the job losses were due to "pressures of market instability caused by the political and economic conditions."[498]

Brompton Bicycle's CEO did not mince his words when he explained the firm's "shit hits the fan planning" decision to spend £50,000 on hiring warehouse space.[499] It intended to stockpile £1 million worth of parts to guard against hard Brexit disruption.

Spirax Salco Engineering plc said in its 2018 annual report that it had adopted several Brexit contingency measures. It is building up a month's buffer stock of raw materials and components in the UK and two weeks of finished goods outside the UK. It anticipated these mitigations to cost approx. £800,000.[500]

Renishaw plc saw revenues decline 7% in FY2019, and adjusted profit before tax fall by 28% to just £103.9 million. Chief executive Will Lee noted that this was "against a backdrop of challenging economic conditions including the impact of trade tensions between the USA and China, and ongoing uncertainty surrounding the potential impacts of Brexit."[501]

Volex plc has been exploring options for an alternate dock in mainland Europe to take delivery of the half of its products it sells to EU customers. This would affect approx. US$7 million worth of sales.[502]

CNH Industrial said in February 2019 that it had stockpiled tractors in Britain in case of a no-deal Brexit, leading to a 27% jump in inventory. The firm estimated the extra inventories cost it £390m. A company spokesperson commented: "We are kind of putting together countermeasures to protect our businesses in case of a no-deal situation."[503] However, by May 2019, the company appeared no longer convinced of the danger, as it indicated that it was selling off the inventory it had previously built up.[504]

The London-based Shadow Robot Company is outsourcing the bulk of its production to Madrid after opening a new office there in response to Brexit.[505] The firm had previously participated in a number of EU-funded projects.[506]

Savoir Beds has doubled its normal stockpile of horsehair (used for manufacturing its mattresses) to £500,000 worth of material. The firm's managing director said it had "rammed our warehouse absolutely full".[507]

Electrocomponents plc said in its 2019 annual report that the firm had invested £26 million in inventory across its European network to "lessen any customer service impact from any potential delays at the UK / EU border". It has also put in place IT systems to automate the customs declarations that will be required post-Brexit. The firm stated that where it was not possible to mitigate the effect of tariffs: "we will look to pass on tariffs and duties in the form of price increases."[508]

Hexstone, a company supplying fixings and fastenings, said it was spending over £3 million on stockpiling additional products in its warehouse, and is also becoming an HMRC Authorised Economic Operator so that it gains access to fast-track clearance at the ports.[509]

Eurocams, an auto parts company, moved most of its distribution operations to the Netherlands. 95% of the firm's revenues comes from Europe. Its owner said: "[This] will mean closing down a majority of what I've got here and going to Holland – not something I wanted to do but it is out of my hands."[510]

Diploma, a FTSE250 firm that supplies components for Formula 1, is stockpiling some of its "faster-moving product lines" in the UK ahead of Brexit.[511]

Law Firms

DLA Piper opened a new office in Dublin. The firm had been evaluating the location for some time, but Brexit clinched things. Senior partner Andrew Darwin said: "Brexit had been the catalyst to take another look and was the additional dimension which tipped the balance of the Dublin business case."[512]

Law firms are seeing a Brexit-driven boom as companies turn to them to help navigate the uncertainty. In 2018, revenues at the top 100 firms came to £24 billion – significantly ahead of their situation just prior to the financial crisis.[513] Salaries at the largest London firms hit a new record high in the 12 months ending April 2019.[514] Regulatory lawyers say that their largest clients are spending upwards of US$10 million each on mitigation actions, with the trend expected to increase.[515]

Law firm, DWF, received a substantial earnings boost from strong demand for Brexit-related litigation. The company's chief executive said: "The current uncertainty we face as a consequence of Brexit means we are seeing a higher incidence of litigation and as over 65 per cent of what we do supports litigation we have seen a significant uptick."[516]

Before 2016, fewer than 50 solicitors from England and Wales were also registered in the Republic of Ireland. Since the referendum, over 2,000 have registered there (11% of named solicitors).[517]

City lawfirm, Lewis Silkin, opened a new office in Dublin in April 2018, citing Brexit as one of the factors prompting it to set up in Ireland.[518]

Education Sector

In February 2019, the University of Surrey offered voluntary redundancy to all its staff in a bid to save £5 million. A letter to employees gave a range of reasons for the decision, including "reduced income due to Brexit".[519]

In August 2017, University College London said up to 95% of its senior researchers from the EU had been contacted with job offers by European institutions.[520]

Within weeks of the referendum, more than 100 prospective EU students withdrew their applications to study at Aberystwyth University. Half pulled out the day after the result was announced.[521] In May 2017, the university announced it would have to make millions of pounds in savings. It said: "Universities also face uncertainties caused by Britain's decision to leave the European Union, as well as tighter visa regulations for international students."[522]

The University for the Creative Arts began implementing a £3.5 million cost-cutting programme in June 2019. Around a hundred positions are at risk. The UCA said in a statement: "The UK higher education sector is facing unprecedented uncertainty, with the outcomes of Brexit and the Augur review likely to impact significantly on how we operate in the future."[523]

The University of South Wales announced in March 2017 that it planned to cut up to 139 jobs. A spokesperson said: "Although we've broadly maintained our UK student numbers, we're in a market where the overall number of people going to university is reducing, and recruitment from overseas will be affected by Brexit."[524]

In October 2018, Imperial College London signed a partnership with the Technical University of Munich. The plan will create academic posts shared by both universities. This would allow UK staff to stay eligible for EU research funding via their Munich connection.[525]

The number of EU students enrolling on courses at Russell Group universities fell 3% in 2018/19. Postgraduate studies were most affected, with declines of 5% for taught students and 9% for research students. This marked a reversal of the strong growth (4-7% per annum) they saw in the years leading up to the referendum. Senior Policy Analyst Dr Hollie Chandler said: "It's fair to assume that uncertainty over Brexit and the UK's future relationship with Europe could be a significant factor."[526]

A survey by the British Council, covering over 1,600 teachers at primary and secondary schools in England, found that the number of students taking language GCSEs has declined by 19% since 2014. According to the British Council: "Two in five teachers say that the implications of Brexit pose a major challenge to providing high-quality language teaching."[527]

Property & Construction

Dawnus, a Welsh construction group, fell into administration in March 2019. It employed around 700 staff. Various factors were blamed, including Brexit. The administrator commented: "Whilst the financial difficulties of the group were not a consequence of Brexit, there is no doubt that Brexit uncertainty impacted the ability to rescue the business."[528]

Property and construction consultant, Gleeds, was forced to cut some staff due to Brexit, mainly at its London office. A spokesperson said: "In line with most of UK industry, the uncertainty over Brexit has affected our strategic thinking, hence we have taken limited action to review departmental resourcing in light of the economic climate."[529]

Lambert Smith Hampton (part of Countrywide plc) saw its transactional revenue in the first six months of 2019 decline 20% compared to 2018. This translated into a £5 million decline in adjusted EBITDA. Countrywide plc's 2019 interim report noted: "With the UK economy experiencing heightened political uncertainty and Brexit postponed until 31 October 2019, the UK investment market has seen a sharp slowing down in the first half of the year."[530]

Nested, a "data-driven" estate agency in London, is laying off 15 staff (20% of its workforce). Its co-founder said: "We have come off a record year and quarter but with continued uncertainty around Brexit market volumes have fallen significantly."[531]

Brexit was blamed as one of the factors behind the axing of the M4 relief road project. Welsh Government director Andrew Slade said: "Brexit has been a huge rock thrown into the pond in the context of what we have been doing in Government generally." The failed project will have cost £61m to £144m, depending on what can be recouped from property sales.[532]

In its 2019 half-year report, a property firm, Savills, stated that income from its UK commercial dealings had fallen 7%. It said: "UK Commercial Transaction fee income decreased 7% to £31.4m (h2 2018: £33.9m), reflecting continued Brexit-related uncertainty." It reported that the UK residential market was also very weak: "UK Residential Transaction market conditions remained challenging with trading volumes at the lowest level since the Global Financial Crisis."[533]

Rogers Stirk Harbour & Partners, an architectural firm, laid off 15 staff, approx. 10% of its workforce, in October 2018. Practice owner Richard Rogers said: "Brexit doesn't help, that's for sure. We have quite a lot of international work but Brexit is bad news in my opinion."[534]

Albion Stone, a supplier of Portland stone, established a 3-month stockpile of machine parts from Sweden and Italy in advance of the 29 March 2019 Brexit date. The firm spent £1.5 million on its overall Brexit preparations, at least £160,000 of which went on stockpiling.[535] However, the company indicated in an interview in August 2019 that it was reluctant to repeat the exercise in advance of the revised Brexit deadline: "I don't think it's worth me wasting another 200,000 pounds, buying in stock, on the very slim possibility there could be a no-deal Brexit."[536]

Make Architects saw its 2017 results impacted by Brexit: "However, revenue decreased by 12 per cent from 2016 due to the fallout from the EU referendum."[537] In 2018, the firm made around 10 staff redundant.

It blamed general uncertainty around Brexit which had led clients to put planned schemes on hold.[538]

In August 2019, new orders in the construction industry fell at the fastest rate since March 2009. Commercial building, house building and civil engineering projects all declined. Customer concerns were "overwhelmingly attributed to domestic political uncertainty".[539]

Travel Sector

Thomas Cook implemented a redundancy programme in April 2019, aimed at cutting cut up to 100 roles in its Peterborough office.[540] The firm announced losses of £1,456 million in May 2019. Chief executive, Peter Fankhauser, cited a number of reasons for the firm's poor performance. He said: "[there] is now little doubt that the Brexit process has led many UK customers to delay their holiday plans for this summer."[541] The firm went bankrupt in September 2019, at a cost of over 9,000 jobs. Over 150,000 British holidaymakers ended up stranded overseas, leading the UK Government to mount the largest peacetime programme of repatriation in history.[542] Hays Travel, an independent travel firm, bought all 555 of Thomas Cook's stores in October 2019, saving around 2,500 jobs.[543]

Saga warned that Brexit was having an impact on its business when it reported its trading figures in April 2019. Lance Batchelor, the group's CEO, said: "Brexit is putting a clear dampener on customers' willingness to commit to holidays in 2019."[544] The firm's lowered profit forecast sent its shares falling nearly 40% following the announcement.[545]

The Holiday Place plc went into administration in May 2019. The firm employed 44 staff, and had an annual turnover of over £30 million. In the statement from the administrator, company representatives covered in extensive detail the trading difficulties it had faced because of Brexit uncertainty. The impact was particularly severe because the firm offered holidays at the high end of the market.[546]

Miscellaneous

UK entities that own .eu domain names will no longer be eligible to renew them post-Brexit. An estimated 300,000 domain registrations will lapse as a result (it's unclear how many belong to live sites). UK registrants will not be permitted to register new .eu domain names in future either.[547] However, special dispensation has been granted to EU citizens resident in the UK, who will be able to keep their domains.[548]

The Government spent £700,000 on the tables and chairs for an office in Leeds set up to deal with Brexit. The office was to have been fully kitted out by the end of December 2018. A thousand staff were expected to be based there.[549]

In Kind Direct, a charity that distributes unwanted company goods, faced a £500,000-worth shortfall compared to its Q1 2019 forecast. It believes this decline in donated products relates to stockpiling ahead of the original Brexit deadline.[550]

Monocle magazine is moving production from Cornwall to Germany to avoid no deal Brexit disruption. Historically, it spent about £1.2 million a year on printing in the UK.[551]

Gay Star News, a specialist news platform, shuttered its operations in July 2019. The founders outlined the reasons for the closure in an open letter: "But the biggest change was the level of confidence brands and businesses in the UK have, due to the uncertainty over Brexit."[552]

Jamm is moving some printing and mailing work to Prague to reassure European customers. Production director Liz Shackleton said: "Our

European clients weren't confident we would still be able to handle their work after Brexit, so we had to act."[553]

Selladoor Worldwide, a West End theatre company, is opening an office in Madrid. Although it plans to focus more on Spanish language productions, the move was partly Brexit related. Executive director David Hutchinson said: "I would be lying if I didn't say that Brexit contingency plans haven't factored into strategic thoughts regarding a mainland Europe hub."[554]

Kent County Council bulldozed flower beds containing 17,000 rare orchids to install a drainage ditch as part of its Brexit preparations. The ditch was intended to protect against flooding if queues built up towards Dover. The council pledged to pay to replant the flowers.[555]

Some art dealers shipped high-value pieces of art out of the UK ahead of the March 2019 Brexit deadline out of concern for the potential for duty being levied on them.[556] (Art can currently be shipped seamlessly around the EU duty-free.) Others sent pieces to European shows early, to guard against them being tied up in congestion at the ports.[557]

In June 2019, banknote maker De La Rue decided to shut a print line in Gateshead, affecting up to 171 jobs. The news came a year after it lost a £450 million deal to print the new blue British passports. (It was beaten to the government contract by a French-Dutch conglomerate.)[558] The firm had originally had to write off £3.7 million in costs after failing to obtain the work.[559]

The MoD had to forego more than £150 million in potential savings when the pound crashed after the referendum. The rapid forex movement forced it to change the budget allocated to purchasing 9 Poseidon P8-A maritime and patrol aircraft.[560]

Many performers attending the 2019 Edinburgh International Festival demanded payment in US dollars or euro. Event director Fergus Linehan said that otherwise: "We'd definitely have people say they just weren't coming." He noted that the firm had hedged around £1 million as the pound weakened.[561]

St Mary's Priory Church in Abergavenny held a special day of prayer for people worried about Brexit. The event was timed to coincide with the UK's original departure date of 29 March 2019. One attendee said: "Hopefully all will be well, but you can only pray for this. And prayer is what we need."[562]

The UK Government announced in October 2018 that it would be producing a special commemorative 50p coin to mark the UK's departure from the EU.[563] In an almost too perfect metaphor for the wider chaos of Brexit, the Treasury confirmed in mid-March 2019 that a handful of prototype coins had been produced with the wrong date on them.[564] (i.e. 29 March 2019, which of course ended up being an ordinary day). The plan twitched back to life in October 2019. Press reports indicated that up to 3 million 50p coins would enter circulation by the end of the month.[565] Each would bear the legend "Peace, prosperity and friendship with all nations". Critics were quick to point out that this appeared to be a list of things we would be surrendering after Brexit.

Blake Envelope invested £2.7 million in a new production site at Yeovil, with a view to protecting itself from Brexit border delays. The plant is expected to be complete in summer 2019. The firm's chief executive said: "The whole basis of this [new] investment was around our concern for Brexit. We are not a company that puts our heads under the cover, we try to plan for every eventuality."[566]

Babcock (the UK's second largest defence contractor) took a one-off charge of £10 million relating to setting up separate subsidiaries across the

EU. It will also incur ongoing Brexit-related costs of £10 million/year from 2020.[567]

Official figures showed that the number of corporate bankruptcies in April-June 2019 was the highest since 2014. While personal insolvencies as a whole fell, the number of full-blown personal bankruptcies over the same period also hit heights not seen since 2014.[568]

Broadcasters have begun to move their licenses to the EU27, since channels licensed in the UK will no longer have the right to broadcast across the EU after Brexit. Viacom and Viceland have secured licenses in the Netherlands.[569] By March 2019, over 130 TV channels had applied for licenses outside the UK.[570]

Go Inspire Group is restructuring its Solutions site in Kettering, and will no longer offer polywrapping there. The firm's chief executive said: "The final nail has been the Brexit uncertainty over the last three months, which really has affected that site. At the end of the day sometimes you have to take costs out." Up to 77 jobs are at risk.[571]

On 21 March 2019, the Parliament petitions website collapsed under the weight of people trying to sign the "Revoke Article 50 and remain in the EU petition."[572] More server capacity was brought online, and the petition passed 6 million signatures in fairly short order.[573] As of August 2019, it is still by far the most popular petition of all time.[574]

In 2017, the UK lost the opportunity to advance the bids for one of its cities to be designated as "European Capital of Culture" in 2023. We had originally been due to be allocated one that year according to a European Parliament decision of 2014.[575] The EU pointed out that the title was only open to cities that were within the EU, which we are of course no longer expected to be by then. This decision nullified formal bids by a number of cities, including Dundee, Nottingham and Milton

Keynes.[576] In the end, Veszprém in Hungary was designated as the sole winner.[577]

In late 2018, hauliers had to turn down lucrative work transporting equipment for bands planning to tour Europe in 2019 due to Brexit uncertainty. Some foregone contracts were worth six figures each.[578]

Figures released by the Department of Trade in June 2019 showed that foreign direct investment fell in the UK in 2018-2019. The number of new projects fell 14%, and the number of new jobs created fell by 24%. The UK remains the top destination in Europe for FDI, but the gap is narrowing.[579]

The Electoral Commission reported that the 2016 referendum cost £129.1 million to stage. This included £94.5 million spent on administration. Statutory grants worth £1.2 million were made to the official Remain and Leave campaigns.[580]

Marrone Bio Innovations changed its trademark plans for its biopesticide Regalia. The firm stated in its 2017 annual report: "We recently withdrew the EU application due to Brexit and plan to resubmit using the Netherlands rather than the UK as the designated rapporteur."[581]

Founded in 1985, the European Union Baroque Orchestra is a training initiative that allows young performers from all over the EU to gain orchestral experience.[582] It auditions around 100 young musicians a year. The EUBO used to be based at Wootton in Oxfordshire. It moved to Antwerp in Belgium in 2017 because of Brexit-related immigration concerns.[583]

Appendix B: Brexit and the automotive industry

The UK automotive sector is a massive industry, employing 186,000 people directly and over 856,000 in associated roles. It generates over £82 billion a year in turnover.[584] Because of its heavy reliance on just-in-time production, it is likely to be severely impacted by any Brexit that leads to queues at the ports. Nissan for instance maintains just half a day's worth of parts in inventory, and aims to keep its plants running 97% of the time.[585] Tolerances this tight turn delay into catastrophe.

The industry faces an unprecedented combination of challenges. Some, such as the fallout from the diesel scandal, the slowdown in China, and the rise of electric vehicles, are regional or global. Self-driving cars seem poised to go from science fiction to a regular presence on our streets. This avalanche of market changes threatens to overwhelm manufacturers. Pressure to adapt, reform and innovate is intense. The risks are huge, as are the rewards.

But other challenges are home-grown, a direct consequence of our relentless pursuit of Brexit. Brexit will impose a raft of new hurdles on UK firms, from tariffs to issues around rules of origin.

Right now, cars made in the UK can be sold anywhere in the EU tariff-free, thanks to our EU membership. But if we leave on WTO terms, the cars we export to the EU will incur 10% tariffs. At a stroke, UK-made cars become more expensive for EU consumers.

As if that wasn't bad enough, the EU signed a huge trade deal with Japan in February 2019. The deal includes a stepped reduction in the tariffs imposed by the EU on cars manufactured in Japan to 0% by 2027. So Japan-made cars will become even cheaper.

That's the big post-Brexit challenge for UK car manufacturers.

The example of Nissan

When delivering bad news about jobs or production, car manufacturers seem reluctant to lay the blame on Brexit. Not surprising. Why antagonise a huge swathe of their potential UK client base if they don't have to? But when you join all the dots, it's clear that Brexit plays a role in their business decisions. Here is an in-depth detailed look at Nissan, the UK's largest auto maker. As you will see, a Brexit thread runs through the firm's announcements, only to peter out towards the end.

- February 2013: Michael Fallon acknowledges the importance of the single market to companies like Nissan: "I visited recently and have spoken to the senior management at Nissan about the Prime Minister's speech to reassure them that we see a future for this country within a protected and enhanced single market. That is what is important for Nissan and many other companies in the sector."[586]

- October 2013: Toshiyuki Shiga, Nissan's chief operating officer, warns of the threat of import tariffs to Nissan's business if the UK were to leave the EU: "The UK is part of the European Union, [that] is very important. From the foreign investor point of view I hope that the UK will remain as an EU member."[587]

- November 2013: Speaking at the launch of the new Nissan Qashqai, the company's chief executive Carlos Ghosn tells the BBC (in the context of a possible referendum on leaving the EU): "If anything has to change, we need to reconsider our strategy and our investments for the future."[588]

- September 2015: John Redwood celebrates Nissan's commitment to UK manufacturing: "The whole House will welcome the great news that Nissan has a very big investment programme for the United Kingdom's biggest car plant, which will carry it through the next five years and beyond with a new model."[589]

- February 2016: Nissan issues a statement indicating the company would prefer to stay in the EU: "Our preference as a business is, of course, that the UK stays within Europe – it makes the most sense for jobs, trade and costs. For us, a position of stability is more positive than a collection of unknowns."[590]
- September 2016: Nissan's CEO warns that some car production could move out of the UK unless the company is protected from likely tariffs after Brexit: "If there are tax barriers being established on cars, you have to have a commitment for carmakers who export to Europe that there is some kind of compensation."[591]
- October 2016: The UK Government provides Nissan with a confidential letter of reassurance. Greg Clark: "[We told Nissan] our objective would be to ensure we have continued access to the markets in Europe and vice versa without tariffs and bureaucratic impediments, and that is how we will approach those negotiations."[592] The Government refuses to publish the letter even as late as December 2018. When it is finally made public, it reveals the promise of an investment of up to £80 million into skills, R&D and innovation.[593]
- October 2016: Nissan makes a fresh commitment to UK manufacturing. Carlos Ghosn: "The support and assurances of the UK government enabled us to decide that the next-generation Qashqai and X-Trail will be produced at Sunderland."[594]
- February 2017: Colin Lawther, Nissan's Senior VP of Manufacturing, gives evidence to the International Trade Committee. He warns that trading on WTO terms would result in a 10% tariff on the 240,000 Nissan vehicles manufactured in the UK and exported to the EU, costing Nissan over £500 million a year. He also notes that the firm would need 100 people just doing customs processing.[595]

- June 2018: Carlos Ghosn warns that Brexit uncertainty is hindering long-term planning. "We don't want to take any decisions in the dark. We don't want to take any decisions we might regret in future."[596]

- October 2018: Nissan postpones wage negotiations with British factory workers until the situation surrounding Brexit is clearer.[597]

- October 2018: Nissan issues a strong warning about the effects of a no deal Brexit on car production in the UK: "As a sudden change from those rules to the rules of the WTO will have serious implications for British industry, we urge UK and EU negotiators to work collaboratively towards an orderly balanced Brexit that will continue to encourage mutually beneficial trade."[598]

- October 2018: Speaking to Paris Motorshow attendees, the CEO of Mercedez-Benz revealed that the firm had been investigating building cars in the UK in partnership with Nissan. He went on to say explicitly that Brexit had put paid to the idea.[599]

- February 2019: A new trade deal between the EU and Japan will see tariffs on cars imported from Japan drop to 0% by 2027. (The UK will participate in this trade deal for as long as it remains an EU member.)[600]

- February 2019: Nissan announces that the next generation X-Trail will be made in Japan, rather than in Sunderland as previously planned. The firm's Europe chairman Gianluca de Ficchy writes to staff: "Today's announcement will be interpreted by a lot of people as a decision related to Brexit. We have taken this decision for the business reasons I've explained, but clearly the uncertainty around the UK's future relationship with the EU is not helping companies like ours to plan for the future."[601]

- March 2019: Nissan indicates it intends to stop producing two Infiniti models in the UK, affecting around 200 jobs. They will instead be manufactured in Japan.[602]
- October 2019: Nissan begins production of the second generation Nissan Juke in Sunderland after investing £100 million in the plant.[603]
- October 2019: The chairman of Nissan Europe warns that "the entire business model for Nissan Europe will be in jeopardy" if the firm faces 10% export duties under a no deal Brexit scenario that left the UK trading on WTO terms.[604]

Appendix C: Brexit – The Theresa May Years

The second series of Brexit began with Boris Johnson in Theresa May's old role. He set about "killing" off familiar characters in a political purge more vicious than the Red Wedding scene in Game of Thrones. Never had so many ministers been fired in so short a time. As we struggle to get to grips with unfamiliar faces, it feels like the perfect opportunity to remind ourselves of what transpired in Season 1.

As the first season opened, an unsuspecting country was waking up on 24 June 2016 to the news that we had voted for Brexit. David Dimbleby delivered the pre-dawn verdict: "Well at twenty minutes to five, we can now say the decision taken in 1975 by this country to join the Common Market has been reversed by this referendum to leave the EU."[605]

A few hours later, Nigel Farage guested on Good Morning Britain. He took the opportunity to disassociate himself from the infamous message on the side of the bus: "No I can't [guarantee that the money will go to the NHS], and I would never have made that claim. I think it's one of the mistakes the people at the Vote Leave campaign made."[606]

Before the day was out, David Cameron, having previously pledged to lead the country no matter the referendum result, announced his resignation outside Number 10: "I was absolutely clear about my belief that Britain is stronger, safer and better off inside the European Union." He concluded his remarks by humming a little tune as the famous black door closed behind him.[607] (He would later invest in a £25,000 shepherd's hut in which to write his memoirs.[608])

Cameron's decision to step down triggered a scramble for the Tory leadership and the prize of steering the country towards Brexit. Five candidates stepped into the ring: Michael Gove, Stephen Crabb, Liam Fox, Andrea Leadsom and Theresa May. (Michael Gove had tripped Boris Johnson on the way in by refusing to back the latter's candidacy at the last minute.) A series of ballots too dull to go into whittled the running down to two: Andrea Leadsom and Theresa May.[609]

After some ill-advised remarks about motherhood, Andrea Leadsom decided to pull out of the contest. Theresa May was the winner. Philip (May, not Hammond) appeared thrilled. Thus began the days of the Maybot.[610]

(Flashbacks showing May's old role as Home Secretary would pepper the rest of the series. From coining the phrase "hostile environment" to championing the Snooper's Charter. From slashing 20,000 officers from police numbers to rejecting compulsory refugee quotas. From introducing new restrictions on non-EEA family migrants to an ad campaign featuring mobile "Go Home" hoardings.[611] Britain under Theresa May's iron fist had never be more welcoming.)

One of Theresa May's first speeches focused on "the precious, precious bond between England, Scotland, Wales and Northern Ireland."[612] Soon after, she popped up to see Nicola Sturgeon and further stressed her intent to hold the Union together. Seemingly unaware of the irony, she would spend the next three years trying to achieve the exact opposite.

In July 2016, on her first overseas trip as Prime Minister, Theresa May met with Angela Merkel. She told the German Chancellor that she would not trigger Article 50 immediately, saying it would take time to negotiate a "sensible and orderly departure."[613] She would later state that the UK would not activate Article 50 in 2016. (It's not unreasonable to expect that decision to have left ample time for intense, detailed planning.)

Brexit leapt back into sharp focus in December 2016 after Parliament voted to allow Theresa May to trigger Article 50 before the end of March 2017. With this momentous decision, the season of goodwill would feel decidedly less friendly. The final bill to support the invocation of Article 50 would pass on 16 March 2017.

On 17 January 2017, Theresa May laid out her negotiating objectives for leaving the EU.[614] In her speech, she addressed EU citizens, telling them: "You will still be welcome in this country as we hope our citizens will be welcome in yours." She also claimed falsely that both sides in the referendum had made it clear that a vote to leave meant a vote to leave the Single Market. So she intended to take the UK out of it, as well as out of the Customs Union, and put an end to freedom of movement. This was anyone's first real inkling that she intended to pursue a hard Brexit. No nice cosy relationship close to the EU for us, like the one enjoyed by Norway, keeping businesses happy and our economy on an even keel. No, the UK would instead cast itself into the outermost void, cutting itself away from the EU Single Market and Customs Union so that it could keep foreigners out. Because that was apparently what absolutely everybody had voted for, even though most people hadn't.[615] [616]

On 24 January 2017, the UK Supreme Court ruled that the Government wasn't allowed to trigger Article 50 without Parliament passing legislation to do so. This was the culmination of a case that had begun a few days after the referendum. The Government had fought tooth and nail to keep Parliament out of the loop, but the Supreme Court's decision shut their argument down.[617]

A brief moment of levity was afforded viewers later in the month. Theresa May had the dubious privilege of being the first foreign leader to grace newly elected US President Donald Trump's presence. A nation smirked as she held his hand to help him navigate some pesky steps.[618]

ElecLink, a £490 million project capable of powering 2 million British homes, kicked off in February 2017. The new interconnect would run through the Channel Tunnel, enabling the UK to tap into France's electricity supply.[619] (As of August 2019, ElecLink was still trying to figure out the rules that would apply in the event of a no-deal Brexit.[620])

On 29 March 2017, Theresa May notified the EU of the UK's decision to begin the Article 50 process. In response, the EU issued a statement: "In these negotiations the [European] Union will act as one and preserve its interests. Our first priority will be to minimise the uncertainty caused by the decision of the United Kingdom for our citizens, businesses and Member States."[621] With that, a glowing timer in the corner of the screen began counting down the 2 years to Brexit Day. Tick, tock, tick, tock. A clear reminder not to waste the time we'd been given.

Three weeks later, Theresa May called the snap General Election she had frequently denied she wanted to hold.

For the next couple of months, campaigning sidelined UK progress on Brexit. The Conservative manifesto promised "Strong and Stable leadership", and positioned the party squarely behind Theresa May's Brexit vision.[622] Labour's manifesto committed it to accepting the referendum result, and stated the party wanted to negotiate its own version of Brexit, one which would magically retain the benefits of the Single Market and the Customs Union while being outside of both.[623]

(Some Brexiters would later claim the Brexit references in the two manifestos "proved" the vast majority of people in the UK wanted to leave the EU. They must have, their reasoning went, because most votes went to the Tories and Labour.)

Throughout the Brexit process, the UK would shroud its plans and related material in secrecy. The EU by contrast took a refreshing "cards on table" stance early on. In May 2017, it released its transparency principles. These committed it to share as much material with the public as possible.[624]

While British politicians were busy kissing babies and making promises they had no intention of keeping, the EU forged ahead, publishing nine position papers setting out its negotiating position on key aspects of Brexit.[625]

Theresa May had misjudged the mood of the country to perfection. She was rewarded on polling day (8 June) with a loss of 13 seats.[626]

With no overall majority, the Tories turned to the DUP to keep them in power. By good fortune, the latter were happy to sell their support for a mere £1 billion, or a trifling £100 million per MP. Theresa May practically bit their hand off sealing the deal.[627]

Brexit talks kicked off in Brussels on 19 June 2017. David Davis concluded this first meeting by announcing that the overall timetable for the negotiations had been agreed. (He had previously promised that it would be the "row of the summer"[628] but gave in to the EU before the day was out.[629])

On 29 June 2017, Theresa May outlined the Government's proposals for the over three million EU citizens who'd made their homes in the UK.[630] Post-Brexit, they would no longer be allowed to stay by default. Instead, they would have to secure "settled status" to keep living here. She claimed this would help put their "anxiety to rest", an odd remark given the that they faced the uncertain prospect of having to apply to retain something they previously enjoyed by right as EU citizens. Many interpreted the new policy as a resurgence of the hostile immigration environment.[631]

Although MPs were off on their summer recess, Brexit negotiations continued. The teams met twice face to face in Brussels.

The Department for International Trade celebrated the EU's new CETA trade agreement with Canada on 21 September 2017. Liam Fox said: "CETA opens the door for UK companies to trade easily and cheaply with a valuable market in which there is considerable demand for British products, skills and expertise."[632] Left unspoken was the fact that the agreement would only apply to us for as long as we remained EU members. (A year later, Liam Fox highlighted the 13.7% increase in UK exports to Canada, which he attributed to CETA.[633])

The next day, Theresa May made a major speech in Florence. In it, she focused on the importance of preserving the Good Friday Agreement, and the Common Travel Area between Ireland and Northern Ireland. She also said that the UK wanted an implementation or transition period after Brexit Day. This would allow time to conclude a new relationship with the EU. During transition, the UK and EU would retain access to each other's markets so that trade could continue uninterrupted.

More rounds of negotiation followed. In October 2017, a summit of EU leaders concluded that the UK had not achieved enough to move on to the next stage of talks. Three matters still needed resolving: the money the UK owed the EU, citizens' rights, and the Irish border. Only with those out of the way could the discussion progress to the subject of the UK's future relationship. The UK's next chance to make its case would be in December.[634]

In November 2017, the EU voted to relocate two key regulatory agencies: the European Medicines Agency and the European Banking Authority. (Both were forced to move because the UK would no longer be an EU member after Brexit.) This was the final step of a long bidding process, which saw dozens of cities compete for the right to host them. Amsterdam won the EMA, while the EBA would transfer to Paris.[635] Over 1,000 jobs would go, and tens of thousands of conference attendees would no longer head to London each year.[636]

The UK made a better fist of things at the second time of asking. In mid-December 2017, the EU agreed to discuss our post-Brexit relationship. Talks on finalising the withdrawal agreement would continue in parallel. But it would not be easy. As Donald Tusk put it: "We all know that breaking up is hard. But breaking up and building a new relation is much harder."[637]

Later in December, David Davis cleared up a mystery that had haunted Brexit for a year by admitting that the Brexit impact assessments didn't exist. At least not in the form he'd described them.[638] (He had first mentioned them in December 2016, and had gone on to talk about them in grandiose terms on a number of occasions. In June 2017, he said: "We've got 50, nearly 60, sectoral analyses already done."[639] Challenged to produce them, he claimed they needed to stay secret for competitive reasons.) The Brexit Committee finally released what little material they had been given just before Christmas.[640]

Brexit negotiations continued during the spring of 2018 to iron out the draft withdrawal agreement, first published on 28 February.[641] Efforts focused on the transition period, and the Irish border. In mid-March, the two sides reached a partial agreement on what the document should say[642]. By April, the post-Brexit trading relationship was also under discussion.

Lots of talk, not much action. Fast forward a few months.

On 6 July 2018, Theresa May held a Cabinet away day at Chequers. Her intention was to get ministers to sign off on her proposed future relationship between the UK and the EU.[643] The assembled press spent a hot summer afternoon reporting from a field. Camera operators grabbed zoom-lens glimpses of ministers as they popped out for fresh air on a terrace. The meeting went on, and on, and on… It was to last almost 12 hours.[644] The fragile consensus it seemingly achieved barely survived longer than that. David Davis resigned over the agreement on 8 July, and his role was given to Dominic Raab. Boris Johnson quit the day after.

The other snag with the Chequers proposal was that it contained many elements the EU was never going to agree to. It was a Santa's wish-list of things it would be nice to have, rather than a realistic negotiating document. The EU broke the bad news to Theresa May at a Salzburg summit in September 2018. Donald Tusk told a press conference: "Everybody shared the view that while there are positive elements in the Chequers proposal, the suggested framework for economic co-operation will not work, not least because it is undermining the single market."[645] French President Emmanuel Macron left his diplomatic gloves at home: "Those who explain that we can easily live without Europe, that everything is going to be all right, and that it's going to bring a lot of money home are liars."[646]

Theresa May dug in her heels and fought back. She insisted her Chequers plan was the only one on the table, and continued to defend it into the Conservative conference season. But opponents of her plan within the Tory party used the EU's rejection to try to undermine her.

Disgruntled Brexiters began to talk openly of mounting a leadership challenge.[647] They lined up to vent their fury in the press. The challenge would go on and off the boil for months. Letters of no confidence went in to the 1922 Committee, and there was a certain frisson within political circles as pundits tried to guess each daily tally.

Mark Francois began his own letter with "She Just Doesn't Listen" in bold. Towards the end of the three page document, he said: "In summary, I believe that Chequers, to which the Prime Minister, (sic) is clearly unbreakably wedded, would not constitute Brexit in any shape or form whatsoever and would therefore betray the spirit of the referendum and the decision of 17.4 million British people."[648]

The high water mark of the ineffectual rebellion came in mid-November. Jacob Rees-Mogg gathered reporters outside Parliament to tell them his letter was with the 1922 Committee. No confidence speculation went into overdrive, then died down again as it became clear the rebels still didn't have the numbers.

The final draft of the Brexit withdrawal agreement was published on 14 November 2018. The next day, Dominic Raab resigned as Brexit Secretary, having only survived a few months in the role. Stepping down, he said that he "cannot in good conscience" support the deal that the Cabinet had agreed.[649] His brief tenure had been unremarkable, save for a speech the previous week in which he'd admitted: "We are, and I hadn't quite understood the full extent of this, but if you look at the UK and if you look at how we trade in goods, we are particularly reliant on the Dover-Calais crossing." Cue a million map jokes.[650] Dominic Raab's departure was followed by those of Esther McVey and Suella Braverman. His successor, Stephen Barclay, would focus on domestic preparations rather than Brexit negotiations.[651]

On 25 November 2018, EU member states approved the Brexit withdrawal agreement alongside the political declaration defining future EU-UK relations. Speaking after the special meeting of the European Council, Donald Tusk said: "Ahead of us is the difficult process of ratification as well as further negotiations. But regardless of how it will all end, one thing is certain: we will remain friends until the end of days, and one day longer."[652]

The EU endorsement paved the way for Theresa May to seek Parliament's approval for the deal. MPs had been due to vote on it on 11 December 2018, following a lengthy debate. However, she pulled the vote with a day's notice after realising she was bound to lose it. Instead it was punted into the new year.

On 12 December 2018, Tory rebels finally mustered their full strength. With the 1922 Committee sitting on enough letters to trigger a no confidence ballot, one was duly organised. Theresa May survived the evening vote, but over a third of all Tory MPs had come out against her. Not a great look, although under Conservative Party rules her survival immunised her against similar challenges for twelve months.[653]

Also on 12 December, the European Parliament agreed a new free trade agreement with Japan. The deal, years in the making, created the world's largest free trade area. Welcoming the announcement, Liam Fox's department said it would "help to boost trade between the UK and Japan and is estimated to increase UK GDP by up to £3 billion [a year] in the longer term."[654] (Of course, the UK will only benefit from the trade deal while we're still EU members.)

A few days later, Jeremy Corbyn decided to get in on the no confidence action. He threatened to declare no confidence in Theresa May as prime minister, rather than in the government in general. (Had he put the matter to a vote and won, this specific form of no confidence wording would have heaped further embarrassment on her. It would not, however, have qualified to bring the government down.[655]) He backed off after the Prime Minister recommitted to holding the Brexit vote in the week beginning 14 January.[656]

Transport Secretary Chris Grayling organised a traffic jam test on 7 January 2019. It called on 150 trucks to help simulate the consequences of post-Brexit delays at Dover. Despite the offer of £550 per driver to take part, only 89 turned up. The exercise was branded a failure and a waste of time, not least because the real thing would involve over 6,000 vehicles.[657]

(Grayling would survive this and countless other humiliations, including awarding a lucrative ferry contract to a company with no ships.[658] He was purged by Boris Johnson on the latter's first day in office.)

Having dodged the vote as long as she dared, Theresa May finally allowed Parliament its say on her withdrawal agreement on 15 January 2019. It was defeated by 432 votes to 202, the largest margin of defeat in parliamentary history for a UK government.[659] She had another try on 12 March, after receiving additional clarifications and reassurances from the EU. Although she managed to avoid setting a new futility record, she still lost by 391 votes to 242.[660] Following this second failure, Parliament voted by a majority of 211 for Theresa May to negotiate a delay to Brexit.[661]

A low point in the UK's Brexit preparations was marked by the announcement in February 2019 that it had secured a trade continuity agreement with the Faroe Islands. The deal preserved £200 million of fish and crustacean trade.[662] Critics pointed out that this represented less that 1/3000th of the UK's overall trade with the EU.

On 20 March 2019, Theresa May asked the EU for an extension of the Article 50 period until 30 June.[663] If granted, the extension would postpone the fateful Brexit Day by three months. Proposals and counter-proposals flew back and forth. On 22 March, the EU agreed to give the UK an extension until 22 May, on condition the withdrawal agreement was signed off before the original Brexit deadline of 29 March. Otherwise the extension would run only until 12 April.[664]

A petition to revoke article 50 and remain in the EU passed a million signatures on 21 March.[665] So many people were trying to sign it that the official Parliament petition website crashed several times. It passed 2 million by 11pm, despite further server crashes. New names were coming on board at a rate of over 1,500 a minute.[666] The next day, it reached 3.6 million signatures, as the sign-up rate peaked at 2,000 a minute.[667] By 24 March, it had passed 5 million signatures to become the most popular petition ever on the parliament website.[668] It hit 6 million signatures by the end of March.[669]

Saturday 23 March saw an estimated one million people (including yours truly) join the "Put it to the People" anti-Brexit march in London. The procession took several hours to cover the distance from Park Lane to Trafalgar Square because of the weight of numbers.[670] No arrests were reported.

On 29 March (ex Brexit Day) MPs voted against the withdrawal deal a third time. Theresa May lost by 344 votes to 286. Although the gap was narrowing each time, it was still a significant defeat. It came even despite the Prime Minister separating the withdrawal agreement from the political declaration, and asking Parliament to vote only on the former.[671] This meant the Article 50 extension would run until 12 April. The UK had only gained a few days breathing space.

As things came to a head inside the House of Commons, Brexit supporters protested in Parliament Square. Their numbers swelled as the day wore on, with tens of thousands blocking nearby streets.[672] They were joined by a hundred or so people from Nigel Farage's March to Leave procession, which had set out from Sunderland two weeks before.[673] The protest brought together Leave Means Leave supporters, English Defence League followers, far-right activists, Trump voters, even French backers of "Frexit".[674] The day passed largely peacefully, but five protesters were arrested in the evening after clashes with police.[675]

Theresa May requested a further Article 50 extension on 5 April. She explained in her letter to the EU that she had reached out to the Opposition to try and secure cross-party consensus. She requested a new deadline of 30 June 2019, i.e. the same one she'd asked for back in March. This, despite not having made the required progress on the withdrawal agreement.[676]

In response, the EU offered a further Article 50 extension until 31 October. (We would be able to leave before Halloween if we agreed the withdrawal agreement before then.) However, the UK would have to participate in the upcoming European elections, or face leaving on 22 May.[677]

Theresa May and Labour redoubled their efforts to try and find common ground, but their talks never progressed to anything concrete. On 7 May, she admitted that it would be impossible to ratify the withdrawal agreement in time to avoid participating in the European elections. This brought new calls for her to resign from Tory rebels.[678]

The Conservative party and Labour were decimated in the European elections on 23 May. The Tories only managed to win 4 seats, losing 14.8% of its vote share compared to the previous European elections. Labour secured 10 seats, but lost 11.3% of its vote share. The Brexit Party and Liberal Democrats were the biggest winners, taking 29 and 16 seats respectively to become the two largest parties in the UK group at the European Parliament. The Greens also advanced, leapfrogging the Tories with 7 MEPs.

Having dodged more political bullets than an action hero, our participation in the European election finally did for Theresa May's career as Prime Minister. The day after the vote, with the results not yet declared, she announced that she would resign as Conservative party leader on 7 June. She said she would stay in office until her successor could be determined.[679]

The new MEPs assembled at the European Parliament on 2 July. Those from the Brexit Party turned their backs during the playing of the EU's anthem, prompting widespread criticism.[680] Liberal Democrat MEPs mounted a protest of a different kind by turning up in matching yellow T-shirts bearing the slogan "Bollocks to Brexit".[681]

With Theresa May having decided to pass the baton, progress on Brexit stopped. Attention turned to who would become the next leader of the Tory Party and Prime Minister. Campaigning had already begun before Theresa May officially quit. Rory Stewart had been the first to tip his hand on 2 May. Others soon followed his lead, including Dominic Raab, Sajid Javid, Michael Gove and Matt Hancock.

The leadership campaign received widespread media coverage, even though only Tory party members could vote, and the general public had no say in who would become our next Prime Minister. (Approximately

159,400 Tory party members were eligible to vote, just 0.34% of the electorate.[682])

The early stages of the campaign descended into something of a drug-off. Michael Gove admitted to having taken cocaine 20 years previously.[683] Rory Stewart said he'd once smoked opium at a wedding in Iran.[684] Several other candidates came forward with their own confessions. By the end of the soul baring exercise, seven out of ten candidates had owned up to a past history of drug taking.[685] (For comparison, around a third of all adults in England and Wales have taken drugs at some point in their lives.[686])

Nominations for party leader closed on 10 June, with ten candidates having secured the backing of enough Tory MPs to progress. A series of internal party ballots whittled the field of candidates down between 13 and 20 June. (Note: Tory MPs were the only ones with any say in the process.) Matt Hancock had the distinction of being the only one of the ten candidates to withdraw proactively, rather than be eliminated in a vote. Rory Stewart caught the public's imagination with his unscripted walkabouts, but Tory MPs were less convinced, and he was eliminated on 19 June. Jeremy Hunt and Boris Johnson were spat out of the back end of this quick-fire process.[687]

With that, the leadership contest moved to its second, more frenetic stage. The two surviving candidates criss-crossed the UK over a three week period. Seven helicopters and a private plane helped ease their journeys.[688] Hunt and Johnson participated in 16 hustings in front of Tory members. They also took part in 4 TV and radio debates (only one was a head-to-head).

The ballot of Tory members closed on 22 July. Boris Johnson won with 92,153 votes, or 66.4% of all votes cast. In the end, less than a hundred thousand people crowned him Tory leader, and therefore Prime Minister.

Season 1 of Brexit ended with Theresa May passing power to her successor on 24 July 2019. The last shot featured Boris Johnson, grinning outside Number 10.

Appendix D: An in-depth look at Article 50

To leave the EU, the UK must follow the rules laid down by Article 50. Article 50 is a short section of the Treaty on European Union, one of the two essential treaties that all member states must sign up to before they can join. Think of them as the Terms and Conditions of EU club membership. (The TEU forms the basis of EU law, and sets out how its institutions are governed.[689] It's an updated version of the Maastricht Treaty. The other core treaty is the Treaty on the Functioning of the European Union, which used to be known as the Treaty of Rome.[690])

Depending on your political viewpoint, Article 50 may look like an escape hatch, or the trap door below a gallows. Either way, it sets out step by step what we have to do to leave. But it is also the root cause of most of the problems of Brexit. Understand Article 50, and you're at least half-way to understanding Brexit.

Aside: Article 50 isn't something the EU cooked up after hearing that we wanted to wave goodbye. It was introduced in 2009, 7 years before the referendum. The UK was fully involved in agreeing it, and a Brit (Lord Kerr) even drafted it.

Since Article 50 will have such a huge impact on the way Brexit plays out, and therefore on our collective futures, it is important to understand the detail.[691] It's short – only 5 brief clauses – but these hide a wealth of complexity. Indeed, Article 50's very briefness has led to a number of disputes over how it should be interpreted.

Let's examine each of the 5 clauses in turn...

1. Any Member State may decide to withdraw from the Union in accordance with its own constitutional requirements.

Clause 1 gives a country permission to exercise its sovereign right to leave the EU. We are not prisoners – the door's always open, should we wish to get out. The "*constitutional requirements*" part is there to guard against a rogue leader disregarding legal due process in their home state because they're so desperate to leave.

2. A Member State which decides to withdraw shall notify the European Council of its intention. In the light of the guidelines provided by the European Council, the Union shall negotiate and conclude an agreement with that State, setting out the arrangements for its withdrawal, taking account of the framework for its future relationship with the Union. That agreement shall be negotiated in accordance with Article 218(3) of the Treaty on the Functioning of the European Union. It shall be concluded on behalf of the Union by the Council, acting by a qualified majority, after obtaining the consent of the European Parliament.

There's a lot to unpick in Clause 2. The first part is easy: tell us if you want to leave. This is what Theresa May did on 29 March 2017, having first secured the permission of Parliament. MPs voted by a majority of 384 to let her get Brexit negotiations under way. Jeremy Corbyn had Labour voting on a 3-line whip to support it.[692] Her invocation of Article 50 started our departure clock ticking. (At this point, we should acknowledge the significance of the Miller Case, a constitutional case decided by the UK's supreme court in January 2017. It concluded that the Government had no right to initiate withdrawal from the EU without Parliament's consent. This crucial ruling paved the way for the round of votes on triggering Article 50.[693])

The next part requires the European Council to draw up guidelines for the negotiations. (As the withdrawing state, we were not allowed to sit in on those meetings, as per clause 4. A very practical restriction, since otherwise we'd have been helping to craft the rules for negotiating with ourselves.)

Now we come to a sticky bit. According to a smattering of Brexiters, "negotiate and conclude" creates a cast-iron obligation on the EU to reach an agreement with us. Most take the view that this interpretation is absurd because, if the EU were genuinely forced to come to terms with us, we could just keep saying "no" again and again and again until we got what we wanted, like a toddler screaming and rolling on the group until its parents give in. In other words, they'd have no choice but to keep putting proposals in front of us, in an infinite loop of mounting despair. In practice, a pragmatic, logical approach was adopted, with both sides trying to work in good faith to find common ground (despite the exchange of hot words on occasions, and constant sniping on the UK side from those not involved in the negotiations). In other words, this was taken to be a best-efforts requirement, which makes sense.

The "arrangements for its withdrawal" is what became known as the Withdrawal Agreement. This covered essential housekeeping matters connected to our departure, such as how much we owed the EU, what would happen to UK citizens in the EU and EU citizens in the UK after Brexit, and so on. It's the equivalent of making a plan to pack up and clean your home, and pay all outstanding bills, prior to moving house. The Withdrawal Agreement, had it been ratified, would have been legally binding on the UK, and the EU.

The "framework for its future relationship with the union" is the Political Declaration. This, together with the Withdrawal Agreement, is intended to define the shape of Brexit as agreed by both sides. The Withdrawal Agreement covers the past, the Political Declaration the future. The Political Declaration does not prescribe a specific type of future relationship. Instead, it's more like a restaurant menu, one listing all the different models we might adopt for our relationship with the EU after we've left. There's the Norway model, in which we stay very close to the EU, keep freedom of movement, and protect frictionless trade. And then there are a series of models of ever-increasing "hardness", each one providing more freedoms, but requiring ever greater sacrifices in return. ("No deal" doesn't figure on the menu. It's the equivalent of storming out of the restaurant because you don't like anything on offer – then going hungry.)

Unlike the Withdrawal Agreement, the Political Declaration doesn't bind us to anything specific. It leaves the tricky matter of agreeing our stance towards the EU until after Brexit day. That's why so many MPs have warned of the dangers of a "blindfold Brexit": we would be out of the EU, but without any real idea of what our relationship would be like afterwards. This was seen as dangerous because there's no rewind button on Article 50. Once we're out, we're out. Afterwards, if we fail to reach an agreement with the EU on our future relationship, there's no plan B. (At least not an easy one. Later, we will see that there is a bumpy route to rejoining.)

Before we leave this clause, it's important to note that the agreement (combined WA and PD package) is to be confirmed by qualified majority vote. In other words, the process can't be held hostage by a single EU member state digging its heels in. Not indefinitely, anyway. So long as a qualified majority are convinced on the EU side, the agreement can go ahead.

> *3. The Treaties shall cease to apply to the State in question from the date of entry into force of the withdrawal agreement or, failing that, two years after the notification referred to in paragraph 2, unless the European Council, in agreement with the Member State concerned, unanimously decides to extend this period.*

Clause 3 is the elephant in the Brexit room. Indeed, it's a herd of pachyderms large enough to fill a cathedral. This is it. The money shot. As the soundtrack swells, it's time to sit up and pay attention…

"*The Treaties shall cease to apply to the State in question*" – this innocuous little phrase is Brexit's Pandora's box. It means that every one of the EU's international treaties, trade agreements, and so on –

the legal gubbins that binds us to the rest of the world via the EU – will no longer apply to us, instantly, as soon as we're no longer a member. Hundreds of legal arrangements established over close to half a century, gone, as surely as if we'd fed each one into a shredder.

- Our participation in the single market and the customs union, which maintains the just-in-time environment manufacturers depend on: gone.
- Our ultimate free trade deal with the EU (no customs, tariffs, or non-tariff barriers): gone.
- Our 40+ trade deals with third party countries by virtue of being EU members: gone.
- Freedom of movement, whether it's the right of UK citizens to live and work in the EU, or for EU citizens to do so here: gone.
- Financial passporting, which enables firms in the UK to sell all over Europe: gone.

The list of what we will lose in that moment is almost endless. Our aircraft will no longer be certified to fly. UK driving licenses will no longer be valid on the Continent. The rules governing the Eurostar, coaches and ferries will change. It will become difficult and costly to take pets on holiday because we will no longer be part of the pet passport regime. Mobile phone charges will apply. UK-certified Doctors, dentists and other professionals will no longer have the right to practice in the EU – and EU professionals won't be able to ply their trade here. The EU's strict food hygiene standards and environmental regulations will no longer apply.

Brexit day is the domino that brings everything we take for granted tumbling down. The loss of our international agreements will have repercussions on most aspect of our lives.

All the consequences of Brexit stem from the loss of the agreements we benefited from as EU members. Every one of them

will have to be replaced merely to get back to the status quo we enjoyed previously.

This process happens automatically. It's the legal consequence of having invoked Article 50. There is nothing more that either the UK or the EU have to do for the UK to leave. Parliament doesn't have to agree anything further. Once we pass the Brexit day deadline, we're out quicker than a finger snap. And that's all down to clause 3.

Incidentally, it's not clear that all our MPs fully understood the final, definitive nature of Article 50 when they agreed to let Theresa May evoke it. Sure, there were warnings at the time about what would happen if no deal could be agreed. But the focus was still very much on reaching one. The negotiations proper had yet to start. Two years may have seemed ample given the apparent willingness by both sides to come to an agreement.

This is not meant to excuse them. (Indeed, there can be no excuse, since they should have insisted on Brexit being planned out in detail before allowing Article 50 to be evoked. Even Vote Leave knew that much.) But it is possible to look for an explanation for something without excusing it. And an initial lack of awareness would certainly tie in with the sense of panic which has descended on Parliament ever since it became clear that "not reaching a deal at all" – i.e. "no deal" – was something the Government is willing to countenance. And that means that, through inattention or oversight, many MPs have become as much of a hostage to fortune as the rest of us.

Time for a change of scene. Imagine you live in a nice house. A picture postcard cottage, with a rambling rose over the front door, and a glimpse of azure sea from the bedroom window.

One sunny morning, you leap out of bed and start ripping the electrical cables out of the walls (having turned the power off first – you're not daft). Next it's the turn of the gas pipes, the phone line, and the cable TV connection. You give the crowbar extra welly on the plumbing. Plaster dust dances like ghosts. Then you mix up a sludgy mound of cement, and pour it down every drain until it oozes across the floor. Finally, you brick up the front and back doors.

Panting, your face puce, you collapse on the sofa in the living room. Deep, gulping breaths. Slowly, you feel the tempo of your heart return to normal.

You close your eyes for an endless moment, then open them and take stock of your handiwork. Everything that made your house a home is gone. With all its connections to the outside world severed, it is little more than a very large and sturdy tent. For practical purposes uninhabitable. As you listen to the gulls calling out to each other as they wheel and dive, the enormity of what you did finally hits you. Fade to black…

Back to clause 3. There are two separate deadlines contained within "*from the date of entry into force of the withdrawal agreement or, failing that, two years after the notification referred to in paragraph 2*".

The one is a fixed length: the two year time-frame that Article 50 grants to complete the negotiation of the withdrawal agreement and the outline of our future relationship. The original Brexit day was 29 March 2019 because Theresa May invoked Article 50 on 29 March 2017.

(Note that the referendum did not create a legally binding obligation to leave, and definitely not to leave on any specific date. The original Brexit day of 29 March 2019 only came about because that was exactly 2 years from the day Theresa May notified the EU of our intent to leave. Any suggestion that we had to leave on 29 March 2019 because the 2016 vote told us to is a false memory after the fact. You will find no reference to that date in relation to Brexit before her Article 50 notification.)

The other is flexible: "*from the date of entry into force of the withdrawal agreement*". This means the two years represent a maximum, not a required duration. If we can reach an agreement with the EU in less than two years, we're free to leave as soon as it's ratified. And the same rule applies to the Article 50 extension we're currently in. Boris Johnson doesn't have to wait until 31 October 2019 to take the UK out of the EU. All he has to do is agree something with the EU sooner.

Speaking of Article 50 extensions, that's what the last part of clause 3 is about: "*unless the European Council, in agreement with the Member State concerned, unanimously decides to extend this period*". In some ways, this is a tougher standard to meet than the one applicable to the actual withdrawal agreement. The latter only needs majority approval. But to extend Article 50, the UK has to request an extension, which must then be signed off by every other EU member. A single hold-out and we don't get more time. To date, the EU have given in twice to our requests. First, there was a blink-and-you'll-miss-it extension until 12 April 2019. That was followed in short order by our current extension, which moved the Brexit deadline to Halloween. The symbolism may not have been intentional, but it's definitely poignant.

The EU may be willing to grant us a further extension should we ask for it, but they will want a good reason for agreeing the request. Time to hold a general election or a second referendum might well qualify. But "sorry, we're still bickering about what sort of Brexit we want" is unlikely to cut the mustard a third time.

You can think of the Article 50 process as the legal equivalent of a conveyor belt. Its far end lies outside the EU. Anyone who clambers onto the conveyor belt will be carried along and find themselves out of the EU and its treaties two years later. If the EU are amenable, they may be willing to bolt extra lengths onto to the conveyor to keep us in a bit longer. But once we reach the end, that's it, we're out out. There are only two ways off the belt. You either climb off it completely. Or you fall off the end and leave the EU.

Clause 3 does a remarkable amount of heavy lifting in a few sentences. Since it's the essence of the entire Brexit debacle, let's take a beat to sum things up. All our international agreements stop the second we leave the EU. We had two years (originally) to negotiate everything, but could leave sooner if we got things done quicker. And the EU can grant us more time, but only if every EU member signs off on it.

> *4. For the purposes of paragraphs 2 and 3, the member of the European Council or of the Council representing the withdrawing*

> *Member State shall not participate in the discussions of the European Council or Council or in decisions concerning it.*
>
> *A qualified majority shall be defined in accordance with Article 238(3)(b) of the Treaty on the Functioning of the European Union.*

Compared to the twists and turns of clause 3, clause 4 is refreshingly straightforward. As we've touched on before, it means we're not allowed to sit on both sides of the table at once. We can't take part in meetings in which the EU's approach to our own future is being thrashed out. The rest of this clause explains how the EU will determine what constitutes a qualified majority of votes.

> *5. If a State which has withdrawn from the Union asks to rejoin, its request shall be subject to the procedure referred to in Article 49.*

Remember the lack of a rewind button on Article 50? We can't magically reverse Brexit once we have left. But clause 5 signposts a roundabout route to readmission. It makes clear that we will have the right to apply to rejoin the EU via Article 49, even after Brexit. (It places no obligation on the EU to accept such an application.)

Article 49 is the standard procedure that all would-be EU member states must follow. We can't expect special treatment, even though we'd be the first state ever to have left the EU and attempted to return. From an administrative standpoint, we would be joining not rejoining. Our new EU membership wouldn't be a continuation of our previous one. It would be a separate instance, with its own distinct conditions. We would have to overcome the same hurdles faced by any applicant.

On paper, at least, our previous status as an EU member would not win us any concessions. But theory is one thing, practice quite another. We might find the process smoother than an applicant that had never been an EU member would. For instance, we would be able to claim that our rules and regulations had once been in harmony with the EU's. That would let us make a credible case that we could harmonise them again.

But we should not forget that the EU has suffered plenty of Brexit upheaval too. And that's on us. We chose to leave. They didn't force us to go. Indeed, they made it clear that they would much rather have us stay. They still want us to, although frustration with our indecision is mounting. So if we do finally leave, they are bound to take a long hard look before letting us back in.

We won't know the specifics of our hypothetical second membership until we apply to rejoin. Our application would trigger a period of intense negotiation, something we have not proven particularly good at.

The EU might well refuse to admit us under the conditions we have today. Without our current rebate, we would have to pay more for EU membership than we do now. The UK also has defined opt-outs from various aspects of EU participation. We have no obligation to adopt the euro, for instance, despite what rabble-rousers claim. And we are not required to be part of the border-free Schengen zone.

It remains to be see what unique benefits, if any, we would be able to wangle second time around. There is no sign of other would-be members being granted any of the privileged terms we currently enjoy. And if the EU did give us back everything, that might tempt other member states to try life outside for a while. So it's likely that our current membership represents the high water mark of the EU's flexibility. We may only be offered standard terms next time.

Every member state has the right to veto the accession of a new country to the EU. That means that we would have to convince 27 other countries to give us another chance. All while negotiating our new membership structure with the EU in parallel. We can expect them to demand a guarantee that we wouldn't seek to leave again a few years down the road. The last thing the EU needs is a reluctant member with a proven track record of being difficult. And individual states are likely to come calling with lists of the concessions they would like in return for letting us back in.

This could leave us in an impossible bind. Unresolved Brexit chaos could make the protective certainty of EU membership essential. Yet the requirements to fulfil to gain readmission to the club could turn out to be too much to bear.

Appendix E:
How politicians manipulate the narrative

(Most of this section is not specifically Brexit-related, but may be of interest to some.)

Politicians gravitate to positive headlines like iron filings drawn to a magnet. They deploy a wide range of tactics in pursuit of friendly column inches. Here are a few of the tricks they use to present themselves and their party in a better light.

1. Ignoring inflation

Prices rise every year, so a policy that promises "the highest amount on record" is meaningless without context. What matters is whether the sum is higher than historic pledges after inflation. For instance, if the Government says it's putting £1.5 billion into the railways, that might be the most ever spent. But if a previous Government ploughed £1.3 billion into track improvements in 1995, that would have paid for much more. Indeed, £1 billion in 1995 is equivalent to £2.5 billion today. So anything under £2.5 billion isn't a record, unless all that matters to you is the raw number of pounds on the table. Or a misleading headline.

2. Focusing on the money being put into a policy while ignoring the cuts that preceded it

Imagine taking £10 from someone every year for 5 years, and then giving them £7 in year 6. That £7 might well be "the largest ever cash increase in real terms". But the person in question will still be down £43 (inflation makes the situation even worse). By drawing attention to the £7 gained, politicians hope to distract from the £43 lost. All too often, it works. The Tories have had a go recently with their promises of extra police staff. While describing the huge 36-month hiring spree they're about to undertake, they have failed to acknowledge that over 20,000 officers have been cut from the force since they came to power. So even on the far side of this recruitment binge, overall police numbers will still be lower than in 2010.

3. Confusing more funding with better outcomes

A journalist confronts a minister with the statistic that adult literacy has fallen 7% in the last 10 years. The MP defends the Government record: "Since coming to office, we have put an extra £11 million into reading programmes." More money may indeed have been spent. But adult literacy still went down. So either the cash was spent on the wrong things, the sum provided was inadequate, or both. The extra money doesn't negate the fact that literacy worsened on the government's watch.

4. Glossing over the time period

"We will be spending an extra £50 million on expanding police stop and search powers." Sounds good, until you dig into the detail and find that the proposed increase is over a decade, with most of the money coming towards the end. An exciting policy shift turns out to be little more than window dressing.

5. Failing to take into account the size of the affected population

"We will be providing an extra £5 million to councils across England to combat the scourge of graffiti." Aha, nice clean walls everywhere. Except that 343 councils will have to share that windfall. So it works out to a rather less headline-friendly £20,408 per council. To be fair, that might pay for a cleaning crew for a couple of months. But it is hardly a revolution.

6. Disregarding the friction inherent in the system

Take the previous example. The money to remove graffiti isn't going to be showered on councils by central government like a singer in a rap video tossing fistfuls of £50 notes out of a moving car. No, councils will have to apply for it, and make a business case. Someone will then have to assess that application, perhaps seek clarifications, and then apportion the loot. All these processes take time, and cost money. What started out as £5 million will be considerably less by the time it's all been distributed. It's like trying to fill a row of glasses from a leaky jug. Everyone gets a bit of water, but there's a lot on the tablecloth too.

7. Ducking the bigger picture

"Our new policy means two million workers will be able to earn £500 more each year before they start paying any income tax". Bingo. Stellar headlines on their way. But will the National Insurance threshold change too? Does the extra income affect eligibility for certain benefits? Will workers outside of the two million contingent lose out? Will the policy be funded by raising a different tax, such as VAT or fuel tax, or by scrapping certain exemptions? In other words, when looking at the situation in its entirety, will people really be better off?

8. Massaging the stats

A politician says: "The local economy is thriving. Take Company X in my constituency. It recently gave its staff an average 2.5% pay rise." Let's rewind, and replay the tape. Company X employs 20 people to patch up cars which have been involved in accidents. Sweaty back-breaking work, barely above minimum wage. At the end of last year, the boss took one worker aside: "Bob, I like you. You're funny, you're conscientious, you play a mean game of darts. I've decided to give you a 50% pay rise." Bob almost shakes his hand off. The rest of the team (were they to ever find out) would rightly be appalled – nobody offered them a penny more. Yet the politician is correct. On average, everyone's now earning 2.5% more. But Bob's living his best life. And everyone else is struggling. It's a bit like photographing your house from just the right angle to miss the coal power plant rising above the treeline. A version of the truth, but is it really the truth?

9. Adjusting the axes on graphs

Your party came top in the local council elections, bagging 24% of the vote. The next highest trailed on 21%. Soon after, you offer to help the campaign team design a new leaflet for a possible snap General Election. They want to include a bar chart that will convey at a glance how far ahead the party's polling. Do you produce one with the vertical axis labelled from 0% to 30%? Or do you only represent a tight range, say from 20% to 25%, which would show your party's result shooting towards the moon next to its rival's wafer thin sliver? Both versions of the illustration rely on the same underlying data, but only one suggestively over-endows your party's prowess.

10. Mistaking correlation for causation

"People who commit violent crimes are more likely to play violent video games. We should therefore ban all video games featuring violence." For the sake of this example, assume that the first statement is true. In other words, those who commit violent crimes really are more likely to play violent video games than the general population are. That doesn't mean that the games are driving them to commit violent crime – or indeed crime of any sort. It could be that people who have a tendency towards criminal violence also happen to enjoy playing games in which they get to rough people up. (People often take their work home.) There's nothing to suggest that if the games weren't available, they'd magically become law-abiding citizens. In other words, more data is needed before drawing a politically self-serving conclusion.

11. Treating a single data point as representative of the whole

"Two postal votes were received from the same address in Camden, even though only one person is registered as living there. Across

England, at least 50,000 postal votes are likely to be fraudulent." Hold on a minute. It may be politically convenient to treat a rare occurrence as typical, rather than exceptional. But just because an instance of apparent voter fraud was detected in Camden, that doesn't mean that voter fraud is equally distributed across the entire country. Indeed, it's possible that Camden's fraudulent voter (if it was even fraud, rather than an administrative error) was the only one in the whole election. We simply don't have enough information to decide. The original assertion was like stepping out of your front door and watching ten people walk past, nine men and a woman. On that basis, you conclude that the population of the UK is 90% male. Or using the example of a stabbing in Leeds to suggest that thousands of people are being killed every day. ("Well, London's twenty times the size of Leeds, so that's already 20 murders...") You simply can't take a tiny sample size and extrapolate it out like that. Not unless you're a politician, anyway.

12. Making a number appear bite-sized, or frighteningly large

A gym subscription seems expensive at £240/year. It becomes a much easier sell when expressed as 66p per day. ("A third of the price of a cup of coffee") Politicians use this reframing tactic all the time. Instead of presenting the electorate with the huge cost of a policy, they'll explain it in terms of how much it will cost each person. "If everyone contributes just £1.50 a week, we can halve the time it takes the NHS to respond to cancer cases." Such a warm and fuzzy sentiment, it seems churlish to point out that amount adds up to over £5 billion a year.

The reverse of this tactic is deployed in the Brexit debate to make the cost of EU membership as scary as possible. About £2.90 per person per week sounds so much worse when recast as £10 billion a year. One figure's a bargain, the other causes outrage. But the amount of money involved is exactly the same in both cases.

By ignoring both the money we never actually send in the first place, and the sum we get back from the EU (as the Leave camp did during the referendum) it's possible to set veins throbbing even harder. And if you stand next to the misleading figure on the side of a bus often enough… you become Prime Minister.

Acknowledgements

They say everyone has a book in them, and this is mine. My heartfelt thanks and gratitude go to…

- Mark B, who turned the brightness down on my purple prose. (The leftover clunkiness is all mine.) His own adventures in publishing inspire me almost as much as our twenty years of friendship.
- The dab hand of Liquid Faerie, for the stunning cover.
- Jo and the Thursday writing group, for humouring my Brexit ramblings in place of fiction for so long. (A special tip of the hat to John for his gracious hosting.)
- My Twitter followers, who turned shouting at the moon into extended conversations.
- And most of all my wife, whose help and encouragement carried me over the finish line.

Endnotes

[1] https://www.mirror.co.uk/news/uk-news/nigel-farage-wants-second-referendum-7985017

[2] https://www.huffingtonpost.co.uk/michael-gove/michael-gove-vote-leave_b_9728548.html

[3] http://news.bbc.co.uk/2/shared/bsp/hi/pdfs/08051604.pdf

[4] https://www.independent.co.uk/news/uk/politics/boris-johnson-eu-referendum-single-market-brexit-a7104846.html

[5] https://www.theguardian.com/politics/2017/jul/20/liam-fox-uk-eu-trade-deal-after-brexit-easiest-human-history

[6] http://www.voteleavetakecontrol.org/briefing_trade.html

[7] http://www.voteleavetakecontrol.org/vote_leave_for_a_fairer_britain.html

[8] https://www.bbc.co.uk/news/business-49290926

[9] https://www.theguardian.com/commentisfree/2018/jun/13/brexit-traitor-trope-hard-right-fantasies-risk

[10] https://www.theguardian.com/politics/2017/apr/02/arron-banks-interview-brexit-ukip-far-right-trump-putin-russia

[11] https://www.politicshome.com/news/uk/political-parties/conservative-party/boris-johnson/news/104838/boris-johnson-vows-deliver

[12] https://www.dailymail.co.uk/news/article-6793015/Vote-Leave-leader-Michael-Gove-warns-rebel-Tory-MPs-48-hours-save-Brexit.html

[13] https://en.wikipedia.org/wiki/The_mother_of_parliaments_(expression)

[14] https://www.ifs.org.uk/publications/14420

[15] https://www.independent.co.uk/news/business/news/austerity-uk-gdp-growth-tax-economy-chancellor-philip-hammond-a8789866.html

[16] https://www.independent.co.uk/news/uk/politics/no-deal-brexit-army-troops-eu-uk-leave-remain-date-vote-tory-party-theresa-may-a8689771.html

[17] http://www.legislation.gov.uk/ukpga/2004/36/contents

[18] https://bylinetimes.com/about/

[19] https://www.bbc.co.uk/news/business-36592782

[20] https://www.bbc.co.uk/news/uk-36505736

[21] https://en.wikipedia.org/wiki/2016_United_Kingdom_European_Union_membership_referendum

[22] http://www.ukpolitical.info/Turnout45.htm

[23] https://www.totalpolitics.com/articles/news/boris-johnson-and-michael-gove-mourning-mode-post-brexit-%E2%80%98funeral%E2%80%99

[24]

http://d3n8a8pro7vhmx.cloudfront.net/themes/55fd82d8ebad646cec000001/attachments/original/1463496002/Why_Vote_Leave.pdf?1463496002

[25] https://whatukthinks.org/eu/questions/if-there-was-a-referendum-on-britains-membership-of-the-eu-how-would-you-vote-2/

[26] https://www.telegraph.co.uk/news/newstopics/eureferendum/11880864/Conservative-Party-to-stay-neutral-during-EU-referendum.html

[27] https://www.bbc.co.uk/news/uk-politics-eu-referendum-35616946

[28] https://www.huffingtonpost.co.uk/entry/faisal-islam-brexit-no-plan_uk_576fe22ee4b0d2571149cffd

[29] https://www.lbc.co.uk/radio/presenters/iain-dale/osborne-must-resign-insists-iain-dale-132772/

[30] https://dominiccummings.com/2015/06/23/on-the-referendum-6-exit-plans-and-a-second-referendum/

[31] https://www.nytimes.com/2016/06/29/world/europe/boris-johnson-brexit-leaders-eu.html

[32] http://www.gov.scot/resource/0043/00439021.pdf

[33] https://www.bbc.co.uk/news/uk-politics-47143135

[34] https://constitution-unit.com/2016/01/19/what-happens-if-we-vote-for-brexit

[35] https://www.channel4.com/news/factcheck/the-culture-secretary-said-the-eu-referendum-was-binding-it-wasnt

[36] http://www.legislation.gov.uk/ukpga/2015/36/contents/enacted

[37] https://researchbriefings.parliament.uk/ResearchBriefing/Summary/CBP-7212

[38] https://publications.parliament.uk/pa/ld200910/ldselect/ldconst/99/9909.htm

[39] https://fullfact.org/europe/was-eu-referendum-advisory/

[40] https://parliamentlive.tv/event/index/a1b65e77-a0e6-4b89-ac09-99d7c5383f45

[41] https://www.electoralcommission.org.uk/i-am-a/journalist/electoral-commission-media-centre/party-and-election-finance-to-keep/leave.eu-fined-for-multiple-breaches-of-electoral-law-following-investigation

[42] https://www.electoralcommission.org.uk/i-am-a/journalist/electoral-commission-media-centre/party-and-election-finance-to-keep/vote-leave-fined-and-referred-to-the-police-for-breaking-electoral-law

[43] https://www.electoralcommission.org.uk/i-am-a/journalist/electoral-commission-media-centre/referendums-to-keep/media-statement-vote-leave

[44] https://ico.org.uk/media/action-weve-taken/mpns/2260051/r-facebook-mpn-20181024.pdf

[45] https://ico.org.uk/action-weve-taken/enforcement/leaveeu-incident-1-monetary-penalty-notice/

[46] https://ico.org.uk/action-weve-taken/enforcement/leaveeu-incident-2-monetary-penalty-notice/

[47] https://ico.org.uk/about-the-ico/news-and-events/news-and-blogs/2019/02/ico-to-audit-data-protection-practices-at-leaveeu-and-eldon-insurance-after-fining-both-companies-for-unlawful-marketing-messages/

[48] https://ico.org.uk/about-the-ico/news-and-events/news-and-blogs/2019/03/ico-fines-vote-leave-40-000-for-sending-unlawful-text-messages/

[49] https://ico.org.uk/media/action-weve-taken/2260271/investigation-into-the-use-of-data-analytics-in-political-campaigns-final-20181105.pdf

[50] https://en.wikipedia.org/wiki/Pax_Europaea

[51] https://metro.co.uk/2013/12/18/a-dog-is-for-life-not-just-for-christmas-puppy-slogan-turns-35-4233581/

[52] https://assets.publishing.service.gov.uk/government/uploads/system/uploads/attachment_data/file/750255/No-deal_EU__exit_step-by-step_guide_to_exporting_Oct_2018.pdf

[53] https://www.gov.uk/government/publications/hmrc-impact-assessment-for-the-movement-of-goods-if-the-uk-leaves-the-eu-without-a-deal/hmrc-impact-assessment-for-the-movement-of-goods-if-the-uk-leaves-the-eu-without-a-deal-third-edition

[54] https://assets.publishing.service.gov.uk/government/uploads/system/uploads/attachment_data/file/831199/20190802_Latest_Yellowhammer_Planning_assumptions_CDL.pdf

[55] https://www.independent.co.uk/news/business/news/brexit-city-of-london-jobs-financial-services-banking-impact-a8975711.html

[56] https://wolfstreet.com/2019/05/07/businesses-in-critical-distress-bankruptcies-surge-in-the-uk/

[57] https://assets.publishing.service.gov.uk/government/uploads/system/uploads/attachment_data/file/831199/20190802_Latest_Yellowhammer_Planning_assumptions_CDL.pdf

[58] https://www.independent.co.uk/news/uk/politics/brexit-secretary-food-supply-dominic-raab-uk-leave-eu-no-deal-a8461771.html

[59] https://www.bbc.co.uk/news/av/uk-politics-49550745/gove-everyone-will-have-the-food-they-need-in-no-deal-brexit

[60] https://uk.reuters.com/article/uk-britain-eu-medicines/no-deal-brexit-could-deepen-europes-shortage-of-medicines-experts-idUKKCN1V20FQ

[61] https://psnc.org.uk/contract-it/brexit-and-community-pharmacy/serious-shortage-protocols-ssps/

[62] https://assets.publishing.service.gov.uk/government/uploads/system/uploads/attachment_data/file/831199/20190802_Latest_Yellowhammer_Planning_assumptions_CDL.pdf

[63] https://www.youtube.com/watch?v=gUtJEfB9Hi4

[64] https://www.bbc.co.uk/news/politics/eu_referendum/results

[65] https://www.moneysavingexpert.com/news/2019/09/duty-free-shopping-for-those-to-travelling-to-the-eu-to-return-i/

[66] https://www.theguardian.com/politics/2019/sep/11/treasury-under-fire-for-promoting-no-deal-brexit-duty-free-shopping

[67] https://www.lexology.com/library/detail.aspx?g=3f4ba661-c438-47c3-87d0-cf119ec016c5

[68] https://researchbriefings.parliament.uk/ResearchBriefing/Summary/CBP-8031

[69] https://www.independent.co.uk/news/uk/politics/brexit-latest-blue-passport-bring-back-home-office-eu-a7249361.html

[70] https://www.gov.uk/government/publications/hmrc-impact-assessment-for-the-movement-of-goods-if-the-uk-leaves-the-eu-without-a-deal/hmrc-impact-assessment-for-the-movement-of-goods-if-the-uk-leaves-the-eu-without-a-deal-third-edition

[71] https://www.ft.com/content/b9cfac7a-836e-11e8-a29d-73e3d454535d

[72] https://www.nhs.uk/using-the-nhs/healthcare-abroad/apply-for-a-free-ehic-european-health-insurance-card/

[73] https://www.independent.co.uk/news/uk/politics/hedge-fund-manager-describes-moment-he-won-220-million-brexit-vote-the-morning-has-gold-in-its-mouth-a7323626.html

[74] https://inews.co.uk/news/tory-donor-bets-300-million-on-losses-for-uk-firms-after-no-deal-brexit-497159

[75] https://www.cityam.com/ma-activity-targeting-uk-slumps-amid-no-deal-brexit-fears/

[76] https://www.ft.com/content/91a7bd42-dace-11e9-8f9b-77216ebe1f17

[77] https://en.wikipedia.org/wiki/Rules_of_origin

[78] https://en.wikipedia.org/wiki/Brexit_and_the_Irish_border

[79] https://www.joe.co.uk/politics/the-irish-border-where-brexit-meets-reality-238887

[80] https://uk.reuters.com/article/uk-irish-tower-idUKL1325533820070213

[81] https://www.parliament.uk/business/committees/committees-a-z/commons-select/exiting-the-european-union-committee/news-parliament-2017/mapping-exercise-documents-published-17-19/

[82] http://www.europarl.europa.eu/factsheets/en/sheet/102/northern-ireland-peace-programme

[83] https://www.gov.uk/government/publications/trading-electricity-if-theres-no-brexit-deal/trading-electricity-if-theres-no-brexit-deal

[84] https://www.belfasttelegraph.co.uk/news/northern-ireland/brexit-government-plan-for-electricity-barges-in-irish-sea-should-northern-ireland-be-cut-off-37108625.html

[85] https://www.rte.ie/news/brexit/2019/0906/1074284-brexit-ireland/

[86] https://blogs.ec.europa.eu/ECintheUK/euromyths-a-z-index/

[87] https://www.thesun.co.uk/news/2727663/now-eurocrats-are-clamping-down-on-colouring-pencils-as-they-tighten-regulations-over-fears-children-could-be-eating-dangerous-levels-of-lead/

[88] https://blogs.ec.europa.eu/ECintheUK/eu-is-acting-on-scientific-evidence-to-cut-lead-in-toys-not-stopping-children-colouring/

[89] https://ec.europa.eu/transparency/regdoc/rep/1/2016/EN/1-2016-560-EN-F1-1.PDF

[90] https://www.telegraph.co.uk/news/uknews/leveson-inquiry/9817625/Leveson-EU-wants-power-to-sack-journalists.html

91 https://blogs.ec.europa.eu/ECintheUK/the-european-commission-does-not-want-to-sack-journalists/

92 https://blogs.ec.europa.eu/ECintheUK/eu-environmetal-plans-lead-to-thousands-of-dumped-fridges/

93 https://blogs.ec.europa.eu/ECintheUK/eu-data-protection-rules-do-not-ban-christmas-wish-lists-in-bavaria-or-elsewhere/

94 https://blogs.ec.europa.eu/ECintheUK/eu-does-not-ban-beaches/

95 https://blogs.ec.europa.eu/ECintheUK/bananas-and-brussels/

96 https://www.gov.uk/guidance/driving-in-the-eu-after-brexit

97 https://www.gov.uk/vehicle-insurance/driving-abroad

98 https://www.theparliamentmagazine.eu/articles/news/threat-no-deal-brexit-intensifies-boris-johnson-refuses-nominate-new-uk-commissioner

99 https://www.politico.eu/article/tory-conservative-leadership-frontrunner-boris-johnson-dismisses-offensive-language-charge/

100 https://www.bbc.co.uk/news/uk-politics-48752222

101 https://www.youtube.com/watch?v=ZeoPfUt2ShQ

102 https://www.independent.co.uk/news/uk/politics/no-deal-brexit-liam-fox-conservative-tory-dunkirk-mps-vote-theresa-may-deal-a8726451.html

103 https://brexitcentral.com/heres-how-ill-get-us-out-of-the-eu-by-october-31st-no-ifs-no-buts-no-excuses/

104 https://en.wikipedia.org/wiki/2019_European_Parliament_election_in_the_United_Kingdom

105 https://www.politicshome.com/news/uk/political-parties/conservative-party/boris-johnson/news/104838/boris-johnson-vows-deliver

106 https://en.wikipedia.org/wiki/Member_states_of_the_World_Trade_Organization

107 https://www.theguardian.com/business/2018/oct/21/brexit-premier-league-side-wanting-to-be-relegated-wto-internal-market

108 https://www.bbc.co.uk/news/business-49425202

109 http://www.pig-world.co.uk/news/ahdb-issues-brexit-no-deal-pork-summary.html

110 https://www.gov.uk/government/news/temporary-tariff-regime-for-no-deal-brexit-published

111 https://www.bbc.co.uk/news/uk-45112872

112 https://www.lexology.com/library/detail.aspx?g=34fe2d57-9b66-4db2-9c5b-2b10e6492bca

113 https://www.youtube.com/watch?v=bgwVEpbb3do

114 https://publications.parliament.uk/pa/cm/cmcode.htm

115 https://publications.parliament.uk/pa/cm200607/cmselect/cmmodern/337/33706.htm

116 https://www.supremecourt.uk/cases/docs/uksc-2019-0192-judgment.pdf

117 http://blogs.sussex.ac.uk/uktpo/publications/most-favoured-nation-clauses-in-eu-trade-agreements-one-more-hurdle-for-uk-negotiators/

118 https://en.wikipedia.org/wiki/List_of_countries_by_GDP_(nominal)

119 https://www.gov.uk/guidance/summary-of-the-uk-faroe-islands-free-trade-agreement-fta

120 https://www.theguardian.com/politics/2018/nov/28/uk-only-30-expert-trade-negotiators-brexit-foreign-affairs-committee-report

121 https://www.open-britain.co.uk/new_research_trade_deals_with_five_key_countries_could_take_26_years_to_negotiate

122 https://trade.ec.europa.eu/doclib/docs/2006/december/tradoc_118238.pdf

123 https://en.wikipedia.org/wiki/Red_Queen%27s_race

124 https://www.theguardian.com/politics/2018/jul/16/michael-gove-admits-leave-was-wrong-to-fuel-immigration-fears

125 https://www.bbc.co.uk/news/uk-politics-46926119

126 https://www.theguardian.com/politics/2016/jun/16/nigel-farage-defends-ukip-breaking-point-poster-queue-of-migrants

[127] https://www.ipsos.com/ipsos-mori/en-uk/economy-and-immigration-key-issues-britons-eu-referendum

[128] https://www.ipsos.com/ipsos-mori/en-uk/economy-and-immigration-key-issues-britons-eu-referendum

[129] https://www.bbc.co.uk/news/uk-wales-48692863

[130] https://assets.publishing.service.gov.uk/government/uploads/system/uploads/attachment_data/file/741926/Final_EEA_report.PDF

[131] https://www.personneltoday.com/hr/no-deal-brexit-could-send-nhs-toppling-over-the-edge/

[132] https://blogs.lse.ac.uk/brexit/2018/11/13/how-eu-migrants-have-propped-up-britains-social-care/

[133] https://www.hospitalityandcateringnews.com/2018/09/without-immigration-hospitality-face-biggest-crisis-yet/

[134] https://www.gov.uk/government/news/uk-announces-2-year-post-study-work-visa-for-international-students

[135] https://uk.reuters.com/article/uk-britain-eu-immigration/uk-miscounted-eu-other-immigrants-before-brexit-vote-idUKKCN1VB215

[136] https://www.bbc.co.uk/news/business-49007700

[137] https://www.theguardian.com/commentisfree/2019/feb/15/brexit-lies-curry-vote-leave-restaurant-industry

[138] https://www.standard.co.uk/news/politics/minister-priti-patel-quit-eu-to-save-our-curry-houses-a3251071.html

[139] https://blogs.lse.ac.uk/brexit/2019/09/13/what-policy-do-british-voters-want-on-eu-immigration-is-there-a-hidden-consensus/

[140] https://www.politicshome.com/news/uk/economy/utilities/news/103676/jeremy-corbyn-plotting-cut-price-takeover-water

[141] https://www.independent.co.uk/news/uk/politics/brexit-eu-railways-eu-rules-nationalise-single-market-restrictions-labour-a8968691.html

[142] https://ec.europa.eu/transport/modes/rail/packages/2013_en

[143] http://theconversation.com/fact-check-do-new-eu-rules-make-it-impossible-to-renationalise-railways-61180

[144] https://www.citymetric.com/transport/would-eu-rules-really-prevent-jeremy-corbyn-s-labour-party-renationalising-railways-3933

[145] https://www.politics.co.uk/comment-analysis/2018/02/27/corbyn-on-state-aid-fact-checked

[146] https://www.ashurst.com/en/news-and-insights/insights/energysource-in-the-shadow-of-nationalisation-in-the-uk/

[147] https://www.whatdotheyknow.com/request/548794/response/1319005/attach/html/3/Scan.pdf.html

[148] https://www.politax.com/post/is-brexit-really-about-tax-avoidance

[149] https://www.oecd.org/ctp/BEPSActionPlan.pdf

[150] https://europa.eu/rapid/press-release_CJE-06-37_en.htm

[151] https://www.bloomberg.com/news/articles/2019-04-02/eu-delivers-u-k-tax-bill-as-brexit-deal-eludes-parliament

[152] https://www.financialsecrecyindex.com/en/

[153] https://europa.eu/rapid/press-release_MEMO-19-1629_en.htm

[154] https://uk.reuters.com/article/uk-eu-tax-blacklist/eu-shrinks-tax-haven-blacklist-removes-uk-dutch-territories-idUKKCN1SN12J

[155] https://euobserver.com/opinion/143552

[156] https://uk.practicallaw.thomsonreuters.com/w-004-6057

[157] https://www.channel4.com/news/factcheck/factcheck-can-we-avoid-paying-the-39-billion-brexit-divorce-bill

[158] https://ec.europa.eu/commission/sites/beta-political/files/essential-principles-financial_settlement_en_0.pdf

[159] https://www.parliament.uk/documents/commons-committees/treasury/Correspondence/2017-19/Correspondence-from-the-Chancellor-of-the-Exchequer-relating-to-the-UK-EU-Withdrawal-financial-settlement-dated-24-January.pdf

[160] https://researchbriefings.parliament.uk/ResearchBriefing/Summary/CBP-8039

[161] https://www.politico.eu/pro/boris-johnson-eu-can-go-whistle-over-brexit-bill/

[162] https://www.telegraph.co.uk/politics/2019/01/30/brussels-orders-britain-pay-brexit-bill-even-no-deal-exit/

[163] https://publications.parliament.uk/pa/ld201617/ldselect/ldeucom/125/12503.htm

[164] https://inews.co.uk/news/brexit/boris-johnson-threatens-withhold-eu-divorce-bill/

[165] https://www.goodreads.com/quotes/390191-cecil-graham-what-is-a-cynic-lord-darlington-a-man

[166] https://www.independent.co.uk/voices/brexit-delay-boris-johnson-extension-cost-article-50-october-31-a9092861.html

[167] https://uk-air.defra.gov.uk/air-pollution/uk-eu-policy-context

[168] https://www.youtube.com/watch?v=c8ZXxDsCbfg

[169] https://assets.publishing.service.gov.uk/government/uploads/system/uploads/attachment_data/file/765518/exemption-relaxation-of-drivers-hours-working-time-rules-2018.pdf

[170] https://www.theguardian.com/politics/2016/dec/07/tory-mps-suggest-firms-draw-up-list-for-bonfire-of-eu-laws-after-brexit

[171] https://www.independent.co.uk/news/uk/politics/brexit-safety-standards-workers-rights-jacob-rees-mogg-a7459336.html

[172] https://www.independent.co.uk/news/uk/politics/brexit-eu-regulations-michael-gove-environment-drugs-a7649041.html

[173] https://citywireselector.com/news/brexit-champion-rees-mogg-blasts-mifid-ii-bureaucracy/a1161078

[174] https://www.fnlondon.com/articles/jacob-rees-mogg-steps-down-from-investment-firm-to-join-cabinet-20190725

[175] https://www.gov.uk/government/publications/pm-letter-to-donald-tusk-19-august-2019

[176] https://www.bbc.co.uk/news/business-50008268

[177] https://www.huffingtonpost.co.uk/entry/the-us-ambassador-is-telling-chlorinated-porkies-about-food-poisoning_uk_5c7fb34ae4b020b54d809fad

[178] https://twitter.com/trussliz/status/1180013827896860673

[179] https://www.youtube.com/watch?v=JMO8W4QnlQQ

[180] https://www.theguardian.com/politics/2019/jan/24/jcb-paid-boris-johnson-10000-three-days-before-speech

[181] https://blogs.sussex.ac.uk/uktpo/2019/05/15/not-just-a-technical-exercise-a-look-at-new-uk-pesticides-regulation/

[182] https://commonslibrary.parliament.uk/science/environment/what-does-brexit-mean-for-the-uks-beaches/

[183] https://www.belfasttelegraph.co.uk/business/northern-ireland/just-10-of-small-firms-prepared-for-nodeal-brexit-says-new-survey-38369710.html

[184] https://blogs.lse.ac.uk/politicsandpolicy/who-will-suffer-most-from-brexit/

[185] https://www.bbc.co.uk/news/uk-politics-49255061

[186] https://www.indy100.com/article/brexit-gove-no-deal-food-andrew-marr-brexit-shortages-watch-video-9087616

[187] https://www.huffingtonpost.co.uk/entry/goves-claim-fresh-food-supplies-unaffected-by-no-deal-brexit-categorically-untrue_uk_5d6bb55ce4b0cdfe05719d77

[188] https://www.huffingtonpost.co.uk/entry/jacob-rees-mogg-lbc-dr-david-nicholl-no-deal-brexit_uk_5d6cdf36e4b09bbc9ef1b480

[189] https://www.theguardian.com/business/2019/jan/14/boris-johnson-dismisses-brexit-claims-of-jaguar-land-rover-boss

[190] https://www.itv.com/news/2019-08-18/government-hits-back-at-leaked-operation-yellowhammer-report-which-suggests-no-deal-will-lead-to-shortages/

[191] https://balkaninsight.com/2019/08/09/democracy-digest-faith-in-the-eu-and-selective-memory/

[192] https://www.independent.co.uk/news/uk/politics/brexit-eu-countries-donald-tusk-president-uk-a8934051.html

[193] https://www.ofx.com/en-gb/forex-news/historical-exchange-rates/

[194] https://www.visitbritain.org/latest-quarterly-data-uk-overall

[195] https://www.theguardian.com/business/2018/jul/20/toblerone-to-revert-to-original-shape-but-with-bigger-size-and-price

[196] https://www.theguardian.com/business/2019/jul/25/us-private-equity-group-snaps-up-cobham-in-4bn-deal

[197] https://news.sky.com/story/greene-kings-4-6bn-takeover-typifies-cheap-uk-assets-11789353

[198] https://www.ft.com/content/fffd7f8c-4456-11e6-b22f-79eb4891c97d

[199] https://www.independent.co.uk/news/uk/home-news/uk-crops-eu-farm-workers-brexit-referendum-rot-manpower-recruitment-numbers-a8194701.html

[200] https://www.itv.com/news/2019-10-04/tonnes-of-british-grown-fruit-wasted-over-shortages-of-eu-workers-amid-no-deal-brexit-fears/

[201] https://www.spectator.co.uk/2008/04/why-hasnt-britain-got-a-sovereign-wealth-fund/

[202] https://en.wikipedia.org/wiki/List_of_countries_by_sovereign_wealth_funds

[203] http://www.conservativehome.com/platform/2016/02/david-davis-britain-would-be-better-off-out-of-the-eu-and-heres-why.html

[204] https://researchbriefings.parliament.uk/ResearchBriefing/Summary/CBP-7851

[205] https://ec.europa.eu/eurostat/documents/2995521/9967985/3-10072019-BP-EN.pdf

[206] https://news.sky.com/story/europe-really-doesnt-need-us-as-much-as-we-need-them-11462776

[207] https://www.bbc.co.uk/news/uk-politics-eu-referendum-36537180

[208] https://assets.publishing.service.gov.uk/government/uploads/system/uploads/attachment_data/file/742793/UK_Sea_Fisheries_Statistics_2017.pdf

[209] https://www.smmt.co.uk/wp-content/uploads/sites/2/SMMT-Motor-Industry-Facts-May-2019-V2.pdf

[210] https://unearthed.greenpeace.org/2018/10/11/fishing-quota-uk-defra-michael-gove/

[211] https://www.gov.uk/government/news/fishing-industry-in-2017-statistics-published

[212] https://www.theguardian.com/business/2019/sep/12/so-long-and-thanks-for-the-fish-eu-trawlers-set-new-course-post-brexit

[213] https://www.gov.uk/guidance/commercial-fishing-and-marketing-of-seafood-if-theres-no-brexit-deal

[214] https://gov.wales/preparing-wales-brexit/fisheries-and-trade

[215] https://www.bbc.co.uk/news/uk-politics-49302778

[216] https://www.independent.co.uk/news/uk/politics/brexit-no-deal-fishing-quotas-eu-boris-johnson-violence-scallop-wars-a9050431.html

[217] https://ukandeu.ac.uk/what-does-a-no-deal-brexit-look-like-for-fishing/

[218] https://www.kluge.no/fagforum/brexit-and-norwegian-fisheries/

[219] https://fishingnews.co.uk/news/brexit-shellfish-threat-no-deal-brexit-shellfish-warning/

[220] https://www.shippo.co.uk/faqs/how-long-do-shipments-take/

[221] https://ec.europa.eu/eurostat/statistics-explained/index.php/Freight_transport_statistics

[222] https://www.raf.mod.uk/aircraft/c-17-globemaster-iii/

[223] https://www.raf.mod.uk/aircraft/c-130j-hercules/

[224] https://www.raf.mod.uk/aircraft/atlas-a400m/

[225] https://www.raf.mod.uk/aircraft/bae146-ccmk2-and-cmk3/

[226] http://www.poferries.com/en/dover-calais/onboard/ships/pride-of-burgundy

[227] https://www.getlinkgroup.com/uk/eurotunnel-group/operations/truck-shuttles/

[228] https://assets.publishing.service.gov.uk/government/uploads/system/uploads/attachment_data/file/762200/port-freight-statistics-2017.pdf

[229] https://en.wikipedia.org/wiki/Year_2000_problem

[230] https://www.gov.uk/government/publications/notice-143-a-guide-for-international-post-users/notice-143-a-guide-for-international-post-users

[231] https://personal.help.royalmail.com/app/answers/detail/a_id/7208/

[232] https://www.parcelforce.com/sites/default/files/Customs%20leaflet.pdf

[233] https://www.gov.uk/government/publications/partnership-pack-preparing-for-a-no-deal-eu-exit/changes-to-customs-excise-and-vat-you-need-to-know-about-if-there-is-no-deal

[234] https://assets.publishing.service.gov.uk/government/uploads/system/uploads/attachment_data/file/650459/customs_bill_white_paper_web.pdf

[235] https://assets.publishing.service.gov.uk/government/uploads/system/uploads/attachment_data/file/831199/20190802_Latest_Yellowhammer_Planning_assumptions_CDL.pdf

[236] https://assets.publishing.service.gov.uk/government/uploads/system/uploads/attachment_data/file/837312/DExEUReportWEB.PDF

[237] https://www.doverport.co.uk/about/performance/

[238] http://en.rfi.fr/europe/20190830-france-starts-brexit-trial-northern-port-calais

[239] https://en.wikipedia.org/wiki/Operation_Brock

[240] https://twitter.com/mikegalsworthy/status/1170990244130414592

[241] https://www.theparliamentmagazine.eu/articles/news/mps-reconsider-brexit-proposal-involving-second-referendum

[242] https://theconversation.com/brexit-deadlock-this-three-way-referendum-design-could-break-it-108217

[243] https://www.instituteforgovernment.org.uk/blog/second-brexit-referendum-practical-questions

[244] https://www.citizensassembly.ie/en/Home/

[245] https://www.independent.co.uk/news/uk/politics/conservative-leader-rory-stewart-brexit-citizens-assembly-archbishop-canterbury-a8933741.html

[246] https://www.politico.eu/article/the-myth-of-the-citizens-assembly-democracy/

[247] https://www.gov.uk/government/news/uk-welcomes-approval-of-new-trade-agreement-with-japan

[248] https://ec.europa.eu/trade/policy/in-focus/eu-mercosur-association-agreement/eu-mercosur-in-your-town/united-kingdom_en.htm

[249] https://www.bbc.co.uk/news/uk-14380936

[250] https://www.gov.uk/guidance/building-digital-uk

[251] https://researchbriefings.files.parliament.uk/documents/SN06193/SN06193.pdf

[252] https://www.gov.uk/government/organisations/office-of-tax-simplification

[253] https://www.bbc.co.uk/news/uk-politics-48199355

[254] https://www.parliament.uk/education/teaching-resources-lesson-plans/

[255] https://ec.europa.eu/unitedkingdom/education/eu-teaching-materials_en

[256] http://www.europarl.europa.eu/unitedkingdom/en/education/teachingresources.html

[257] https://www.gov.uk/government/publications/national-curriculum-in-england-citizenship-programmes-of-study/national-curriculum-in-england-citizenship-programmes-of-study-for-key-stages-3-and-4

[258] https://www.independent.co.uk/news/uk/politics/brexit-no-deal-eu-immigration-control-vote-leave-latest-a9102686.html

[259] https://www.theguardian.com/politics/2019/aug/08/uk-to-ease-visa-restrictions-on-top-scientists-post-brexit

[260] https://www.gov.uk/government/news/uk-announces-2-year-post-study-work-visa-for-international-students

[261] https://fullfact.org/economy/trident-nuclear-cost/

[262] https://www.gov.uk/government/news/chancellor-announces-billions-to-turbo-charge-no-deal-preparations

[263] https://www.theguardian.com/politics/2018/dec/29/brexit-more-than-100m-spent-on-extra-ferries-in-case-of-no-deal

[264] https://www.theguardian.com/uk-news/2019/may/01/chris-grayling-cancels-ferry-contracts-at-extra-50m-cost-

to-taxpayers-brexit

[265] https://www.theguardian.com/politics/2019/feb/11/incompetent-grayling-must-quit-over-brexit-ferry-deal-says-labour

[266] https://www.nao.org.uk/wp-content/uploads/2019/05/Out-of-court-settlement-with-Eurotunnel.pdf

[267] https://lloydslist.maritimeintelligence.informa.com/LL1128635/UK-reopens-controversial-Brexit-ferry-tender

[268] https://www.gov.uk/government/publications/department-for-exiting-the-european-union-monthly-workforce-management-information-for-2017-and-2018

[269] https://www.bbc.co.uk/news/business-49189377

[270] https://www.bbc.co.uk/news/uk-england-kent-42885595

[271] https://www.independent.co.uk/voices/no-deal-brexit-theresa-may-chris-grayling-m20-fake-traffic-jam-a8715351.html

[272] https://www.parliament.uk/written-questions-answers-statements/written-question/commons/2018-10-25/183831

[273] https://www.politico.eu/article/uk-plan-to-use-m26-motorway-as-parking-lot-port-dover-if-no-brexit-deal/

[274] https://www.nao.org.uk/wp-content/uploads/2019/05/Departments-use-of-consultants-to-support-preparations-for-EU-Exit.pdf

[275] https://www.bbc.co.uk/news/business-48181004

[276] https://www.parliament.uk/business/committees/committees-a-z/commons-select/public-accounts-committee/inquiries/parliament-2017/inquiry30/

[277] https://www.bbc.co.uk/news/uk-politics-47128398

[278] https://www.kentonline.co.uk/kent/news/hotels-for-officers-running-operation-brock-could-cost-1000s-202094/

[279] https://www.bbc.co.uk/news/uk-england-kent-47899266

[280] https://www.accountancydaily.co/hmrc-blames-brexit-shortcomings-service-delivery

[281] https://www.bbc.co.uk/news/uk-politics-49255061

[282] https://scramnews.com/boris-johnson-100m-no-deal-brexit-advertising-campaign-us-firms/

[283] https://www.gov.uk/government/publications/uk-governments-preparations-for-a-no-deal-scenario/uk-governments-preparations-for-a-no-deal-scenario

[284] https://www.gov.uk/government/uploads/system/uploads/attachment_data/file/734352/defra-ara-2017-2018-web.pdf

[285] https://www.theguardian.com/politics/2019/apr/11/uk-stands-down-6000-no-deal-brexit-staff-after-spending-15bn

[286] https://www.civilserviceworld.com/articles/news/2000-civil-servants-moving-departments-brexit-roles-%E2%80%93-report

[287] https://metro.co.uk/2019/04/05/extreme-brexit-stockpilers-22-tons-baked-beans-huge-numbers-toilet-roll-9120619/

[288] https://www.politicshome.com/news/uk/home-affairs/news/105725/mps-blast-governments-%C2%A320m-no-deal-brexit-council-spending-pledge

[289] https://www.politico.eu/article/uk-officials-summer-holidays-canceled-to-prepare-for-no-deal-brexit/

[290] https://civilserviceworld.com/articles/news/departments-push-fill-hundreds-brexit-roles-eu-departure-approaches

[291] https://www.bbc.co.uk/news/uk-wales-46127592

[292] https://www.handyshippingguide.com/shipping-news/uk-customs-declarations-changes-will-affect-all-freight-customers-eventually_11982

[293] https://www.theguardian.com/society/2018/nov/10/hospital-food-at-risk-no-deal-brexit

[294] https://www.theguardian.com/politics/2018/dec/13/civil-service-seeks-staff-for-no-deal-brexit-crisis-centre

[295] https://www.bbc.co.uk/news/uk-northern-ireland-49824526

[296] https://www.irishmirror.ie/news/irish-news/politics/government-offering-businesses-up-60000-18858140

297 https://www.irishtimes.com/business/transport-and-tourism/this-is-the-border-dublin-port-ireland-s-ground-zero-for-brexit-1.3762725

298 http://www.xinhuanet.com/english/2019-04/05/c_137950963.htm

299 https://www.rha.uk.net/news/press-releases/2018-11-november/don%E2%80%99t-let-m26-motorway-plans-divert-christmas-says-rha

300 https://www.gov.uk/settled-status-eu-citizens-families

301 https://www.parliament.uk/business/publications/written-questions-answers-statements/written-question/Commons/2019-04-25/247657/

302 https://news.sky.com/story/eu-settled-status-launch-sparks-fears-of-a-new-windrush-11613355

303 https://www.gov.uk/government/publications/eu-settlement-scheme-private-beta-1

304 https://www.gov.uk/government/publications/eu-settlement-scheme-private-beta-2/eu-settlement-scheme-private-beta-testing-phase-2-report

305 https://www.gov.uk/government/news/over-50000-applications-to-the-eu-settlement-scheme-on-opening-weekend

306 https://www.theguardian.com/politics/2019/oct/10/eu-nationals-lacking-settled-status-could-be-deported-minister-says

307 https://www.gov.uk/guidance/eu-settlement-scheme-application-fee-refunds

308 https://www.theguardian.com/politics/2019/oct/10/eu-nationals-lacking-settled-status-could-be-deported-minister-says

309 https://www.bbc.co.uk/news/business-49290926

310 https://www.thetimes.co.uk/article/sterling-deposits-are-cut-as-fears-rise-over-no-deal-g33xmc5db

311 https://www.uktech.news/news/industry-analysis/the-eus-investment-in-uk-tech-plunges-post-brexit-20180423

312 https://www.ft.com/content/a62c82f8-6052-11e9-b285-3acd5d43599e

313 https://www.independent.co.uk/news/uk/politics/uk-brexit-cost-referendum-eu-finance-eib-lords-transport-a8754656.html

314 https://www.accountancyage.com/2019/07/08/brexit-uncertainty-sees-city-jobs-dramatically-fall/

315 https://www.consilium.europa.eu/en/policies/relocation-london-agencies-brexit/

316 https://www.forbes.com/sites/francescoppola/2019/05/31/the-european-banking-authority-leaves-london/#232999a81715

317 https://www.bloombergquint.com/markets/marathon-s-richards-is-waiting-in-wings-for-u-k-brexit-slowdown

318 https://bylinetimes.com/2019/09/11/brexit-disaster-capitalism-8-billion-bet-on-no-deal-crash-out-by-boris-johnsons-leave-backers/

319 https://inews.co.uk/news/tory-donor-bets-300-million-on-losses-for-uk-firms-after-no-deal-brexit/

320 https://www.independent.co.uk/news/uk/politics/hedge-fund-manager-describes-moment-he-won-220-million-brexit-vote-the-morning-has-gold-in-its-mouth-a7323626.html

321 https://www.bbc.co.uk/news/business-47060676

322 https://www.hsbc.com/-/files/hsbc/investors/hsbc-results/2017/annual/hsbc-holdings-plc/180220-annual-report-and-accounts-2017.pdf

323 https://www.reuters.com/article/us-britain-eu-hsbc/hsbc-shifts-european-branches-to-french-unit-control-ahead-of-brexit-idUSKBN1KT1FX

324 https://www.bloomberg.com/news/articles/2019-04-12/what-brexit-will-cost-some-of-britain-s-leading-companies

325 https://inews.co.uk/news/business/hsbc-staff-job-cuts-london-paris-restructuring-brexit-uk-finance/

326 https://de.reuters.com/article/us-rbs-results/britains-rbs-sets-128-million-aside-to-cover-brexit-uncertainty-idUSKCN1N00M3

327 https://www.ftadviser.com/investments/2018/05/09/columbia-threadneedle-moves-uk-funds-over-brexit-fears/

328 https://www.rte.ie/news/business/2019/0213/1029338-bank-of-america-brexit-bill/

[329] https://www.risk.net/our-take/5831041/clearing-up-deutsches-swaps-shift

[330] https://www.bnnbloomberg.ca/london-loses-a-us-240b-month-market-thanks-to-brexit-1.1163913

[331] https://www.thetradenews.com/cme-group-approved-amsterdam-entity-ahead-brexit/

[332] https://www.fca.org.uk/publication/business-plans/business-plan-2018-19.pdf

[333] https://www.proactiveinvestors.co.uk/companies/news/200459/tp-icap-plunges-as-ceo-quits-amid-warning-that-brexit-related-costs-will-see-it-missing-2018-profit-expectations-200459.html

[334] https://www.prnewswire.co.uk/news-releases/canaccord-genuity-group-inc-announces-a-restructuring-of-its-uk-capital-markets-business-837810684.html

[335] https://www.insurancebusinessmag.com/uk/news/breaking-news/ms-amlin-gets-green-light-for-brexit-move-102565.aspx

[336] https://www.reuters.com/article/internaxx-ma-swissquote/update-1-swissquote-to-buy-luxembourgs-internaxx-to-bypass-brexit-idUSL5N1UY2GZ

[337] https://www.wsj.com/articles/standard-chartered-hopes-no-deal-brexit-planning-will-boost-growth-11559655491

[338] https://www.uk.daiwacm.com/site-tools/brexit-faqs

[339] https://www.bank-abc.com/world/ABCIB/En/AboutABC/Media/Press/Pages/Brexit_Update-Bank_ABC_in_Europe.aspx

[340] https://www.ft.com/content/d1e5af80-9ce3-38f3-805b-2e13646bdc22

[341] https://www.thetradenews.com/marketaxess-gains-approval-dutch-operation/

[342] https://www.reuters.com/article/uk-britain-eu-jpmorgan-paris/jpmorgan-plans-temporary-paris-hub-for-200-staff-if-no-deal-brexit-idUSKCN1Qh305

[343] https://www.fnlondon.com/articles/jpmorgan-has-spent-more-than-100m-on-brexit-as-it-primes-staff-to-leave-the-uk-20190325

[344] https://citywireselector.com/news/architas-bolsters-dublin-operations-as-part-of-brexit-plans/a1244109

[345] https://www.irishtimes.com/business/markets/goldcore-targets-brexit-fears-with-dublin-gold-vault-1.3696238

[346] https://www.usinenouvelle.com/article/la-plate-forme-d-echanges-xtx-choisit-paris-pour-l-apres-brexit.N762559

[347] https://www.credit-suisse.com/media/assets/investment-banking/docs/financial-regulatory/milan/ibcm-brexit-planning-with-credit-suisse.pdf

[348] https://www.nomuraholdings.com/investor/library/sec/20f/190625/190625_e.pdf

[349] https://www.itv.com/news/2018-08-08/nomura-contacts-eu-clients-about-frankfurt-migration-ahead-of-hard-brexit/

[350] https://www.man.com/documents/download/kdmwd-sMiRH-S2ozi-Qw5A2/Corporate_Annual_Report_For_the_year_ended_31_December_2018_English_31-12-2018.pdf

[351] https://www.man.com/documents/download/nnHwO-iogvq-aYTLU-NPhZC/Corporate_Interim_Report_For_the_six_months_ended_30_June_2019_English_30-06-2019.pdf

[352] https://techcrunch.com/2019/03/05/fintexit/

[353] https://uk.reuters.com/article/uk-britain-eu-mufg/japans-mufg-says-picks-amsterdam-as-eu-investment-banking-base-idUKKCN1BO013

[354] https://www.financemagnates.com/institutional-forex/regulation/mufg-securities-opens-european-subsidiary-in-amsterdam/

[355] https://www.bloomberg.com/news/articles/2019-07-03/mufg-targets-50-job-cuts-in-london-voluntary-redundancy-plan

[356] https://www.thetradenews.com/hermes-implements-brexit-mitigation-plan-new-irish-entity/

[357] https://www.smbc.co.jp/news_e/e600486_01.html

[358] https://otp.tools.investis.com/clients/uk/standard_life/rns/regulatory-story.aspx?cid=65&newsid=1141631

[359] https://www.insurancejournal.com/news/international/2018/11/13/507321.htm

[360] https://www.bbc.co.uk/news/business-44805565

[361] https://info.stmgroupplc.com/stm-life-brexit-planning/

[362] https://www.rsagroup.com/support/brexit-information-and-documents-for-rsa-europe-policy-holders/

[363] https://www.thisismoney.co.uk/wires/reuters/article-6781077/Insurer-Admiral-warns-economic-disruption-hard-Brexit.html

[364] https://uk.reuters.com/article/uk-britain-eu-idUKKCN1Q81YW

[365] https://www.independent.ie/business/brexit/royal-londons-ireland-brexit-move-to-cost-21m-37790666.html

[366] https://www.hiscoxgroup.com/about-hiscox/partvii

[367] http://www.markelinternational.com/brexit/

[368] https://www.libertyspecialtymarkets.com/press-releases/liberty-announces-intention-headquarter-post-brexit-eu-operations-luxemboug/

[369] https://www.libertyspecialtymarkets.com/press-releases/liberty-redomicile-uk-insurance-company-luxemboug/

[370] https://www.insurancebusinessmag.com/uk/news/breaking-news/liberty-specialty-markets-granted-licence-for-brexit-hub-118789.aspx

[371] https://www.aig.be/microsites/brexit

[372] http://www.tokiomarinekiln.com/news-views/news-releases/tokio-marine-group-receives-approval-to-complete-its-part-vii-transfer-ahead-of-brexit/

[373] https://calvinayre.com/2019/05/23/business/bet365-shifting-gibraltar-ops-malta-brexit-uncertainty/

[374] https://timesofmalta.com/articles/view/uk-gambling-giant-bet365-moving-to-malta-post-brexit.679462

[375] https://www.irishexaminer.com/breakingnews/business/ladbrokes-eyes-back-office-switch-to-ireland-908957.html

[376] https://www.sbcnews.co.uk/retail/2019/03/05/brexit-upheaval-sees-gvc-shift-focus-to-ireland-and-malta/

[377] https://londonlovesbusiness.com/888-holdings-prepares-for-a-disruptive-brexit/

[378] https://psnc.org.uk/wp-content/uploads/2019/08/PSNC-Briefing-023.19-Serious-Shortage-Protocols-FINAL-PUBLISHED-v2.0.pdf

[379] https://pharmaphorum.com/news/ema-cuts-services-amid-brexit-staff-exodus/

[380] https://www.ema.europa.eu/en/news/ema-now-operating-amsterdam

[381] https://www.rcplondon.ac.uk/news/490-million-question-new-cost-overseas-health-workers-post-brexit

[382] https://www.fiercebiotech.com/cro/recardio-puts-brakes-new-heart-drug-trials-u-k-over-brexit-concerns

[383] https://www.gsk.com/media/5349/annual-report-2018.pdf

[384] http://d18rn0p25nwr6d.cloudfront.net/CIK-0000078003/7f755a1d-48c9-45fd-808e-773f05f764be.pdf

[385] https://www.irishtimes.com/business/health-pharma/brexit-pushes-steris-to-move-again-to-ireland-1.3695410

[386] https://www.wasdell.co.uk/news/2370/

[387] https://www.wasdell.co.uk/news/operations-commence-at-wasdell-groups-eu-headquarters/

[388] https://uk.reuters.com/article/uk-britain-eu-astrazeneca/astrazeneca-will-keep-uk-investment-freeze-if-no-brexit-clarity-idUKKCN1MP1Q9

[389] https://www.biopharmadive.com/news/astrazeneca-duplicating-uk-testing-as-brexit-looms/542084/

[390] https://www.supplychaindive.com/news/AstraZeneca-supply-chain-adjustment-Brexit/548694/

[391] https://www.england.nhs.uk/wp-content/uploads/2019/07/ongoing-eu-exit-preparations-letter-kw.pdf

[392] https://www.boydconsultants.com/new-dublin-office-in-ireland-for-boyds/

[393] https://www.accu-chek.co.uk/filedownload/25626

[394] https://www.almacgroup.com/news/almac-group-announces-further-expansion-at-its-european-campus-in-dundalk/

[395] https://uk.reuters.com/article/uk-dechra-pharma-brexit/dechra-pharma-says-to-implement-hard-brexit-plan-idUKKCN1LJ0MP

[396] https://www.ft.com/content/d4ac54e6-4310-11e9-b168-96a37d002cd3

[397] https://www.theguardian.com/society/2019/may/08/nhs-nursing-crisis-worsened-by-brexit-exodus

[398] https://www.thetimes.co.uk/article/safety-giant-bsi-bets-on-holland-wbhm5m9kl

[399] https://www.bloomberg.com/news/articles/2018-09-13/brexit-a-five-year-curve-of-pain-as-costs-set-to-surge-j-j-says

[400] https://www.sheffieldtelegraph.co.uk/news/aps3m-cost-of-brexita-a-drain-on-sheffield-healthcare-firma-187847

[401] https://www.theguardian.com/business/2019/aug/06/dominos-stockpiles-toppings-to-beat-any-no-deal-brexit

[402] https://www.uk.saputo.com/news/2019/trading-update-for-the-nine-months-ended-31-december-2018/

[403] https://www.thisismoney.co.uk/money/markets/article-7032343/Pub-group-Marstons-stockpiled-6m-worth-beer-Brexit.html

[404] https://www.bbc.co.uk/news/business-49258852

[405] https://www.pressandjournal.co.uk/fp/business/farming/1762096/qms-beefs-up-its-coffers-in-event-of-no-deal-brexit/

[406] https://www.irishtimes.com/business/retail-and-services/bewley-s-posts-loss-after-taking-12m-brexit-goodwill-write-down-1.3706102

[407] https://www.thedrinksbusiness.com/2019/07/irish-company-cc-to-move-listing-to-london/

[408] https://harpers.co.uk/news/fullstory.php/aid/25184/Romanian_group_pulls_out_of_LWF_as_Brexit_hits_funding.html

[409] https://www.just-drinks.com/news/uks-pirates-grog-rum-battles-brexit-with-bottling-switch-to-netherlands_id127357.aspx

[410] https://www.blackpoolgazette.co.uk/news/business/triple-blow-causes-fylde-meats-firm-to-close-1-9325393

[411] https://beta.companieshouse.gov.uk/company/01356795/filing-history/MzE5MTg2MDQzNmFkaXF6a2N4/document?format=pdf&download=0

[412] https://www.dailyrecord.co.uk/news/business-consumer/brexit-blow-scotlands-biggest-turkey-13770399

[413] https://news.sky.com/story/nestle-warns-of-very-severe-no-deal-brexit-11565092

[414] https://www.fnlondon.com/articles/nestle-ceo-mark-schneider-brexit-will-not-leave-our-cupboards-bare-20190708

[415] https://www.nestle.be/fr/lentreprise/faq/lentreprise/brexit

[416] https://www.thegrocer.co.uk/wholesalers/nhs-hot-meals-supplier-apetito-invests-in-brexit-stockpiling/596894.article

[417] https://www.bbc.co.uk/news/business-46191729

[418] https://www.lbc.co.uk/news/lidl-warns-british-suppliers-of-the-rising-costs-o/

[419] https://www.theguardian.com/world/2019/sep/12/no-deal-brexit-likely-to-push-up-price-of-bread-in-ireland

[420] https://amp.independent.ie/business/farming/agri-business/flour-power-meet-the-cereal-growers-driving-a-25m-flour-mill-project-37634153.html

[421] https://www.theguardian.com/politics/2018/nov/05/brexit-metropolitan-police-rush-set-up-no-deal-safety-net-unit

[422] https://inews.co.uk/news/brexit/brexit-no-deal-traffic-dover-lorries-hauliers/

[423] https://www.scotland.police.uk/whats-happening/news/2019/july/police-scotlands-brexit-contingency-plans-reactivated

[424] https://www.bbc.co.uk/news/uk-scotland-scotland-politics-49387542

[425] https://www.thescottishsun.co.uk/news/4139042/brexit-police-scotland-2-5m-bill-eu/

[426] https://www.thelocal.es/20190329/spain-takes-over-eu-anti-piracy-mission-from-britain-due-to-brexit

[427] https://www.thejournal.ie/ship-launching-celine-dublin-port-3969187-Apr2018/

[428] https://afloat.ie/port-news/dublin-port/item/42098-new-brexit-buster-sister-ship-mv-laureline-expands-dublin-port-s-direct-route-cargo-sailings-to-europe

[429]

https://assets.publishing.service.gov.uk/government/uploads/system/uploads/attachment_data/file/785497/shipping-fleet-statistics-2018.pdf

430 https://theloadstar.com/uncertainty-over-brexit-driving-shipowners-to-run-down-the-uk-flag/

431 https://www.irishexaminer.com/breakingnews/ireland/ringaskiddy-boosts-customs-capacity-under-brexit-plan-942234.html

432 https://www.rte.ie/news/munster/2019/0709/1061031-waterford-port-rotterdam/

433 https://www.bbc.co.uk/news/uk-england-47845057

434 https://www.transport-network.co.uk/Declining-car-industry-pleads-No-deal-Brexit-would-cause-devastation/15905

435 https://www.autonews.com/article/20181025/COPY01/310259922/jaguar-land-rover-launches-slovak-plant-amid-brexit-jobs-fears

436 https://news.sky.com/story/uk-car-firms-have-spent-330m-on-no-deal-brexit-plans-11773871

437 https://www.theguardian.com/business/2019/jul/09/bmw-engine-production-uk-brexit-fears

438 https://news.sky.com/story/brexit-pain-blamed-as-car-store-owner-cuts-300-jobs-11812786

439 https://www.bbc.co.uk/news/uk-northern-ireland-36656558

440 http://www.irishnews.com/business/2018/06/06/news/95-more-jobs-going-at-wrightbus—and-brexit-is-being-blamed-1348577/

441 https://www.bbc.co.uk/news/uk-northern-ireland-49818156

442 https://www.bbc.co.uk/news/business-44614352

443 https://www.shropshirestar.com/news/uk-news/2019/06/27/heathrow-owner-hikes-earnings-outlook-after-slashing-brexit-contingency-costs/

444 https://www.theguardian.com/business/2019/jul/28/uk-aerospace-industry-steps-up-no-deal-brexit-plan-to-leave-regulator

445 http://corporate.easyjet.com/~/media/Files/E/Easyjet/pdf/investors/results-centre/2018/easyjet-h2-2018-results.pdf

446 https://www.dartgroup.co.uk/uploadedFiles/Dart_Group_Plc/Shared_Resources_(Images,_docs_etc)/Documents/Report_And_Accounts/Dart-AR2019.pdf

447 https://www.airlineratings.com/news/flybmi-files-bankruptcy-blames-brexit/

448 https://www.thelocal.de/20181212/rolls-royce-to-switch-work-to-germany-over-brexit

449 https://www.rolls-royce.com/~/media/Files/R/Rolls-Royce/documents/annual-report/2018/2018-full-annual-report.pdf

450 https://www.theguardian.com/business/2019/aug/06/chief-says-rolls-royce-spent-100m-preparing-for-no-deal-brexit

451 https://ec.europa.eu/inea/connecting-europe-facility/cef-transport

452 https://ec.europa.eu/inea/sites/inea/files/cefpub/eu_investment_in_transport_in_uk.pdf

453 https://www.gov.uk/government/news/space-sector-to-benefit-from-multi-million-pound-work-on-uk-alternative-to-galileo

454 https://www.theregister.co.uk/2018/08/28/uk_may_go_it_alone_on_galileo/

455 https://www.esa.int/Our_Activities/Navigation/Galileo_s_ground_control_segment_contracted_for_upgrade

456 https://www.halfordscompany.com/media/2565/halfords-fy19-interim-results-rns.pdf

457 https://news.artnet.com/market/david-zwirner-gallery-paris-1598059

458 https://metro.co.uk/2019/03/14/body-shop-announces-jobs-to-go-to-germany-in-wake-of-brexit-8898082/

459 http://nationaltechnology.co.uk/Panasonic_Moves_EU_HQ_Amsterdam.php

460 https://asia.nikkei.com/Business/Companies/Sony-to-move-European-base-to-Holland-as-Brexit-nears

461 https://www.bristolpost.co.uk/news/business/bristol-sports-company-moving-europe-2343320

462 https://cyclingindustry.news/freestyle-extreme-ceases-trading-seemingly-blaming-brexit/

[463] https://www.bbc.co.uk/news/business-47071874

[464] https://www.theguardian.com/business/2018/sep/13/john-lewis-profits-dive-99-percent

[465] https://uk.reuters.com/article/uk-johnlewis-results/john-lewis-cuts-staff-bonus-ahead-of-brexit-idUKKCN1QO103

[466] https://www.standard.co.uk/news/politics/nodeal-brexit-alert-as-john-lewis-unveils-first-loss-in-155-years-a4234826.html

[467] https://www.swissinfo.ch/eng/in-case-of-brexit-emergency—a-stockpile-of-luxury-swiss-watches/44834166

[468] https://www.thelocal.ch/20190327/why-luxury-watchmakers-are-worried-about-brexit-switzerland-baseland

[469] https://www.belfasttelegraph.co.uk/business/uk-world/ao-world-founder-condemns-brexit-costs-as-wasted-money-38035717.html

[470] https://www.retail-week.com/electricals/aocom-boss-we-wasted-millions-on-brexit-non-event/7032077.article

[471] https://www.standard.co.uk/news/uk/pets-at-home-stockpiles-millions-of-pounds-worth-of-stock-so-families-dont-run-out-food-for-animals-a4001636.html

[472] https://www.retailgazette.co.uk/blog/2019/05/pets-at-home-warns-on-further-stockpiling-amid-no-deal-brexit-threat/

[473] https://www.retail-insight-network.com/news/majestic-wine-assets-sale-bidco/

[474] https://www.independent.ie/business/brexit/bisto-owner-sees-irish-sales-sink-as-brexit-stocks-unwind-38322393.html

[475] https://www.bbc.co.uk/news/av/uk-england-birmingham-49258311/parcel-firm-dpd-has-no-deal-brexit-warehouse-in-oldbury

[476] https://www.confectionerynews.com/Article/2018/09/11/Mondelez-prepares-for-a-no-deal-Brexit-by-stockpiling-chocolate

[477] https://www.bbc.co.uk/news/business-46107834

[478] https://www.elektron-technology.com/wp-content/uploads/2019/07/Elektron-Technology-plc-Annual-Report-and-Accounts-2019.pdf

[479] https://www.theregister.co.uk/2018/10/18/scisys_sidesteps_brexit_with_a_proposed_irish_listing_to_keep_eu_space_work_rolling_in/

[480] https://www.theregister.co.uk/2018/12/17/galileo_scisys/

[481] https://www.theregister.co.uk/2019/02/20/apples_reseller_pulls_down_the_shutters_calls_in_the_administrators/

[482] https://beta.companieshouse.gov.uk/company/02994117/filing-history/MzIwMTg0ODc1M2FkaXF6a2N4/document?format=pdf&download=0

[483] https://www.diyweek.net/new-safety-mark-replacement-could-cost-uk-manufacturers-millions

[484] https://publications.parliament.uk/pa/ld201719/ldselect/ldeucom/215/215.pdf

[485] https://www.northantstelegraph.co.uk/news/loss-of-110-jobs-as-wellingborough-manufacturing-site-closes-1-8478831

[486] https://investors.eurocell.co.uk/media/1213/eurocell-interim-results-2019-rns.pdf

[487] https://www.kidderminstershuttle.co.uk/news/regional/17481308.brexit-blamed-for-hereford-factorys-closure/?ref=twtrec

[488] https://www.eadt.co.uk/business/companies-leaving-the-uk-because-of-brexit-uncertainty-1-5855954?fbclid=IwAR33RxCileBvuMFnEORcvDLncjbNcJu6x5QlJn7mRzQ0SNmmiQyxeRU9gUw

[489] https://www.newsandstar.co.uk/news/17690070.dmack-tyre-boss-scraps-plan-new-200m-factory-carlisle—-blames-brexit/

[490] https://www.tirebusiness.com/news/uk-race-tire-company-dmack-administration

[491] https://www.waterloo.co.uk/news/brexit-contingency-planning/

[492] http://www.aztecoils.co.uk/default.aspx?pageid=2720&catid=53&topicid=1066

493 https://www.gwp.co.uk/news/new-warehouse-to-support-jit-service/

494 https://www.nytimes.com/2019/01/31/business/brexit-european-union.html

495 https://www.pressandjournal.co.uk/fp/business/north-of-scotland/1754588/robotics-company-cites-brexit-in-european-expansion/

496 https://www.foodingredientsfirst.com/news/bracing-for-brexit-diverse-and-secure-supply-chain-is-vital-for-mitigating-no-deal-difficulties-says-ulrick-short.html

497 https://www.reuters.com/article/us-britain-eu-aerospace-analysis/brexit-race-to-stockpile-pushes-some-of-uks-aerospace-suppliers-to-the-brink-idUSKCN1NR1QB

498 https://www.itv.com/news/wales/2019-04-17/car-parts-manufacturer-calsonic-kansei-announces-95-job-losses-at-llanelli-site/

499 https://www.theguardian.com/business/2019/jan/07/brompton-bike-parts-hard-brexit

500 http://www.spiraxsarcoengineering.com/Investors/Documents/Spirax-Sarco%20Engineering%20plc%20Annual%20Report%202018.pdf

501 https://www.renishaw.com/media/pdf/en/3ff4aac5ec7e489aa5042f2738efe3e4.pdf

502 https://www.londonstockexchange.com/exchange/news/market-news/market-news-detail/VLX/13860975.html

503 https://www.fginsight.com/news/news/farm-machinery-manufacturers-stockpile-tractors-due-to-brexit-fears-79532

504 https://www.bloomberg.com/news/articles/2019-05-09/lingering-trade-tension-is-poison-for-us-tractor-maker-says

505 https://www.uktech.news/news/british-robot-firm-moves-production-madrid-maintain-eu-base-post-brexit-20170525

506 https://www.roboticsbusinessreview.com/legal/london-robotics-company-considers-options-brexit/

507 https://www.huffingtonpost.co.uk/entry/business-stockpiling-no-deal-brexit_uk_5d52aaa1e4b05fa9df04b47

508 https://www.electrocomponents.com/investor-centre/annual-report-2019

509 https://torque-expo.com/hexstone-puts-contingencies-in-place-ahead-of-brexit/

510 https://www.msn.com/en-gb/money/business/small-businesses-steel-themselves-for-no-deal-brexit/ar-BBU2vor

511 https://www.standard.co.uk/business/diploma-starts-to-stockpile-parts-ahead-of-brexit-a3993891.html

512 https://www.legalbusiness.co.uk/blogs/dla-becomes-latest-firm-to-make-post-brexit-dublin-move-after-lengthy-consideration/

513 https://llm-guide.com/articles/as-uk-law-firms-enjoy-the-boom-times-how-can-you-become-a-lawyer-in-the-uk

514 https://www.forbes.com/sites/oliverwilliams1/2019/07/31/theres-a-brexit-bonus-boom-for-these-professionals/#1e19093943fd

515 https://www.nytimes.com/2019/03/31/business/law-firms-brexit.html

516 https://www.cityam.com/listed-law-firm-dwf-riding-high-on-brexit-related-litigation/

517 https://www.breakingnews.ie/ireland/tsunami-rise-in-number-of-solicitors-from-england-and-wales-registering-in-ireland-886563.html

518 http://www.lex100.com/index.php/news/news-2/1465-real-opportunity-in-ireland-lewis-silkin-becomes-fourth-firm-to-open-in-dublin-post-brexit-vote

519 https://www.getsurrey.co.uk/news/surrey-news/university-surrey-cut-staff-citing-15885247?fbclid=IwAR2Zxl5epw3FmY0PQ3cPl5Xn5hUM8vDRw_H5arUDx4GkwYgA55CAUp8z7bM

520 https://www.theguardian.com/education/2017/aug/29/universities-abroad-headhunting-ucl-eu-researchers-brexit

521 https://www.bbc.co.uk/news/uk-wales-36799951

522 https://www.itv.com/news/wales/2017-05-09/aberystwyth-university-writes-to-members-of-staff-requesting-voluntary-redundancies-in-bid-to-make-savings/

523

https://www.downsmail.co.uk/news_sport/News/JOB_LOSSES_College_staff_in_strike_ballot_over_3.5m_in_cuts/

524 https://www.bbc.co.uk/news/uk-wales-south-east-wales-39441926

525 https://www.bbc.co.uk/news/business-45789503

526 https://russellgroup.ac.uk/news/fall-in-eu-student-numbers/

527 https://www.britishcouncil.org/research-policy-insight/insight-articles/language-trends

528 https://www.theconstructionindex.co.uk/news/view/dawnus-administrators-cite-brexit

529 https://www.building.co.uk/news/gleeds-blames-brexit-for-job-cuts/5099753.article#.XPI8AJu5BqU.twitter

530 https://www.countrywide.co.uk/corporate/investor-relations/reports-presentations/2019/countrywide-interim-report-2019.pdf/

531 https://techcrunch.com/2019/03/14/nested-brexit/

532 https://www.walesonline.co.uk/news/politics/m4-relief-road-newport-brexit-16587653

533 https://otp.tools.investis.com/clients/uk/savills-plc/rns/regulatory-story.aspx?newsid=1320536&cid=181

534 https://www.bdonline.co.uk/news/richard-rogers-confirms-job-losses-at-rshp/5096012.article

535 https://www.msn.com/en-gb/money/business/small-businesses-steel-themselves-for-no-deal-brexit/ar-BBU2vor

536 https://www.bloomberg.com/news/articles/2019-08-02/many-u-k-companies-are-taking-their-chances-with-a-no-deal-brexit

537 https://architectprojects.co.uk/make-architects-blames-brexit-uncertainty-for-12-revenue-fall-in-2017/

538 https://www.bdonline.co.uk/news/make-blames-brexit-for-job-losses/5096714.article

539 https://www.cityam.com/construction-industry-orders-decline-at-fastest-rate-in-a-decade/

540 https://www.peterboroughtoday.co.uk/business/thomas-cook-to-axe-100-jobs-at-its-peterborough-office-as-it-seeks-to-cut-costs-1-8926697

541 https://www.peterboroughtoday.co.uk/business/peterborough-s-thomas-cook-reveals-a-1-5-billion-loss-as-brexit-hits-holiday-bookings-1-8929471

542 https://www.businessinsider.com/thomas-cook-bankrupt-airline-stranded-rescue-2019-9

543 https://www.theguardian.com/business/2019/oct/09/hundreds-of-thomas-cook-jobs-saved-as-uk-stores-bought-up

544 http://www.travelweekly.co.uk/articles/328459/saga-warns-brexit-a-clear-dampener-on-2019-holiday-bookings

545 https://uk.reuters.com/article/uk-saga-results/saga-shares-plunge-as-older-britons-cut-back-on-european-travel-idUKKCN1RG0L8

546 https://beta.companieshouse.gov.uk/company/01555368/filing-history/MzIzOTU1NjIxMWFkaXF6a2N4/document?format=pdf&download=0

547 https://eurid.eu/en/register-a-eu-domain/brexit-notice/

548 https://eurid.eu/en/news/brexit-and-eu-rules-for-eu-citizens/

549 https://www.politico.eu/article/uk-splashes-out-700000-on-furniture-for-brexit-office/

550 https://www.thirdsector.co.uk/brexit-stockpiling-hits-charities-relying-donated-goods/policy-and-politics/article/1592101

551 https://www.bloomberg.com/news/articles/2019-02-01/jetsetter-magazine-monocle-shifts-printing-to-germany-on-brexit

552 https://www.gaystarnews.com/article/gay-star-news-is-closing-you-deserve-the-full-story-all-our-thanks-and-love/#gs.t7lskc

553 https://www.printweek.com/print-week/news/1167076/jamm-sets-up-in-prague-due-to-brexit

554 https://www.theolivepress.es/spain-news/2019/04/10/west-end-theatre-company-behind-fame-and-little-shop-of-horrors-moves-to-spain-over-brexit-fears/

555 https://www.kentonline.co.uk/maidstone/news/rare-orchids-dug-up-in-brexit-preparations-202728/

556 https://www.aljazeera.com/news/2019/03/brexit-fears-art-dealers-ship-work-uk-190310125947106.html

557 https://news.artnet.com/market/brexit-london-art-galleries-1495789

558 https://news.sky.com/story/de-la-rue-cuts-jobs-after-loss-of-post-brexit-passport-work-11748748

559 https://www.chroniclelive.co.uk/business/business-news/north-east-business-news-live-14718605

560 https://www.pressandjournal.co.uk/fp/news/moray/1629669/brexit-costs-ministry-of-defence-155m-in-raf-lossiemouth-poseidon-savings/

561 https://www.thestage.co.uk/news/2019/edinburgh-international-festival-performers-reject-sterling-payments-over-brexit-fears/

562 https://www.itv.com/news/wales/2019-03-29/church-in-abergavenny-opens-its-doors-for-a-special-day-of-brexit-prayers/

563 https://www.bbc.co.uk/news/business-46016359

564 https://www.thesun.co.uk/news/8659312/special-50p-coins-celebrating-brexit-produced-with-wrong-date-on-them/

565 https://uk.finance.yahoo.com/news/more-than-10-million-commemorative-brexit-50-p-coins-will-be-minted-095319489.html

566 https://www.printweek.com/print-week/news/1166720/blake-reshores-production-ahead-of-brexit

567 https://www.ft.com/content/dcd098e4-3997-11e9-b72b-2c7f526ca5d0

568 https://uk.reuters.com/article/us-britain-economy-bankruptcy/uk-company-insolvencies-hit-five-year-high-in-second-quarter-idUKKCN1UP1AN

569 https://www.tvbeurope.com/business/broadcasters-begin-moving-licences-away-from-uk

570 https://tbivision.com/2019/03/22/tbi-weekly-brexit-fallout-signals-more-competition-for-uk-businesses/

571 https://www.printweek.com/print-week/news/1167456/go-inspire-restructures-kettering-solutions-site

572 https://www.bbc.co.uk/news/uk-politics-47652071

573 https://petition.parliament.uk/petitions/241584

574 https://en.wikipedia.org/wiki/UK_Parliament_petitions_website

575 https://eur-lex.europa.eu/legal-content/EN/TXT/?uri=uriserv:OJ.L_.2014.132.01.0001.01.ENG

576 https://www.theguardian.com/politics/2017/nov/23/eu-rules-british-cities-cannot-be-capitals-of-culture

577 https://ec.europa.eu/programmes/creative-europe/actions/capitals-culture_en

578 https://www.thesun.co.uk/news/7676717/brit-haulier-outraged-no-deal-fears/

579 https://www.bbc.co.uk/news/business-48776125

580 https://inews.co.uk/news/politics/brexit/brexit-referendum-cost-2016-electoral-commission-187554

581 https://www.sec.gov/Archives/edgar/data/1441693/000149315218004788/form10-k.htm

582 https://en.wikipedia.org/wiki/European_Union_Baroque_Orchestra

583 https://www.theguardian.com/politics/2017/feb/18/baroque-orchestra-eu-britain-brexit-immigration-free-movement

584 https://www.smmt.co.uk/industry-topics/uk-automotive/

585 http://data.parliament.uk/writtenevidence/committeeevidence.svc/evidencedocument/international-trade-committee/uk-trade-options-beyond-2019/oral/48155.pdf

586 https://hansard.parliament.uk/Commons/2013-02-07/debates/13020759000029/TopicalQuestions?highlight=nissan#contribution-13020759000169

587 https://www.telegraph.co.uk/finance/newsbysector/industry/10364535/Britain-must-stay-in-the-EU-says-Nissan-boss.html

588 https://www.coventrytelegraph.net/news/uk-world-news/nissan-boss-leave-eu-leave-6285353

589 https://hansard.parliament.uk/Commons/2015-09-07/debates/15090723000001/EuropeanUnionReferendumBill?highlight=nissan#contribution-1509083001343

590 http://nissaninsider.co.uk/nissan-it-makes-sense-for-uk-to-remain-in-eu/

591 https://www.theguardian.com/business/2016/sep/30/nissan-hard-brexit-compensation-new-uk-investment-

tariffs

592 https://www.politicshome.com/news/uk/economy/manufacturing/news/80319/greg-clark-reveals-government-assurances-secure-nissan

593 https://assets.publishing.service.gov.uk/government/uploads/system/uploads/attachment_data/file/776095/Letter-from-BEIS-Secretary-of-State-to-Carlos-Ghosn-October_2016.pdf

594 https://www.bbc.co.uk/news/business-37787890

595 http://data.parliament.uk/writtenevidence/committeeevidence.svc/evidencedocument/international-trade-committee/uk-trade-options-beyond-2019/oral/48155.pdf

596 https://www.bbc.co.uk/news/live/business-44574865?ns_mchannel=social&ns_source=twitter&ns_campaign=bbc_live&ns_linkname=5b33a6bb26200f067b046175%26%27We%20have%20no%20clue%20how%20Brexit%20will%20play%20out%27%26&ns_fee=0#post_5b33a6bb26200f067b046175

597 https://asia.nikkei.com/Business/Companies/Nissan-wants-UK-pay-talks-pushed-to-2019-awaiting-Brexit-impact

598 https://www.itv.com/news/tyne-tees/2018-10-04/nissan-warns-hard-brexit-will-have-serious-implications-on-sunderland-factory/

599 https://www.independent.co.uk/news/business/news/mercedes-benz-brexit-production-move-nissan-plant-sunderland-a8568331.html

600 http://ec.europa.eu/trade/policy/in-focus/eu-japan-economic-partnership-agreement/

601 https://www.itv.com/news/tyne-tees/2019-02-03/nissan-confirm-to-make-new-x-trail-suv-in-japan-scrapping-original-plans-to-build-in-sunderland/

602 https://fortune.com/2019/03/13/brexit-nissan-infiniti-sunderland/

603 https://www.autocar.co.uk/car-news/new-cars/nissan-juke-production-begins-sunderland-plant

604 https://www.theguardian.com/politics/2019/oct/10/nissan-no-deal-brexit-would-jeopardise-entire-european-business-model

605 https://www.express.co.uk/news/uk/682947/eu-referendum-bbc-brexit

606 https://www.independent.co.uk/news/uk/politics/eu-referendum-result-nigel-farage-nhs-pledge-disowns-350-million-pounds-a7099906.html

607 https://www.youtube.com/watch?v=fXNV3Ad0qQ0

608 https://www.bbc.co.uk/news/uk-politics-39761410

609 https://en.wikipedia.org/wiki/2016_Conservative_Party_leadership_election_(UK)

610 https://en.wiktionary.org/wiki/Maybot

611 https://en.wikipedia.org/wiki/Theresa_May

612 https://www.bbc.co.uk/news/uk-northern-ireland-36789572

613 https://www.politicshome.com/news/europe/eu-policy-agenda/brexit/news/77524/angela-merkel-backs-theresa-mays-plan-not-trigger

614 https://www.gov.uk/government/speeches/the-governments-negotiating-objectives-for-exiting-the-eu-pm-speech

615 https://en.wikipedia.org/wiki/Causes_of_the_vote_in_favour_of_Brexit

616 https://www.rand.org/pubs/external_publications/EP67713.html

617 https://en.wikipedia.org/wiki/R_(Miller)_v_Secretary_of_State_for_Exiting_the_European_Union

618 https://www.theguardian.com/us-news/video/2017/jan/27/trump-may-hold-hands-white-house-video

619 https://www.gov.uk/government/news/new-electricity-connection-to-france-gets-go-ahead

620 https://www.newpower.info/2019/08/eleclink-interconnector-consults-on-no-deal-brexit-trading-rules/

621 https://www.consilium.europa.eu/en/press/press-releases/2017/03/29/euco-50-statement-uk-notification/

622 https://www.conservatives.com/manifesto

623 https://labour.org.uk/wp-content/uploads/2017/10/labour-manifesto-2017.pdf

624 http://data.consilium.europa.eu/doc/document/XT-21023-2017-INIT/en/pdf

625 https://ec.europa.eu/commission/brexit-negotiations/negotiating-documents-article-50-negotiations-united-kingdom_en

626 https://en.wikipedia.org/wiki/2017_United_Kingdom_general_election

627 https://www.telegraph.co.uk/news/2017/06/26/arlene-foster-meet-theresa-may-finalise-dup-deal-prop-tory-minority/

628 https://www.ft.com/content/01396086-38ae-11e7-821a-6027b8a20f23

629 https://www.theguardian.com/politics/2017/jun/20/row-of-the-summer-with-the-eu-over-brexit-timetable-ends-in-uk-climbdown

630 https://www.gov.uk/government/publications/safeguarding-the-position-of-eu-citizens-in-the-uk-and-uk-nationals-in-the-eu

631 https://www.bbc.co.uk/news/uk-politics-40403431

632 https://www.gov.uk/government/news/canada-trade-deal-offers-boost-to-british-business-and-opens-the-door-for-future-trade

633 https://www.gov.uk/government/news/uk-trade-with-canada-up-14-since-new-free-trade-agreement-introduced

634 https://www.bbc.co.uk/news/uk-politics-41733429

635 https://www.bbc.co.uk/news/business-42050742

636 https://www.politico.eu/article/brexit-ema-eba-european-banking-authority-european-medicines-agency-everything-you-need-to-know-about-the-eu-agencies-leaving-london-because-of-brexit/

637 https://www.theguardian.com/politics/2017/dec/08/sufficient-progress-in-brexit-talks-announced-after-mays-dash-to-brussels

638 https://www.businessinsider.com/government-publishes-39-brexit-sectoral-reports-2017-12?r=US&IR=T

639 https://www.newstatesman.com/politics/staggers/2017/12/many-times-david-davis-talked-about-brexit-analysis-he-says-doesn-t-exist

640 https://www.parliament.uk/business/committees/committees-a-z/commons-select/exiting-the-european-union-committee/news-parliament-2017/sectoral-analyses-published-evidence-17-19/

641 https://ec.europa.eu/commission/sites/beta-political/files/draft_withdrawal_agreement.pdf

642 https://ec.europa.eu/commission/publications/draft-agreement-withdrawal-united-kingdom-great-britain-and-northern-ireland-european-union-and-european-atomic-energy-community-0_en

643 https://www.gov.uk/government/publications/the-future-relationship-between-the-united-kingdom-and-the-european-union

644 https://www.bbc.co.uk/news/uk-politics-44749993

645 https://inews.co.uk/news/brexit/theresa-may-faces-brexit-crisis-at-eu-leaders-reject-her-chequers-proposals/

646 https://www.theguardian.com/politics/2018/sep/20/donald-tusk-demands-answer-to-irish-border-question-next-month

647 https://www.bbc.co.uk/news/uk-politics-45488136

648 https://www.express.co.uk/news/politics/1046208/theresa-may-no-confidence-vote-brexit-mark-francois-letter-brexit-deal

649 https://www.theguardian.com/politics/2018/nov/15/dominic-raab-quits-as-brexit-secretary-over-eu-withdrawal-deal

650 https://www.bbc.co.uk/news/uk-politics-46142188

651 https://www.bbc.co.uk/news/uk-46241693

652 https://www.consilium.europa.eu/en/meetings/european-council/2018/11/25/

653 https://www.theguardian.com/politics/2018/dec/12/theresa-may-defeats-leadership-challenge-by-83-votes

654 https://www.gov.uk/government/news/uk-welcomes-approval-of-new-trade-agreement-with-japan

655 https://www.bbc.co.uk/news/uk-politics-46599895

656 https://www.standard.co.uk/news/politics/corbyn-to-table-no-confidence-vote-in-theresa-may-if-she-fails-to-

announce-date-of-mps-vote-on-her-a4019676.html

657 https://www.standard.co.uk/news/uk/lorries-queue-in-fake-traffic-jam-in-test-of-no-deal-brexit-border-chaos-a4031926.html

658 https://www.theguardian.com/uk-news/2019/may/01/chris-grayling-cancels-ferry-contracts-at-extra-50m-cost-to-taxpayers-brexit

659 https://www.parliament.uk/business/news/2019/parliamentary-news-2019/meaningful-vote-on-brexit-resumes-in-the-commons/

660 https://www.parliament.uk/business/news/2019/march/key-brexit-vote-as-meaningful-vote-returns-to-the-commons/

661 https://www.theguardian.com/politics/2019/mar/14/mps-vote-by-majority-of-210-to-extend-article-50-and-delay-brexit

662 https://www.gov.uk/government/news/uk-and-faroe-islands-sign-trade-continuity-agreement

663 https://data.consilium.europa.eu/doc/document/XT-20005-2019-INIT/en/pdf

664 https://data.consilium.europa.eu/doc/document/XT-20006-2019-INIT/en/pdf

665 https://metro.co.uk/2019/03/21/petition-revoke-article-50-cancel-brexit-smashes-target-8958623/

666 https://www.theguardian.com/politics/2019/mar/21/petitions-site-crashes-after-thousands-back-call-to-revoke-article-50

667 https://www.standard.co.uk/news/politics/petition-to-cancel-brexit-altogether-hits-25m-signatures-and-rising-but-theresa-may-says-it-doesnt-a4098266.html

668 https://www.theguardian.com/politics/2019/mar/24/brexit-petition-to-revoke-article-50-reaches-5m-signatures

669 https://www.independent.co.uk/news/uk/politics/brexit-petition-article-50-revoke-signatures-six-million-latest-a8847506.html

670 https://www.bbc.co.uk/news/uk-politics-47678763

671 https://www.euractiv.com/section/uk-europe/news/pivotal-vote-on-29-march-the-brexit-day-that-wasnt/

672 https://www.bbc.co.uk/news/uk-politics-47751805

673 https://en.wikipedia.org/wiki/March_to_Leave

674 https://www.theguardian.com/politics/2019/mar/29/pro-brexiters-block-roads-westminster-chanting-bye-bye-eu

675 https://metro.co.uk/2019/03/29/pro-brexit-march-turns-ugly-as-police-arrest-five-protesters-9062221/

676 https://assets.publishing.service.gov.uk/government/uploads/system/uploads/attachment_data/file/793058/PM_letter_to_His_Excellency_Mr_Donald_Tusk__1_.pdf

677 https://www.consilium.europa.eu/media/39042/10-euco-art50-conclusions-en.pdf

678 https://www.bbc.co.uk/news/uk-politics-48188951

679 https://www.bbc.co.uk/news/uk-politics-48379730

680 https://www.bbc.co.uk/news/uk-politics-48839829

681 https://www.bbc.co.uk/news/uk-politics-48857811

682 https://en.wikipedia.org/wiki/2019_Conservative_Party_leadership_election_(UK)

683 https://inews.co.uk/news/politics/michael-gove-deeply-regrets-cocaine-tory-leadership/

684 https://news.sky.com/story/smoking-opium-in-iran-was-stupid-mistake-pm-hopeful-rory-stewart-admits-11731525

685 https://www.theguardian.com/politics/2019/jun/09/high-tories-how-the-leadership-candidates-drug-pasts-compare

686 https://assets.publishing.service.gov.uk/government/uploads/system/uploads/attachment_data/file/728754/drug-misuse-2018-hosb1418-infographic.pdf

687 https://en.wikipedia.org/wiki/2019_Conservative_Party_leadership_election_(UK)

688 https://www.standard.co.uk/news/politics/tory-leadership-contest-party-chairman-brandon-lewis-under-fire-

for-hiring-seven-helicopters-and-a4180356.html

689 https://en.wikipedia.org/wiki/Treaty_on_European_Union

690 https://en.wikipedia.org/wiki/Treaty_on_the_Functioning_of_the_European_Union

691 https://eur-lex.europa.eu/eli/treaty/teu_2012/oj

692 https://www.bbc.co.uk/news/uk-politics-38833883

693 https://en.wikipedia.org/wiki/R_(Miller)_v_Secretary_of_State_for_Exiting_the_European_Union

Printed in Great Britain
by Amazon

55467634R00158